JAINISM

OR

THE EARLY FAITH OF ASOKA

JAINISM

OR

THE EARLY FAITH OF ASOKA;

WITH

ILLUSTRATIONS OF THE ANCIENT RELIGIONS OF THE EAST,

FROM

THE PANTHEON OF THE INDO-SCYTHIANS

(*Read at the Meeting of the Royal Asiatic Society, Feb. 26, 1877.*)

To which is Prefixed a Notice on Bactrian Coins and Indian Dates

BY

EDWARD THOMAS, F.R.S.,

CORRESPONDANT DE L'INSTITUT DE FRANCE;
CORRESPONDING MEMBER GERMAN ORIENTAL SOCIETY; HON. MEMBER ASIATIC SOCIETY BENGAL;
VICE-PRESIDENT NUMISMATIC SOCIETY.

GYAN

Published by

Gyan Publishing House
5, Ansari Road
Daryaganj, New Delhi-110002
Phone: 011-47034999, 9811692060
E-mail: books@gyanbooks.com

Distribution Network
gyanbooks.com
India, USA, Canada, UK, Australia, France

ISBN : 978-81-212-2806-0 (HB)
First Published, 1877

2nd Impression 2021

Printed at: Gyan Press, Delhi.

Jainism or The Early Faith of Asoka
Author: Edward Thomas

JAINISM,

OR

THE EARLY FAITH OF ASOKA;

WITH

ILLUSTRATIONS OF THE ANCIENT RELIGIONS OF THE EAST,

FROM

THE PANTHEON OF THE INDO-SCYTHIANS.

(*Read at the Meeting of the Royal Asiatic Society, Feb.* 26, 1877.)

TO WHICH IS PREFIXED A NOTICE ON BACTRIAN COINS AND INDIAN DATES.

BY

EDWARD THOMAS, F.R.S.,

CORRESPONDANT DE L'INSTITUT DE FRANCE; CORRESPONDING MEMBER GERMAN ORIENTAL SOCIETY; HON. MEMBER ASIATIC SOCIETY BENGAL; VICE-PRESIDENT NUMISMATIC SOCIETY.

LONDON:
TRÜBNER & CO., 57 AND 59, LUDGATE HILL.

1877.

PREFATORY NOTICE.

THE publishers of the JOURNAL OF THE ROYAL ASIATIC SOCIETY—under the impression that there are many points of unusual interest in the articles named on the title-page—have resolved to issue a small edition, as a separate brochure, which may be available to Orientalists at large, who do not happen to be Members of the SOCIETY, to the pages of whose JOURNAL these essays would otherwise be confined.

CONTENTS.

ARTICLE I. (From J.R.A.S. Vol. IX. pp. 1–21.)

ARTICLE II. (J.R.A.S. Vol. IX. pp. 155–234.)

BACTRIAN COINS AND INDIAN DATES.

BY

EDWARD THOMAS, F.R.S.

A SHORT time ago, a casual reference to the complicated Greek monograms stamped on the earlier Bactrian coins suggested to me an explanation of some of their less involved combinations by the test of simple Greek *letter* dates, which was followed by the curious discovery that the Bactrian kings were in the habit of recognizing and employing *curtailed* dates to the optional omission of the figure for *hundreds*, which seems to have been the immemorial custom in many parts of India. My chief authority for this conclusion was derived from a chance passage in Albírúní,[1] whose statement, however, has since been independently supported by the interpretation of an inscription of the ninth century A.D. from Kashmír,[2] which illustrates the provincial use of a cycle of *one hundred* years, and has now

[1] Albírúní, writing in India in 1031 A.D., tells us, "Le vulgaire, dans l'Inde, compte par siècles, et les siècles se placent l'un après l'autre. On appelle cela le Samvatsara du cent. Quand un cent est écoulé, on le laisse et l'on en commence un autre. On appelle cela Loka-kâla, c'est-à-dire comput du peuple." —Reinaud's Translation, *Fragments Arabes*, Paris, 1845, p. 145.

[2] This second inscription ends with the words *Ṣaka Kálagatavdah* 726—that is, "Ṣaka Kâla years elapsed 726," equivalent to A.D. 804, which is therefore the date of the temple. This date also corresponds with the year 80 of the local cycle, which is the *Loka-kdla* of Kashmír or cycle of 2,700 years, counted by centuries named after the twenty-seven *nakshatras*, or lunar mansions. The reckoning, therefore, never goes beyond 100 years, and as each century begins in the 25th year of the Christian century, the 80th year of the local cycle is equivalent to the 4th year of the Christian century.—General A. Cunningham, *Archæological Report*, 1875, vol. v. p. 181.

been definitively confirmed by information obtained by Dr. Bühler[1] as to the origin of the Kashmírí era and the corroboration of the practice of the omission of "*the hundreds* in stating dates" still prevailing in that conservative kingdom.[2]

Since Bayer's premature attempt to interpret the mint-monogram ΙΡ, on a piece of Eucratides, as 108,[3] Numismatists have not lost sight of the possible discrimination of dates as opposed to the preferential mint-marks so abundant on the surfaces of these issues, though the general impression has been adverse to the possibility of their fulfilling any such functions.[4]

[1] "Dr. Bühler has found out the key to the Kashmirean era: it begins in the year of the Kaliyug 25, or 3076 B.C., when the Saptarshis are said to have gone to heaven. The Kashmír people often omit the hundreds in stating dates. Thus the year 24 (Kashmír era) in which Kalhana wrote his Râjataranginí, and which corresponded with Ṣaka 1070, stands for 4,224."—*Athenæum*, Nov. 20, 1875, p. 675.

[2] Since this was written, General Cunningham's letter of the 30th March, 1876, has appeared in the *Athenæum* (April 29th, 1876), from the text of which I extract the following passages. These seem to establish the fact that the optional omission of the hundreds was a common and well-understood rule so early as about the age of Asoka. "The passage in which the figures occur runs as follows in the Sahasarâm text:—

> iyam cha savane vivuthena dutesa
> paṅnalâti satâvivuthati 252.

The corresponding passage in the Rûpnâth text is somewhat different:—

> ahâle sava vivasetavâya ati vyathena
> sâvane kaṭesu 52 satavivasâta.

The corresponding portion of the Bairât text is lost. My reason for looking upon these figures as expressing a date is that they are preceded in the Rûpnâth text by the word kaṭesu, which I take to be the equivalent of the Sanskrit *krânteshu*=(so many years) 'having elapsed.'"

I do not stop to follow General Cunningham's arguments with regard to the value of the figures which he interprets as 252. The sign for 50, in its horizontal form, has hitherto been received as 80, but that the same symbol came, sooner or later, to represent 50, when placed perpendicularly, is sufficiently shown by Prof. Eggeling's Plate, p. 52, in Vol. VIII. of our Journal. I should, however, take great exception to the rendering of the *unit* as 2, which, to judge by Mr. Bayley's letter, in the same number of the *Athenæum*, Gen. Cunningham and Dr. Bühler had at first rightly concurred in reading as 6.

[3] *Hist. Reg. Græcorum Bactriani*, St. Petersburg, 1738, p. 92: "Numus Eucratidis, quem postea copiosius explicabo, annum 108. habet, sine dubio epochae Bactrianae, qui annus ex nostris rationibus A.V.C. 606. Septembri mense iniit. Igitur cum hoc in numo victoriae ejus Indicae celebrantur, quibus ut Justinus ait, *Indiam in potestatem redegit*." See also pp. 38, 56, 134.

[4] H. H. Wilson, Ariana Antiqua, pp. 235, 238. General A. Cunningham, Numismatic Chronicle, vol. viii. o.s. p. 175; and vol. viii. N.S. 1868, p. 183; vol. ix. N.S. 1869, p. 230.

In 1858 I published, in my edition of "Prinsep's *Essays on Indian Antiquities*," a notice of the detached letters *OΓ* as occurring on a coin of Eucratides (No. 3, p. 184, vol. ii.), and *ΠΓ* as found on the money of Heliocles (No. 1, p. 182), which letters, in their simple form, would severally represent the figures 73 and 83; but the difficulty obtruded itself that these numbers were too low to afford any satisfactory elucidation of the question involved in their application as dynastic dates.

Among the later acquisitions of Bactrian coins in the British Museum is a piece of Heliocles bearing the full triliteral date, after the manner of the Syrian mints, of *PΠΓ* or 183, which, when tested by the Seleucidan era (*i.e.* 311—183), brings his reign under the convenient date of B.C. 128, authorizing us to use the coincident *abbreviated* figures, under the same terms, as *OΓ*=73 for 173 of the Seleucidan era= B.C. 138 for Eucratides, and the repeated *ΠΓ* = 83 for 183 Seleucidan=B.C. 128, for Heliocles,[1] a date which is further supported by the appearance of the exceptionally combined *open* monogram ꟷΑꟷ (*ΠA*), or 81 for 181=B.C. 130 on his other pieces.

The last fully-dated piece, in the Bactrian series, is the unique example of the money of Plato (bearing the figured letter date *PMZ* = 147 of the Seleucidæ, or B.C. 165). We have two doubtful dates Ξ=60 and Ξ*E*=65, on the coins of Apollodotus; but if these letters were intended for dates, they will scarcely fit-in with the Seleucidan scheme. Menander dates his coins in *regnal* years. I can trace extant examples from 1 to 8. But this practice by no means necessitates the disuse of the Seleucidan era in ordinary reckonings, still less its abandonment in State documents where more formal precision was

[1] General Cunningham was cognizant of the date ΠΓ = 83 as found on the coins of Heliocles, which he associated with the year B.C. 164, under the assumption that he had detected the true initial date of the Bactrian era, which he had settled to his own satisfaction, "as beginning in B.C. 246."—Num. Chron. N.S. vol. viii. 1868, p. 266; N S. vol. ix. 1869, pp. 35, 230. See also Mr. Vaux's note, N.C. 1875, vol. xv. p. 3.

required. Subjoined is a rough facsimile and technical description of the coin of Plato.[1]

Silver. *Size* 1·2. *Wt.* 258 *grains.*

Obv. Head of king to the right, with helmet ornamented with the peculiar ear and horn of a bull, so marked on the coins of Eucratides.

Rev. Apollo driving the horses of the Sun. Monogram No. 46*a*, Prinsep's Essays.

Legend. ΒΑΣΙΛΕΩΣ ΕΠΙΦΑΝΟΥΣ ΠΛΑΤΩΝΟΣ.

Date at foot, ΡΜΖ=147 Selucidæ (or B.C. 165).

My first impression on noticing the near identity of the obverse head with the standard Numismatic portraits of Eucratides, and the coincidence of the date with that assumed, by our latest authority,[2] as the year of the decease of that monarch, was that Plato must have succeeded him; but the advanced interpretation of the dates, above given, puts any such assignment altogether out of court, and necessitates a critical reconstruction of all previous speculative epochal or serial lists of the Bactrian succession.

In the present instance the adoption of the helmet of the Chabylians[3] by Eucratides and Plato may merely imply that

[1] The woodcut here given was prepared for Mr. Vaux's original article on this unique coin of Plato, in the Numismatic Chronicle, vol. xv. p. 1.

[2] Gen. Cunningham, N.C. vol. viii. o.s. 1843, p. 175, and vol. ix. N s. 1869, p. 175.

[3] "The Chabylians had small shields made of raw hides, and each had two javelins used for hunting wolves. Brazen helmets protected their heads, and above these they wore the ears and horns of an ox fashioned in brass. They had also crests on their helms."—Herodotus vii. 76; Rawlinson, vol. iv. p. 72; Xenophon Anab. v.

they both claimed kindred with that tribe, or at some time held command in their national contingent—and Plato may, with equal possibility, have introduced the device, in the first instance, as have copied the more abundant obverses of similar character from the coins of Eucratides. On the other hand, the identity of the helmet may indicate an absolute borrowing of a ready prepared device. The singular and eccentric combination of Bactrian Mint dies has from the first constituted a difficulty and a danger to modern interpreters. I have for long past looked suspiciously upon the too facile adaptations of otherwise conscientious mint masters, leading them to utilize, for reasons of their own, the available die-devices in stock for purposes foreign to the original intent under which they were executed. However, in the present instance, the imperfect preservation of the single coin of Plato available does not permit of our pronouncing with any certainty upon the identity of the features with those of the profile of Eucratides.

To revert to our leading subject. In addition to the value of the data quoted above as fixing definitively, though within fairly anticipated limits, the epochs of three prominent Bactrian kings, their conventional use of the system of abbreviated definitions points, directly, to the assimilation of local customs, to which the Greeks so readily lent themselves, in adopting the method of reckoning by the Indian *Loka Kála*, which simplified the expression of dates, even as we do now, in the civilized year of our Lord, when we write 76 for 1876.

The extension of the Seleucidan era eastwards, and its amalgamation of Indian methods of definition within its own mechanism, leads further to the consideration of how long this exotic era maintained its ground in Upper India, and how much influence it exerted upon the chronological records of succeeding dynasties. I have always been under the impression that this influence was more wide-spread and abiding than my fellow-antiquaries have been ready to admit,[1] but

[1] Journal Royal Asiatic Society, Vol. XII. p. 41; Journal Asiatic Society Bengal, 1855, p. 565, and 1872, p. 175; Prinsep's Essays, vol. ii. p. 86; Journal Asiatique, 1863, p. 388.

I am now prepared to carry my inferences into broader channels, and to suggest that the Indo-Scythian "Kanishka" group of kings continued to use the Seleucidan era, even as they retained the minor sub-divisions of the Greek months, which formed an essential part of its system: and under this view to propose that we should treat the entire circle of dates of the "Hushka, Jushka, and Kanishka" *family*, mentioned in the Rája Taranginí, which their inscriptions expand from ix. to xcviii., as pertaining to the fourth century of the Seleucidan era, an arrangement which will bring them into concert with our Christian reckoning from 2 B.C. to 87 A.D. A scheme which would, moreover, provide for their full possession of power up to the *crucial* "Saka" date of 78–79 A.D., and allow for the subsequent continuance of a considerable breadth of sway outside the limited geographical range of Indian cognizance.

There are further considerations which add weight to the conclusion that the Kanerki Scythians adopted, for public purposes, the Seleucidan era; they may be supposed, like the Parthians and other Nomads, to have achieved but scant culture till conquest made them masters of civilized sections of the earth.

In the present instance, these new invaders are seen to have ignored or rejected the Semitic-Bactrian writing employed by the Kadphises horde in parallel concert with the traditional monumental Greek, and to have relied exclusively on the Greek language in their official records [1] till the later domestication of some of the members of the family, at Mathurá, led to an exceptional use of the Devanágarí alphabet, in subordination to the dominant Greek, on the coins of Vásudeva. In no case do we find them recognizing the Semitic type of character, though the inscriptions quoted

[1] Prof. Wilson's Plates, in his Ariana Antiqua, arranged 35 years ago, and altogether independently of the present argument, will suffice to place this contrast before the reader. The Kadphises group extend from figs. 5 to 21 of plate x. All these coins are *bilingual*, Greek and Semitic-Bactrian. The Kanerki series commence with No. 15, plate xi., having nothing but Greek legends, either on the obverse or on the reverse, and follow on continuously through plates xii. xiii. and xiv. down to fig. 11. After that, the Greek characters become more or less chaotic, till we reach No. 19.

below will show how largely that alphabet had spread in some portions of their dominion. But beyond this, their adherence, or perhaps that of their successors, to Greek, continues mechanically till its characters merge into utter incoherence on the later mintages.[1] All of these indications lead to the inference that, as far as the Court influences were concerned, the tendency to rely upon Greek speech would have carried with it what remained *in situ* of the manners and customs of their Western instructors.[2]

There are two groups or varieties of Indo-Scythian Inscriptions of the Kanishka family. The one in the Indian *proper* or Láṭ alphabet, all of which are located at Mathurá. The published Mathurá inscriptions of this group (excluding the two quotations placed within brackets) number 20 in all; as a rule they are merely records of votive offerings on the part of "pious founders," and contain only casual references to the ruling powers. Twelve of these make no mention of any monarch, though they are clearly contemporaneous with the other dedicatory inscriptions. Throughout the whole

[1] Ariana Antiqua, pl. xiv. Nos. 12, 13, 14, 16, 17.

[2] The circumstances bearing upon the battle of Karór (or كدور) are of so much importance in the history of this epoch, that I reproduce Albírúní's account of that event: "On emploie ordinairement les ères de Sri-Harcha, de Vikramáditya, de Ṣaka, de Ballaba, et des Gouptas. . . . L'ère de Vikramáditya est employée dans les provinces méridionales et occidentales de l'Inde. . . L'ère de Ṣaka, nommée par les Indiens 'Ṣaka-kála,' est postérieure à celle de Vikramáditya de 135 ans. Ṣaka est le nom d'un prince qui a régné sur les contrées *situées entre l'Indus et la mer.* Sa résidence était placée au centre de l'empire, dans la contrée nommée Aryavartha. Les Indiens le font naître dans une classe autre que celle des Sakya; quelques-uns prétendent qu'il était Soudra et originaire de la ville de Mansoura; il y en a même qui disent qu'il n'était pas de race indienne, et qu'il tirait son origine des régions occidentales. Les peuples eurent beaucoup à souffrir de son despotisme, jusqu'à ce qu'il leur vînt du secours de l'Orient. Vikramáditya marcha contre lui, mit son armée en déroute, et le tua sur le territoire de Korour, situé entre Moultan et le château de Louny. Cette époque devint célèbre, à cause de la joie que les peuples ressentirent de la mort de Ṣaka, et on la choisit pour ère principalement chez les astronomes."—Reinaud's translation.

General Cunningham has attempted to identify the site of Karór with a position "50 miles S.E. of Multán and 20 miles N.E. of Baháwalpúr," making the "castle of Loni" into "*Ludhan*, an ancient town situated near the old bed of the Sutlej river, 44 miles E.N.E. of Kahror and 70 miles E.S.E. of Multán."—*Ancient Geography of India* (Trübner, 1871), p. 241. These assignments, are, however, seriously shaken by the fact that Albírúní himself invariably places these two sites far north of Multán, *i.e.* according to his latitudes and longitudes, *Multán* is 91°—29° 30′ N., while *Kadór*, as he writes it, is 92°—31° N., and Loni (variant *Loi*) is 32° N.—Sprenger's Maps, No. 12, etc.

series of twenty records the dates are confined to numbers below *one hundred:* they approach and nearly touch the end of a given century, in the 90 and 98; but do not reach or surpass the crucial *hundred* discarded in the local cycle.

The two inscriptions, Nos. 22, 23, from the same locality, dated, severally, Samvat 135 with the Indian month of Paushya, and Samvat 281, clearly belong to a different age, and vary from their associates in dedicatory phraseology, forms of letters, and many minor characteristics, which General Cunningham readily discriminated.[1]

Indo-Scythian Inscriptions.

In the Indo-Páli Alphabet.

At Mathurá.	KANISHKA.	*Mahárája Kanishka. Samvat* 9.
		[*Kanishka. Samvat* 28.]
		[*Huvishka. Samvat* 33.][2]
	HUVISHKA.	*Mahárája* DEVAPUTRA *Huvishka.* Hemanta, *S.* 39.
		Mahárája RÁJATIRÁJA DEVAPUTRA *Huvishka.* Grishma, *S.* 47.[3]
		Mahárája Huvishka. Hemanta, *S.* 48.
	VÁSUDEVA.	*Mahárája Rájátirája* DEVAPUTRA *Vásu(deva).* Varsha, *S.* 44.
		Mahárája Vásudeva. Grishma, *S.* 83.
		Mahárája Rájatirája, SHÁHI, *Vásudeva.* Hemanta, *S.* 87.
		Rája Vásudeva. Varsha, *S.* 98.[4]

[1] Arch. Rep. vol. iii. p. 38.

[2] These two dates are quoted from Gen. Cunningham's letter to the *Athenæum* of 29 April, 1876, as having been lately discovered by Mr. Growse, B.C.S.

[3] The 47th year of the Monastery of Huvishka.

[4] I was at first disposed to infer that the use of the Indian months in their full development indicated a period subsequent to the employment of the primitive three seasons, but I find from the Western Inscriptions, lately published by Prof. Bhandarkar, that they were clearly in contemporaneous acceptance. While a passage in Hiouen Thsang suggests that the retention of the normal terms was in a measure typical of Buddhist belief, and so that, in another sense, *the months* had a confessed conventional significance.

"Suivant la sainte doctrine de Jou-laï (du Tathágata), une année se compose de trois saisons. Depuis le 16 du premier mois, jusqu'au 15 du cinquième mois, c'est la saison chaude. Depuis le 16 du cinquième mois, jusqu'au 15 du neuvième mois, c'est la saison pluvieuse (Varchás). Depuis le 16 de neuvième mois, jusqu'au 15 du premier mois, c'est la saison froide. Quelquefois on divise l'année en quatre saisons, savoir: le printemps, l'été, l'automne et l'hiver."—Hiouen Thsang, vol. ii. p. 63. The division into three seasons is distinctly *non-Vedic.*—Muir, vol. i. p. 13; Elliot, Glossary, vol. ii. p. 47.

"There are two summers in the year and two harvests, while the winter intervenes between them."—Pliny vi. 21; Diod. Sic. I. c. i.

The parallel series are more scattered, and crop up in less direct consecutive association, these are indorsed in the *Bactrian* or Aryan adaptation of the Ancient Phœnician alphabet.

Indo-Scythian Inscriptions.

In the Bactrian-Páli Alphabet.

Baháwalpúr. *Maharaja Rajadiraja* Devaputra *Kanishka.*
Samvat 11, on the 28th of the (Greek) month of Dæsius.

Manikyála Tope. *Maharaja Kaneshka,* Gushana *vaṣa samvardhaka.*
"Increaser of the dominion of the Gushans" (Kushans).
Samvat 18.

Wardak Vase. *Maharaja rajatiraja Huveshka. Samvat* 51, 15th of Artemisius.[1]

[1] Besides these inscriptions, there is a record of the name of Kanishka designated as *Raja Gandharya*, on "a rough block of quartz," from Zeda, near Ohind, now in the Láhore Museum. This legend is embodied in very small Bactrian letters, and is preceded by a single line in large characters, which reads as follows: *San* 10 + 1 (=11) *Ashadasa masasa di* 20, *Udeyana gu.* 1. *Isachhu nami.*" I do not quote or definitively adopt this date, as the two inscriptions appear to me to be of different periods, and vary in a marked degree in the forms as well as in the size of their letters.—Lowenthal, J.A.S.B. 1863, p. 5; Gen. Cunningham, Arch. Report, vol. v. p. 57.

In addition to the above Bactrian Páli Inscriptions, we have a record from Taxila, by the "Satrap Liako Kusuluko," in "the 78th year of the great king, the Great Moga, on the 5th day of the month Panæmus" (J.R.A.S. xx. o.s. p. 227; J.A.S.B. 1862, p. 40). And an inscription from Takht-i-Bahi of the Indo-Parthian king Gondophares, well known to us from his coins (Ariana Antiqua, p. 340, Prinsep's Essays, vol. ii. p. 214), and doubtfully associated with the *Gondoferus* of the Legenda Aurea, to the following tenor: "*Maharayasa Gudupharasa Vasha* 20 + 4 + 2 (=26) *San . . . Satimae* 100 + 3 (=103) *Vesakhasa masasa divase* 4." (Cunningham, Arch. Rep. vol. v. p. 59.) And to complete the series of regal quotations, I add the heading of the inscription from Panjtar of a king of the Kushans: "*Sam* 100 + 20 + 2 (=122) *Sravanasa masasa di prathame* 1, *Maha rayasa Gushanasa Ra . . .*" (Professor Dowson, J.R.A.S. Vol. XX. o.s. p. 223; Cunningham, Arch. Rep. vol. v. p. 61.)

This is an inscription which, in the exceptional character of its framework, suggests and even necessitates reconstructive interpretations. The stone upon which it is engrossed was obviously fissured and imperfectly prepared for its purpose in the first instance; so that, in the opening line, Gondophares' name has to be taken over a broken gap with space for two letters, which divides the *d* from the *ph*. The surface of the stone has likewise suffered from abrasion of some kind or other, so that material letters have in certain cases been reduced to mere shadowy outlines. But enough remains intact to establish the name of the Indo-Parthian King, and to exhibit a double record of dates, giving his regnal year and the counterpart in an era the determination of which is of the highest possible importance. The *vasha* or year of the king, expressed in figures alone, as 26, is not contested. The *figured* date of the leading era presents no difficulty whatever to those who are conversant with Phœnician notation, or who may hereafter choose to consult the ancient coins of Aradus. The symbol for *hundreds* is incontestable. The preliminary stroke ı, to the right of the sign, in

The above collection of names and dates covers, in the latter sense, a period of from An. 9 to An. 98, or eighty-nine years in all. The names, as I interpret them, apply to two individuals, only, out of the triple brotherhood mentioned in the *Rája Tarangini*. After enumerating the reigns of (1) Aṣoka, (2) Jaloka, and (3) Dámodhara, Professor Wilson's translation of that chronicle continues:—

"Dámodhara was succeeded by three princes who divided the country, and severally founded capital cities named after themselves. These princes were called Hushka, Jushka, and Kanishka,[1] of Turushka or Tatar extraction. . . . They are considered synchronous, but may possibly be all that are preserved of some series of Tatar princes who, it is very likely, at various periods, established themselves in Kashmír."[2] I

the Western system, marks the simple number of *hundreds*; in India an additional prolongation duplicates the value of the normal symbol. Under these terms the adoptive Bactrian figures are positive as 103. Before the *figured* date there is to be found, *in letters*, the word *ṣatimae* "in one hundred" or "hundredth," in the reading of which all concur. It is possible that the exceptional use of the figure for 100, which has not previously been met with, may have led to its definition and repetition *in writing* in the body of the inscription, in order that future interpreters should feel no hesitation about the value of the exotic symbol. There was not the same necessity for repeating the 3, the three fingers of which must always have been obvious to the meanest capacity. I have no difficulty about the existence and free currency of the Vikramáditya era *per se* in its own proper time, which some archæologists are inclined to regard as of later adaptation. But I am unable to concur in the reading of *Samvatsara*, or to admit, if such should prove the correct interpretation, that the word *Samvatsara* involved or necessitated a preferential association with the Vikramáditya era, any more than the *Samvatsara* (J.R.A.S., Vol. IV. p. 500) and *Samvatsaraye* (*ibid.* p. 222), or the abbreviated *Sán* or *Sam*, which is so constant in these Bactrian Pali Inscriptions, and so frequent on Indo-Parthian coins (Prinsep's Essays, vol. ii. p. 205, Coins of Azas, Nos. 1, 2, 6, 7, 12; Azilisas, Nos. 1, etc.; Gondophares, p. 215, No. 4.

[1] Abulfazl says "brothers." Gladwin's Translation, vol. ii. p. 171; Calcutta Text, p. 574. هشکک - زشکک - کنشکک هرسه برادر آئین بوده داشتند.

General Cunningham considers that he has succeeded in identifying all the three capitals, the sites of which are placed within the limits of the valley of Kashmír, *i.e.*,

"*Kanishka-pura* (Kanikhpur) hod. Kâmpur, is ten miles south of Sirinagar, known as Kámpur Sarai.

"*Hushka-pura*, the Hu-se-kia-lo of Hiuen Thsang—the Ushkar of Albírúní—now surviving in the village of *Uskara*, two miles south-east of Baráhmula.

"*Jushka-pura* is identified by the Brahmans with Zukru or Zukur, a considerable village four miles north of the capital, the *Schecroh* of Troyer and Wilson."—Ancient Geography of India (London, 1871), p. 99.

[2] Prof. H. H. Wilson, "An Essay on the Hindu History of Kashmír," Asiatic Researches, vol. xv. p. 23; and Troyer's Histoire des Rois du Kachmir (Paris, 1840-52), vol. i. p. 19. See also Hiouen-Thsang (Paris, 1858), vol. ii. pp. 42, 106, etc.

assume *Vásu Deva* (Krishṇa's title) to have been the titular designation of Kanishka,[1] while *Devaputra* was common to both brothers, and the *Sháhi*[2] was perhaps optional, or devoted to the senior in the joint brotherhood[3] or head of the more extensive tribal community of the Kanerki.

The Mathurá inscriptions, as we have seen, distinguish the subdivisions of the year by the old triple seasons of *Grishma*, *Varsha*, and *Hemanta*, while the Bactrian Páli inscriptions ordinarily define the months by their Macedonian designations;[4] the question thus arises as to whether this latter

[1] Coin of Vásu Deva struck in his Eastern dominions. *Trésor de Numismatique.* Gold. Pl. lxxx., figs. 10, 11.

Obverse.—Scythian figure, standing to the front, casting incense into the typical small Mithraic altar. To the right, a trident with flowing pennons: to the left, a standard with streamers.

Legend, around the main device, in obscure Greek, the vague reproduction of the conventional titles of PAO NANO PAO KOPANO.

Below the left arm व *Va* सु *su* } = VASU, in the exact style of character found in his Mathurá Inscriptions.

Reverse.—The Indian Goddess Párvatí seated on an open chair or imitation of a Greek throne, extending in her right hand the classic regal fillet; Mithraic monogram to the left.

Legend, APΔOXPO, Ard-Ugra = "half Ṣiva," *i.e.* Párvatí.

Those who wish to examine nearly exact counterparts of these types in English publications may consult the coins engraved in plate xiv., Ariana Antiqua, figs. 19, 20. The latter seems to have an imperfect rendering of the व *va* on the obverse, with सु *su* (formed like *pu*) on the reverse. [For corresponding types see also Journ. As. Soc. Beng. vol. v. pl. 36, and Prinsep's Essays, pl. 4. General Cunningham, Numismatic Chronicle, vol. vi. o.s. pl. i. fig. 2.] The *u* is not curved, but formed by a mere elongation of the downstroke of the स *s*, which in itself constitutes the vowel. The omission of the consecutive *Deva* on the coins is of no more import than the parallel rejection of the *Gupta*, where the king's name is written *downwards*, Chinese fashion, in the confined space below the arm. See also General Cunningham's remarks on Vásudeva, J.R.A.S. Vol. V. pp. 193, 195. Gen. Cunningham proposes to amend Prof. Wilson's tentative reading of Baraono on the two gold coins, Ariana Antiqua, pl. xiv. figs. 14, 18 (p. 378), into PAO NANO PAO BAZOΔHO KOPANO. The engraving of No. 14 certainly suggests an initial B in the name, and the AZ and O are sufficiently clear. We have only to angularize the succeeding O into Δ to complete the identification. These coins have a reverse of Ṣiva and the Bull.—Arch. Rep. vol. iii. p. 42. Dr. Kern does not seem to have been aware of these identifications when he proposed, in 1873 (Révue Critique, 1874, p. 291), to associate the Mathurá Vásudeva with the Indo-Sassanian *Pehlvi* coin figured in Prinsep, pl. vii. fig. 6. Journ. Roy. Asiatic Soc. Vol. XII. pl. 3; Ariana Antiqua, pl. xvii. fig. 9.

[2] The full Devaputra Shahán Sháhi occurs in the Samudra Gupta inscription on the Allahábád Láṭ. It may possibly refer to some of the extra Indian successors of these Indo-Scythians.

[3] Troyer translates paragraph 171, "Pendant le long règne de ces rois," vol. i. p. 19.

[4] "The Macedonian months, which were adopted by the Syro-Macedonian

practice does not imply a continued use of the Seleucidan era, in association with which the names of these months must first have reached India?[1] and which must have been altogether out of place in any indigenous scheme of reckoning. Tested by this system, the years 9–98 of the fourth century of the Seleucidan era (B.C. 311–12) produce, as I have elsewhere remarked, the singularly suitable return of B.C. 2 to A.D. 87. And a similar process applied to the third century of the newly-discovered Parthian era (B.C. 248)[2] would represent B.C. 39 and A.D. 50. But this last method of computation seems to have secured a mere local and exceptional currency, and the probabilities of its extension to India are as zero compared with the wide-spread and enduring date[3] of the Seleucidæ, which the Parthians themselves continued to use on their coinage in conjunction with the old

cities, and generally by the Greek cities of Asia, after the time of Alexander, were *lunar* till the reformation of the Roman calendar of *Cæsar* (by inserting 67+23 =90 days in this year). After that reformation the Greek cities of Asia, which had then become subject to the Roman Empire, gradually adopted the Julian year. But although they followed the Romans in computing by the solar Julian year of 365d. 6h. instead of the lunar, yet they made no alteration in the season at which their year began (ΔΙΟΣ=Oct. Nov.), or in the order of the months." —Clinton, Fast. Hell. vol. iii. pp. 202, 347.

[1] Some importance will be seen to have attached to the use of the contrasted terms for national months in olden time, as we find Letronne observing: "Dans tous les exemples de doubles ou triples dates que nous offrent les inscriptions rédigées en Grèce, le mois qui est énoncé le premier est toujours celui dont fait usage la nation à laquelle appartient celui qui parle."—Letronne, Inscriptions de l'Egypte (Paris, 1852), p. 263.

[2] Assyrian Discoveries, by George Smith, London, 1875, p. 389. From the time of the Parthian conquest it appears that the tablets were dated according to the Parthian style. There has always been a doubt as to the date of this revolt, and consequently of the Parthian monarchy, as the classical authorities have left no evidence as to the exact date of the rise of the Parthian power. I, however, obtained three Parthian tablets from Babylon; two of them contained double dates, one of which, being found perfect, supplied the required evidence, as it was dated according to the Seleucidan era, and according also to the Parthian era, the 144th year of the Parthians being equal to the 208th year of the Seleucidæ, thus making the Parthian era to have commenced B.C. 248. This date is written: "Month . . . . 23rd day 144th year, which is called the 208th year, Arsaces, King of kings."

Clinton, following Justin and Eusebius, etc., 250 B.C., Fasti Romani, vol. ii. p. 243, and Fasti Hellenici, vol. iii. p. 311; Moses Chorenensis, 251 or 252 B.C.; Suidas, 246 B.C.

[3] "Antiochus, *surnamed* Epiphanes, son of Antiochus the king, . . . reigned in the 137th year of the kingdom of the Greeks."—Maccabees I. i. 10 —ii. 70, et. seq. "In the 143rd year of the kingdom of the Seleucidæ."— Josephus, Ant. xii. 3. "It came to pass . . in the 145th year on the 25th of that month which is by us called *Chasleu*, and by the Macedonians *Apelleus*,

Macedonian *months*,[1] whose importance in their bearing upon the leading era I have enlarged upon in the parallel Indo-Scythic instance immediately under review. So that, as at present advised, I hold to a preference for the Seleucidan test, which places the Indo-Scythians in so satisfactory a position both relatively to their predecessors and successors. I have at the same time no reserve in acknowledging the many difficulties surrounding the leading question; but if we can but get a second "pied à terre," a fixed date-point, after the classical testimony to the epoch of the great Chandra Gupta, we may check the doubts and difficulties surrounding many generations both before and after any established date that we may chance to elicit from the present and more mature inquiries.

The comparative estimates by the three methods of computation immediately available stand roughly as follows:—

Seleucidan .	[1st Sept., 312 B.C.]	B.C. 2 to A.D. 87.
Vikramáditya . .	[57 B.C.[2]] . .	B.C. 48 to A.D. 41.
Ṣaka . .	[14th March, 78 A.D.[3]]	A.D. 88 to A.D. 177.

Before taking leave of the general subject of Indian methods of defining dates, I wish to point out how much the conventional practice of the suppression of the *hundreds* must have impaired the ordinary continuity of record and

in the 153rd Olympiad, etc."—xii. 4. "Seleucus cognominatus *Nicator* regnum Babelis, totiusque Eraki, et Chorasanæ, Indiam usque, Ab initio imperii ipsius orditur æra, quæ Alexandri audit, ea nempe qua tempora computant Syri et Hebræi."—Bar-Hebræus, Pococke, p. 63.

"The Jews still style it the *Æra of Contracts*, because they were obliged, when subject to the Syro-Macedonian princes, to express it in all their contracts and civil writings."—Gough's Seleucidæ, p. 3.

The Syriac text of the inscription at Singanfu is dated "in 1093d year of the Greeks" (A.D. 782).—A. Kircher, La Chine, p. 43; Yule, Marco Polo, vol. ii. p. 22; see also Mure's History of Greece, vol. iv. pp. 74–79.

[1] The dates begin to appear on the Syro-Macedonian coins under Seleucus IV., Trésor de Numismatique, ϛΛΡ = 136; Mionnet, vol. v. p. 30, ΡΛΖ = 137. Cleopatra and Antiochus VIII. also date their coins in the Seleucidan era. See Mionnet, vol. v. pp. 86, 87.

The Parthian coin dates commence with A.S. ΠΣ = 280 (B.C. 31), ΑΡΤΕ, *Artemisius*, and continue to A.S. 539, Trés. de Num. Rois Grecs, pp. 143–147; Lindsay, Coinage of the Parthians (Cork, 1852), pp. 175–179.

[2] Luni-solar year. [3] Solar or Sidereal year. Prinsep, Useful Tables, pp. 153-7.

affected the resulting value of many of the fragmentary data that have been preserved to our time.

The existence of such a system of disregarding or blotting-out of centuries—persevered in for ages—must naturally have led to endless uncertainties among subsequent home or foreign inquirers, whose errors and misunderstandings were occasionally superadded to the normal imperfections of their leading authorities. Something of this kind may be detected in the illustrative works both of Hiuen Thsang and Albírúní, wherever the quotation refers to hundreds in the gross. Apart from the improbabilities of events adapting themselves to *even* numbers *in hundreds*, it is clear that, where hundreds alone are given, the date itself must be looked upon as more or less vague and conjectural, elicited, in short, out of uncertain and undefined numbers, and alike incapable of correction from minor totals; such a test must now be applied to Hiuen Thsang's oft-quoted open number of 400 as marking the interval between Buddha and Kanishka.[1]

So also one of Albírúní's less-consistently worked-out dates is liable to parallel objection, such, for instance, as the *even* "400 before Vikramáditya," which constitutes his era of "Ṣrí Harsha," and which he is frank enough to confess *may* perchance pertain to the other Ṣrí Harsha of 664 after Vikramáditya (or 57+664=607-8 A.D.). His clear 400 of the era of Yezdegird is, however, a veritable conjuncture, a singular and unforced combination of independent epochs,[2]

[1] "Dans les quatre cents ans qui suivront mon *Nirváṇa*, il y aura un roi qui s'illustrera dans le monde sous le nom de Kia-ni-se-kia (Kanishka)."—Mémoires sur les Contrées occidentales (Paris, 1857), i. p. 106. "Dans la 400e année après le Nirváṇa" (p. 172). This 400 is the sum given in the Lalita Vistára, but the Mongol authorities have 300. Foe-koue Ki, chapter xxv., and Burnouf's Intr. Hist. Bud., vol. i. p. 568, "trois cent ans," p. 579, "un peu plus de quatre cent ans après Çakya, au temps de Kanichka." Hiuen Thsang confines himself to obscure hundreds in other places. "Dans la centième année après le Nirváṇa de Jou-laï, Aṣoka, roi de Magadha," p. 170. "La six centième année après le Nirváṇa," p. 179. Nágárjuna is equally dated 400 years after Buddha. "Nágárjuna is generally supposed to have flourished 400 years after the death of Buddha."—As. Res. vol. xx. pp. 400, 513. Csoma de Koros, Analysis of the Gyut. See also As. Res. vol. ix. p. 83; xv. p. 115; and Burnouf, vol. i. p. 447, and J.A.S.B. vol. vii. p. 143. M. Foucaux, in his Tibetan version of the Lalita Vistára, speaks of Nágárjuna as flourishing "cent ans après le mort de Çakya Mouni, p. 392, note.

[2] Reinaud, *loc. cit.* pp. 137, 139. Albírúní here rejoices, that "cette époque s'exprime par un nombre rond et n'est embarrassée ni de dizaines ni d'unités," which seems to show how rarely, in his large experience, such a phenomenon had been met with.

approximately marked by the date of the death of Mahmúd of Ghazní,[1] in an era that had not yet been superseded in the East by the Muhammadan Hijrah.

I conclude this paper with a reproduction of the unique coin of the Ṣaka King Heraüs, which, on more mature examination, has been found to throw unexpected light on the chief seat of Ṣaka-Scythian power,[2] and to supply incidentally an approximate date, which may prove of considerable value in elucidating the contemporaneous history of the border lands of India.

I have recently had occasion to investigate the probable age of this piece by a comparison of its reverse device with the leading types of the Imperial Parthian mintages, with which it has much in common, and the deduction I arrived at, from the purely Numismatic aspect of the evidence, was

[1] The era of Yezdegird commenced 16th June, 632 A.D. The date on Mahmúd's tomb is 23rd Rabí' the second, A.H. 421 (30th April, A.D. 1030).

[2] Albírúní was naturally perplexed with the identities of Vikramáditya and Sáliváhana, and unable to reconcile the similarity of the acts attributed alike to one and the other. He concludes the passage quoted in note 2, p. 9, in the following terms :—" D'un autre côté, Vikramáditya, reçut le titre de *Srí* (grand) à cause de l'honneur qu'il s'était acquis. Du reste, l'intervalle qui s'est écoulé entre l'ère de Vikramáditya et la mort de Saka, prouve que le vainqueur n'était pas le célèbre Vikramáditya, mais un autre prince du même nom."—Reinaud, p. 142.

Major Wilford, in like manner, while discussing the individualities of his " 8 or 9 Vikramádityas," admitted that " the two periods of Vikramáditya and Sáliváhana are intimately connected, and the accounts we have of these two extraordinary personages are much confused, teeming with contradictions and absurdities to a surprising degree."—As. Res., vol. ix. p. 117; see also vol. x. p. 93.

A passage lately brought to notice by Dr. Bühler throws new light upon this question, for, in addition to supplying chronological data of much importance in regard to the interval of 470 years which is said to have elapsed between the great *Jaina Mahávíra* (the 24th *Tírthankara*) and the first *Vikramáditya* of B.C. 57, it teaches us that there were Ṣaka kings holding sway in India in B.C. 61–57, which indirectly confirms the epoch of the family of Heraüs, and explains how both Vikramádityas, at intervals of 135 years, came to have *Ṣaka* enemies to encounter, and consequently equal claims to titular *Ṣakári* honours.

"1. Pálaka, the lord of Avanti, was anointed in that night in which the Arhat and Tírthankara Mahávíra entered Nirváṇa. 2. 60 are (the years of King Pálaka, but 155 are (the years) of the Nandas; 108 those of the Mauryas, and 30 those of *Púsamitta* (Pushyamitra). 3. 60 (years) ruled Balamitra and Bhánumitra, 40 Nabhovahana. 13 years likewise (lasted) the rule of Gardabhilla, and 4 are (the years) of Ṣaka."—From the Prakrit Gáthás of Merutunga, etc.

"These verses, which are quoted in a very large number of Jaina commentaries and chronological works, but the origin of which is not clear, give the adjustment between the eras of Víra and Vikrama, and form the basis of the earlier Jaina chronology."—Dr. Bühler, Indian Antiquary, vol. ii. p. 363.

that, recognizing the imitative adoption of certain details of the main devices of the suzerain rulers, and supposing such adoption to have been immediate and contemporaneous, the dates B.C. 37 to A.D. 4 would "mark the age of Heraüs."[1] This epoch singularly accords with the date of Isidore of Charax,[2] from whose text of the 'Stathmi Parthici' we likewise gather that the recognized seat of the Ṣaka-Scythians, then feudatories of the Parthian Empire, was located in the valley of the Helmund,[3] and was known by the optional

[1] Records of the Gupta Dynasty (Trübner, 1876), p. 37.

"It is in regard to the typical details, however, that the contrast between the pieces of Mauas and Heraüs is most apparent. Mauas has no coins with his own bust among the infinite variety of his mint devices, nor has Azas, who imitates so many of his emblems. But, in the Gondophares group, we meet again with busts and uncovered heads, the hair being simply bound by a fillet, in which arrangement of the head-dress Pakores, with his bushy curls, follows suit. But the crucial typical test is furnished by the small figure of victory crowning the horseman on the reverse, which is so special a characteristic of the Parthian die illustration.

"We have frequent examples of Angels or types of victory extending regal fillets in the Bactrian series, but these figures constitute as a rule the main device of the reverse, and are not subordinated into a corner, as in the Parthian system. The first appearance of the fillet in direct connexion with the king's head in the Imperial series, occurs on the coins of Arsaces XIV., *Orodes* (B.C. 54–37), where the crown is borne by an eagle (Lindsay, *History of the Parthians*, Cork, 1852, pl. iii. fig. 2, pp. 146-170; *Trésor de Numismatique*, pl. lxviii. fig. 17); but on the reverses of the copper coinage this duty is already confided to the winged figure of Victory (Lindsay, pl. v. fig. 2, p. 181). Arsaces XV., Phrahates IV. (37 B.C.-4 A.D.), continues the eagles for a time, but progresses into single (*Ibid.*, pl. iii. fig. 60; v. fig. 4, pp. 148, 170; *Trésor de Numismatique*, pl. lxviii. fig. 18; pl. lxix. fig. 5), and finally into double figures of Victory eager to crown him (*Ibid.*, pl. iii. figs. 61-63), as indicating his successes against Antony and the annexation of the kingdom of Media (Lindṣay, p. 46; Rawlinson, *The Sixth Monarchy*, p. 182).

"Henceforth these winged adjuncts are discontinued, so that, if we are to seek for the prototype of the Heraüs coin amid Imperial Arsacidan models, we are closely limited in point of antiquity, though the possibly deferred adoption may be less susceptible of proof."

[2] The period of Isidore of Charax has been the subject of much controversy. The writer of the notice in Smith's Dictionary contents himself with saying, "He seems to have lived under the early Roman Emperors." C. Müller, the special authority for all Greek geographical questions, sums up his critical examination of the evidence to the point: "Probant scriptorem nostrum Augusti temporibus debere fuisse proximum."—Geog. Grec. Min. vol. i. p. lxxxv.

[3] 17. Ἐντεῦθεν Ζαραγγιανὴ, σχοῖνοι κα΄. Ἔνθα πόλις Πάριν καὶ Κορὸκ πόλις. 18. Ἐντεῦθεν Σακαστανὴ Σακῶν Σκυθῶν, ἣ καὶ Παραιτακηνὴ, σχοῖνοι ξγ΄. Ἔνθα Βαρδὰ πόλις καὶ Μὶν πόλις καὶ Παλακεντὶ πόλις καὶ Σιγὰλ πόλις· ἔνθα βασίλεια Σακῶν· καὶ πλησίον Ἀλεξάνδρεια πόλις (καὶ πλησίον Ἀλεξανδρόπολις πόλις)· κῶμαι δὲ ἕξ. Isidore of Charax, "Stathmi Parthici," ed. C. Müller, Paris, pp. 253, lxxxv. and xciii., map No. x. The text goes on to enumerate the stages up to *Alexandropolis* μητρόπολις Ἀραχωσίας, and concludes: Ἄχρι τούτου ἐστὶν ἡ τῶν Πάρθων ἐπικράτεια. I annex for the sake of comparison Ptolemy's list of the cities of Drangia, after the century and a half which is roughly estimated as the interval between the two geographers. Sigal and Sakastanè seem

names of *Sakastanè* or *Paraitakenè* with a capital city entitled *Sigal.*

The ancient Sigal may perhaps be identified with the modern site of *Sekooha*, the metropolis of a district of that name, which, in virtue of its position, its walls, and its wells, still claims pre-eminence among the cities of Seistán.[1]

And to complete the data, I now find on the surface of the

alike to have disappeared from the local map. 1. Προφθασία. 2. Ῥοῦδα. 3. Ἵννα. 4. Ἀρικάδα. 5. Ἄστα. 6. Ξαρξιάρη. 7. Νοστάνα. 8. Φαραζάνα. 9. Βιγίς. 10. Ἀριάσπη. 11. Ἀράνα.—Ptolemy, lib. vi. cap. 19; Hudson, vol. iii. p. 44; Journ. R A.S. Vol. X. p. 21, and Vol. XV. pp. 97, 150, 206; Darius' Inscription, Persian "Saka," Scythic "Sakka." The old term of سکان is preserved in all the intelligent Persian and Arabian writers. Majmal Al Tawáríkh, Journ. Asiatique, 1839 سکان شاه; Hamza Isfaháni سکان شاه p. 50; وسکان اسم لسجستان p. 51. And the Armenians adhere to the *Sakasdan.*—Moses of Khorene, French edition, vol. ii. p. 143; Whiston, pp. 301, 364; St.-Martin, L'Arménie, vol. ii. p. 18. "سجستان. Les villes principales sont: *Zalek*, *Kerkouyah*, *Hissoum*, *Zaranj*, et *Bost*, où l'on voit les ruines de l'écurie de Roustam, le Héros."—B. de Meynard, La Perse, p. 303. Other references to the geography of this locality will be found in Pliny vi. 21; Ouseley's Oriental Geography, p. 205; Anderson's Western Afghánistan, J.A.S. Bengal, 1849, p. 586; Leech (*Sekwa*), J.A.S.B., 1844, p. 117; Khanikoff, 'Asie Centrale,' Paris, 1861, p. 162 (*Sékouhé*); Ferrier's Travels, p. 430; Malcolm's Persia, vol. i. p. 67; Pottinger's Beloochistán, pp. 407–9; Burnouf's Yaçna, p. xcix.

[1] "This fortress is the strongest and most important in Seistán, because, being at 5 parasangs from the lake, water is to be obtained only in wells which have been dug within its *enceinte.* The intermediate and surrounding country being an arid parched waste, devoid not only of water, but of everything else, the besiegers could not subsist themselves, and would, even if provisioned, inevitably die of thirst. It contains about 1200 houses. . . . I have called it the capital of Seistán, but it is impossible to say how long it may enjoy that title."—Caravan Journeys of J. P. Ferrier, edited by H. D. Seymour, Esq., Murray, 1857, p. 419. "On the 1st February, 1872, made a 30 mile march to *Sekuha*, the more modern capital of Seistán . .; finally we found Sekuha itself amid utter desolation."—Sir F. J. Goldsmid. From R. Geog. Soc. 1873, p. 70. See also Sir H. Rawlinson's elaborate notes on Seistán, p. 282, "Si-koheh" [three hills], in the same volume. I may add in support of this reading of the name of the capital, that it very nearly reproduces the synonym of the obscure Greek Σιγάλ, in the counterpart Pehlvi ددول = سیکر Sí *gar* or *gal*, which stands equally for "three hills." Tabarí tells us that in the old language, "*guer* a le sens de montagne" (Zotenberg, vol. i p. 5), and Hamza Isfahání equally recognizes the *ger* as "colles et montes" (p. 37). The interchange of the *r*s and *l*s did not disturb the Iránian mind any more than the indeterminate use of *g*s and *k*s. See Journ. R.A.S. Vol. XII. pp. 265, 268, and Vol. XIII. p. 377. We need not carry on these comparisons further, but those who wish to trace identities more completely may consult Pictet, vol. i. p. 122, and follow out the Sanskrit *giri*, Slave *gora*, etc. Since the body of this note was set up in type, Sir F. Goldsmid's official report upon "Eastern Persia" has been published, and supplies the following additional

original coin, after the final A in ΣΑΚΑ, the Greek monogram [monogram], which apparently represents the ancient province, or provincial capital, of *Drangia*.[1]

HERAÜS, ṢAKA KING.

Silver. British Museum. *Unique.*

Obv. "Bust of a king, right, diademed and draped; border of reels and beads.

Rev. ΤΥΙΑΝΝΟΥΝΤΟΣ ΗΙΑΟΥ

ΣΑΚΑ

ΚΟΙΙΑΝΟΥ.

(Τυραννοῦντος Ἡράου Σάκα κοιράνου.)

A king, right, on horseback; behind, NIKE, crowning him.[2]"

details as to the characteristics of Sikoha:—"The town, . . . which derives its name from three clay or mud hills in its midst, is built in an irregular circular form around the base of the two principal hills. The southernmost of these hills is surmounted by the *ark* or citadel, an ancient structure known as the citadel of Mir Kuchak Khân. . . . Adjoining this, and connected with it, is the second hill, called the Búrj-i-Falaksar, on which stands the present Governor's house; and about 150 yards to the west is the third hill, not so high as the other two, undefended. . . . The two principal hills thus completely command the town lying at their base, and are connected with one another by a covered way." "Sekuha is quite independent of an extra-mural water supply, as water is always obtainable by digging a few feet below the surface anywhere inside the walls, which are twenty-five feet in height, strongly built."—Major E. Smith, vol. i. p. 258.

[1] The progressive stages of this Monogram are curious. We have the normal [monogram].—Mionnet, pl. i. No. 12; Lindsay, Coins of the Parthians, pl. xi. No. 7. Next we have the Bactrian varieties [monogram], [monogram], and [monogram], entered in Prinsep's Essays, pl. xi. c. No. 53; Num. Chron. vol. xix. O.S. Nos. 48, 52, and vol. viii. N.S. pl. vii. Nos. 71, 72, and 76; and likewise Mionnet's varieties, Nos. 156, 299: Ariana Antiqua, pl. xxii. No. 118.

[2] I am indebted to Mr. P. Gardner for this woodcut. I retain his description of the coin as it appeared in the Numismatic Chronicle, 1874, vol. xiv. N.S. p. 161. It will be seen that Mr. Gardner failed to detect the worn outline of the Monogram.

Colonel Pearse, R.A., retains a single example of an exceptionally common class of small *silver* coins displaying the obverse head in identical form with the outline in the woodcut. The reverse type discloses an ill-defined, erect figure, to the left, similar in disjointed treatment to some of the reverses in the Antiochus-Kodes class,[1] accompanied by two parallel legends in obscure Greek. The leading line, *giving the title*, is altogether unintelligible; but its central letters range ×□ΙΔΙΙΝ× or ×□ΙΑΙΙΚ×. The second line gives a nearer approach to "Moas" in a possible initial M, followed by the letters ꟻ□ΙΙΔΗL=*μοιιδης*, *μοπρης*, *μοιιαης*, etc. All these specimens, in addition to other Kodes associations, give outward signs of debased metal, or the Nickel, which was perchance, in those days, estimated as of equal value with silver.[2]

The interest in this remarkable coin is not confined to the approximate identifications of time and place, but extends itself to the tenor of the legend, which presents us with the unusual titular prefix of *Τυραννοῦντος*, which, as a synonym of *Βασιλεύοντος*, and here employed by an obvious subordinate, may be held to set at rest the disputed purport of the latter term, in opposition to the simple *Βασιλεύς*, which has such an important bearing upon the relative positions of the earlier Bactrian Kings. The examples of the use of the term *Βασιλεύοντος* in the preliminary Bactrian series are as follows[3]:—

1. Agathocles in subordination to Diodotus	Obv. ΔΙΟΔΟΤΟΥ ΣΩΤΗΡΟΣ. Rev. ΒΑΣΙΛΕΥΟΝΤΟΣ ΑΓΑΘΟΚΛΕΟΥΣ ΔΙΚΑΙΟΥ.
2. Agathocles in subordination to Euthydemus	Obv. ΕΥΘΥΔΗΜΟΥ ΘΕΟΥ. Rev. ΒΑΣΙΛΕΥΟΝΤΟΣ ΑΓΑΘΟΚΛΕΟΥΣ ΔΙΚΑΙΟΥ.
3. Agathocles in subordination to Antiochus	Obv. ΑΝΤΙΟΧΟΥ ΝΙΚΑΤΟΡΟΣ. Rev. ΒΑΣΙΛΕΥΟΝΤΟΣ ΑΓΑΘΟΚΛΕΟΥΣ ΔΙΚΑΙΟΥ.
4. Antimachus Theus in subordination to Diodotus	Obv. ΔΙΟΔΟΤΟυ ΣΩΤΗΡΟΣ. Rev. ΒΑΣΙΛΕΥΟΝΤΟΣ ΑΝΤΙΜΑΧΟΥ ΘΕΟΥ.

[1] Num. Chron. vol. iv. N.S. p. 209, pl. viii. fig. 7.

[2] J.R.A.S., Vol. IV. N.S. p. 504; Records of the Gupta Dynasty, p. 38.

[3] M. de Bartholomæi, Koehne's Zeitschrift, 1843, p. 67, pl. iii. fig. 2; Reply to M. Droysen, Zeitschrift für Münz, 1846; my papers in Prinsep's Essays (1858), vol. i. p. xvi., vol. ii. pp. 178–183; in the Numismatic Chronicle, vol. ii. 1862, p. 186; and Journ. R. A. S., Vol. XX. 1863, p. 126; M. Raoul Rochette, Journal des Savants, 1844, p. 117; Droysen, Geschichte des Hellenismus, Hamburg,

The whole question as to the relative rank of the princes, whose names figure conjointly in the above legends, reduces itself concisely to this contrast, that the sub-king invariably calls himself *βασιλεύς* on his own proper coins, but on these exceptional tributary pieces, where he prefixes the image and superscription of a superior, he describes himself as *βασιλεύοντος*. These alien Satraps were effective kings within their own domains, but clearly bowed to some acknowledged head of the Bactro-Greek confederation, after the manner of their Indian neighbours, or perchance included subjects, who so especially regarded the gradational import of the supreme *Mahárajadhirája*, in contradistinction to the lesser degrees of regal state implied in the various stages of *rája*, *mahárája*, *rájádhirája*, etc. These binominal pieces are rare, and, numismatically speaking, "occasional," *i.e.* coined expressly to mark some public event or political incident, like our modern *medals*; coincident facts, which led me long ago to suggest[1] that they might have been struck as nominal tribute money or fealty pieces, in limited numbers, for submission with the annual *nazaráná*, or presentation at high State receptions, to the most powerful chief or general of the Græco-Bactrian oligarchy for the time being.

There is a curious feature in these binominal coins, which, as far as I am aware of, has not hitherto been noticed. It is, that the *obverse* head, representing the portrait of the superior king, seems to have been adopted directly from his own ordinary mint-dies,[2] which in their normal form presented

1843; Lassen, Ind. Alt., 1847; Gen. Cunningham, Numismatic Chronicle, vol. viii. N.S. 1868, p. 278, et seq., ix. 1869, p. 29; Mr. Vaux, Numismatic Chronicle, vol. xv. N.S. p. 15.

[1] Journal Royal Asiatic Society, Vol. XX. p. 127; Numismatic Chronicle, N.S. vol. ii. p. 186.

[2] I have long imagined that I could trace the likeness of Antiochus Theos on the obverse of the early gold coins of Diodotus (Prinsep's Essays, pl. xlii. 1; Num. Chron. vol. ii. N.S. pl. iv. figs. 1–3). I suppose, however, that in this case the latter monarch used his suzerain's ready-prepared die for the one face of his precipitate and perhaps hesitating coinage, conjoined with a new reverse device bearing his own name, which might have afforded him a loophole of escape on his "right to coin" being challenged. Apart from the similarity of the profile, the contrast between the high Greek art and perfect execution of the obverse head, and the coarse design and superficial tooling of the imitative reverse device, greatly favours the conclusion of an adaptation, though the motive may have been merely to utilize the *obverses* of existing mint appliances of such high merit.

the profile of the monarch without any surrounding legend, his name and titles being properly reserved for their conventional position on the *reverse* surface of his current coins. In the novel application of the head of the suzerain to a place on the *obverse* of a coin bearing the device and designations of his confessed subordinate on the *reverse*, it became necessary to add to the established obverse-device a specification of the name and titles of the superior, whose identification would otherwise have remained dependent upon the fidelity and the public recognition of the likeness itself. Hence, under the new adaptation, it likewise became requisite to engrave on the old die, around the standard Mint head, the suzerain's superscription in the odd corners and spaces in the field, no provision having been made, in the first instance, for any legend at all, and no room being left for the ordinary circular or perpendicular arrangement of the words, such as would have been spaced out under ordinary circumstances. In the majority of the instances we are able to cite, the Greek letters on the *adapted obverse* vary materially in their forms and outlines from those of the associated legends on the *reverse*, which still further proves the independent manipulation applied to the obverses of the compound pieces.

In addition to these indications as bearing upon the Bactrian proper coinage, the title of *Τυραννοῦντος* is highly suggestive in its partial reappearance on the coins of the leading Sáh Kings Nahapana and Chastana, connecting the Scythic element geographically to the southward with the province of Guzerát, for a full *résumé* of which I must refer my readers to the Archæological Report of Western India,[1] for 1875.

[1] See also the short copies of my Essay on the Records of the Gupta Dynasty, London, 1876, p. 31.

THE EARLY FAITH OF AṢOKA.

BY

E. THOMAS, F.R.S.

In most of the modern discussions on the ancient religions of India, the point at issue has been confined to the relative claims to priority of Buddhism and Brahmanism, a limitation which has led to a comparative ignoring of the existence of the exceptionally archaic creed of the Jainas.

This third competitor for the honours of precedence has lately been restored to a very prominent position, in its archæological *status*, by the discovery of numerous specimens of the sculptures and inscriptions of its votaries on the sacred site of Mathurá, the *Μόδουρα ἡ τῶν Θεῶν* of the Greeks,[1] that admit of no controversy, either as to the normal date or the typical import of the exhumed remains.

This said Mathurá on the Jumna constituted, from the earliest period, a "high place" of the Jainas, and its memory[2] is preserved in the southern capital of the same name, the *Μόδουρα, βασίλειον Πανδίονος* of Ptolemy, whence the sect, in after-times, disseminated their treasured knowledge, under the peaceful shelter of their *Matams* (colleges)[3] in aid of

[1] Ptolemy, Μέθορα, Arrian (quoting Megasthenes), Indica viii. *Methora*, Pliny, vi. 22.

[2] F. Buchanan, Mysore, iii. 81, "Uttara Madura, on the Jumna."

[3] The modern version of the name of the city on the Jumna is मथुरा *Mathurá*. Babu Rajendralála has pointed out that the old Sanskrit form was मधुरा *Madhurá* (J.A.S. Bengal, 1874, p. 259), but both transcriptions seem to have missed the true derivative meaning of मठ *Maṭha* (hodie مٹھ), "a monastery, a convent or college, a temple," etc., from the root मठ् "to dwell,"

local learning and the reviving literature of the Peninsula.[1]

The extended geographical spread of Jaina edifices has lately been contrasted, and compactly exhibited, in Mr. Fergusson's Map of the architectural creeds of India;[2] but a more important question regarding the primary origin of their buildings is involved in the sites chosen by their founders: whence it would appear that the Jainas must have exercised the first right of selection, for the purposes of their primitive worship, of the most striking and appropriate positions, on hill-tops and imperishable rocks,[3] whose lower sections were honey-combed with their excavated shrines—from which vantage-ground and dependent caves they were readily displaced, in after-days, by appropriating Buddhists on the

as a hermit might abide in his cave. The southern revenue terms have preserved many of the subordinate forms, in the shape of taxes for "Maṭhs." Rajputána and the N.W. Provinces exhibit extant examples in abundance of the still conventional term, while the distant Himálayas retain the word in Joshi-*Math*, Bhairava-*Math*, etc. The Vishnu Puráṇa pretends to derive the name from *Madhu*, a local demon (i. 164), while the later votaries of Kṛishna associate it with the Gopí's "churn" *math*.—Growse, Mathurá Settlement Report, 1874, vol. i. p. 50.

[1] "The period of the predominance of the Jainas (a predominance in intellect and learning—rarely a predominance in political power) was the Augustan age of Tamil literature, the period when the Madura College, a celebrated literary association, appears to have flourished, and when the Kuraḷ, the Chintámaṇi, and the classical vocabularies and grammars were written."—Caldwell, p. 86. See also p. 122. "The *Jaina cycle*. I might perhaps have called this instead *the cycle of the Madura Sangam or College*."—p. 128. Dr. Caldwell, Grammar of the Dravidian Languages, London, 1875.

[2] History of Indian and Eastern Architecture; Murray, London, 1876, Map, p. 47.

[3] The late Mr. G. W. Traill has preserved an illustration of the innate tendency of the aboriginal mind to revert to primitive forms of worship, which almost reminds us of the party-coloured Pigeons of Norfolk Island, which, when left to their own devices, reverted to the normal type of Blue Rock. He observes: "The sanctity of the Himalaya in Hindu mythology by no means necessarily implies the pre-existence of the Hindu religion in this province (Kumaon), as the enormous height and grandeur of that range, visible from the plains, would have been sufficient to recommend it as a scene for the penances of gods and heroes. . . . The great bulk of the population are now Hindus in prejudices and customs, rather than in religion. Every remarkable mountain, peak, cave, forest, fountain and rock has its presiding demon or spirit, to which frequent sacrifices are offered, and religious ceremonies continually performed by the surrounding inhabitants at small temples erected on the spot. These temples are extremely numerous throughout the country, and new ones are daily being erected; while the temples dedicated to Hindu deities, in the interior, are, with few exceptions, deserted and decayed."—G. W. Traill, As. Res., xvi. p. 161. See also J.R.A.S. Vol. VIII. p. 397; Vol. XIII. "Khond Gods," pp. 233-6; "Aboriginal Gods," p. 285. Hunter's Rural Bengal, pp. 130, 182, etc.

one part, or ousted and excluded by the more arrogant and combative Brahmans on the other.

The introductory phase in the consecutive order of the present inquiry involves the consideration of the conflicting claims to priority of the Jainas and the Buddhists. Some half a century ago, Colebrooke, echoing the opinions of previous commentators, seems to have been fully prepared to admit that Buddhism was virtually an emanation from anterior Jainism. We have now to examine how far subsequent evidence confirms this once bold deduction. Unquestionably, by all the laws of religious development, of which we have lately heard so much, the more simple faith, *per se*,[1] must be primarily accepted as the precursor of the more complicated and philosophical system,[2] confessing a common origin.

Colebrooke summarized his conclusions to the following effect:

"It is certainly probable, as remarked by Dr. Hamilton and Major Delamaine,[3] that the Gautama of the Jainas and of the Bauddhas is the same personage: and this leads to the further surmise, that both sects are branches of one stock. According to the Jainas, only one of Mahávíra's eleven disciples left spiritual successors: that is, the entire succession of Jaina priests is derived

[1] "The ritual of the Jainas is as simple as their moral code. The *Yati*, or devotee, dispenses with acts of worship at his pleasure, and the lay votary is only bound to visit daily a temple where some of the images of the *Tírthankaras* are erected, walk round it three times, and make an obeisance to the images, with an offering of some trifle, usually fruit or flowers, and pronounce some such *Mantra* or prayer as the following: '*Namo Arihantánam, Namo Siddhánam*,' . . 'Salutation to the *Arhats*,' etc. A morning prayer is also repeated: . . 'I beg forgiveness, O Lord, for your slave, whatever evil thoughts the night may have produced—I bow with my head.' . . The reader in a Jaina temple is a *Yati*, or religious character; but the ministrant priest, the attendant on the images, the receiver of offerings, and conductor of all usual ceremonies, is a *Brahmán*."—Wilson's Essays, vol i. p. 319. "I may remark, parenthetically, with a view to what is still to be established—that the Khandagiri Inscription opens with the self-same invocation, 'NAMO ARAHANTÁNAM, NAMO SAVA SIDHÁNAM,' 'Salutation to the *arhantas*, glory to all the saints' (or those who have attained final emancipation!)."—Prinsep, J.A.S.B. vol. vi. p. 1080.

[2] "Buddhism (to hazard a character in a few words) is monastic asceticism in morals, philosophical scepticism in religion; and whilst ecclesiastical history all over the world affords abundant instances of such a state of things resulting from gross abuse of the religious sanction, that ample chronicle gives us no one instance of it as an original system of belief. Here is a legitimate inference from sound premises; but that Buddhism was, in very truth, a reform or heresy, and *not* an original system, can be proved by the most abundant direct testimony of friends and enemies."—B. H. Hodgson, J.R.A.S. (1835), Vol. II. p. 290.

[3] Major J. Delamaine, Trans. R.A.S. Vol. I. pp. 413–438.

from one individual, Sudharma-swámí. Two only out of eleven survived Mahávíra, viz. Indrabhúti and Sudharma: the first, identified with Gautama-swámí, has no spiritual successors in the Jaina sect. The proper inference seems to be, that the followers of this surviving disciple are not of the sect of Jina, rather than that there have been none. . . . .

"I take Párṣwanátha to have been the founder of the sect of Jainas, which was confirmed and thoroughly established by Mahávíra and his disciple Sudharma. . . . . A schism, however, seems to have taken place, after Mahávíra, whose elder disciple, Indrabhúti, also named Gautama-swámí, was by some of his followers raised to the rank of a deified saint, under the synonymous designation of Buddha (for Jina and Buddha bear the same meaning, according to both Buddhists and Jainas)."—Transactions of the R.A.S. (1826), Vol. I. p. 520; and Prof. Cowell's edition of Colebrooke's collected Essays, vol. ii. p. 278.[1]

At the time when Colebrooke wrote, the knowledge of the inner history of Buddhism was limited in the extreme. Our later authorities contribute many curious items and suggestive coincidences, tending more fully to establish the fact that Buddhism was substantially an offshoot of Jainism. For example, Ananda is found, in some passages of recognized authority, directly addressing Gotama *himself* in his own

[1] Professor Wilson, writing in 1832 on the "Religious Sects of the Hindus," objected to this inference of Colebrooke's, on the ground of the supposed contrast of the *castes* of the two families. It is, however, a question, now that we know more of the gradual developments of *caste* in India, whether the divisions and subdivisions, relied upon by Prof. Wilson, had assumed anything like so definite a form, as his argument would imply, at so early a period as the date of the birth of Sákya Muni. Professor Wilson's observations are as follows:—"When Mahávíra's fame began to be widely diffused, it attracted the notice of the *Brahmans* of *Magadha*, and several of their most eminent teachers undertook to refute his doctrines. Instead of effecting their purpose, however, they became converts, and constituted his *Gaṇadharas*, heads of schools, the disciples of Mahávíra and teachers of his doctrines, both orally and scripturally. It is of some interest to notice them in detail, as the epithets given to them are liable to be misunderstood, and to lead to erroneous notions respecting their character and history. This is particularly the case with the first Indrabhúti, or Gautama, who has been considered as the same with the Gautama of the Bauddhas, the son of Máyádeví, and author of the Indian metaphysics. That any connexion exists between the *Jain* and the Bráhmaṇa Sage is, at least, very doubtful; but the Gautama of the *Bauddhas*, the son of Ṣuddhodana and Máyá, was a *Kshattriya*, a prince of the royal or warrior caste. All the Jain traditions make their Gautama a *Brahman* originally of the *gotra*, or tribe of Gotama *Rishi*, a division of the *Brahmans* well known and still existing in the South of India. These two persons therefore cannot be identified, whether they be historical or fictitious personages."—H. H. Wilson's Essays, vol. i. p. 298; Asiatic Res. vol. xvii.

proper person, and speaking of the "twenty-four Buddhas, who had immediately preceded him."[1] On other occasions the twenty-four Jaina *Tírthankaras* are reduced in the sacred texts of their supplanters to the six authorized antecedent Buddhas, or expanded at will into 120 *Tathágatas* or Buddhas, with their more deliberately fabulous multiplications.[2]

The Maháwanso, in like manner, has not only allowed the reference to the "twenty-four supreme Buddhos" to remain in its text,[3] but has given their conventional names—which however have little in common with the Jaina list—in the order of succession. Mahanámo's Tíká[4] has preserved the catalogue, in its more complete form, specifying the parentage, place of birth and distinctive "*Bo-trees*"[5] of each of the "twenty-four *Buddhos*," and concluding, after a reference to Kassapo (born at *Benares*), with Gotamo (a Brahman named Jotipálo at Wappula), "the *Buddho* of the present system, and *Mettéyo* [who] is still to appear." This amplification and elaborate discrimination of sacred trees has also a suspicious air of imitation about it, as we know that Ward was only able to discover six varieties of Indian trees nominally sacred to the gods,[6] and Mr. Fergusson's exami-

1 Spence Hardy, Manual of Buddhism, pp. 88, 94, 311.

2 B. Hodgson, Asiatic Researches, vol. xvi. p. 444, "Sarvárthasiddha observes, he has given so many [120] names *exempli gratia*, but his instructors were really no less in number than 80 crores." In other places Mr. Hodgson expresses his doubts "as to the historical existence of Ṣâkya's six predecessors."—Works, p. 135, and J.R.A.S. Vol. II. p. 289. See also Csoma de Körös, J.A.S.B. vol. vii. p. 143. "Immense is the number of such Buddhas that have appeared in former ages in several parts of the universe."

3 Cap. i. p. 1.

4 Maháwanso, Turnour's Introduction, Ceylon, 1837, p. xxxii.

5 The "Bo-trees of the twenty-four Buddhos" are given in the following order (Maháwanso, p. xxxii):

1. Pippala.	9. Sonaka.	17. Assana.
2. Sálakalyána.	10. Salala.	18. Amalaka.
3. Nága.	11. Nipa.	19. Pátali.
4. Do.	12. Welu.	20. Pundariko.
5. Do.	13. Kakudha.	21. Sála.
6. Do.	14. Champá.	22. Sirísa.
7. Ajjuna.	15. Bimbajála.	23. Udumbara.
8. Sonaka.	16. Kanihâni.	24. Nigrodha.

As this list is quoted merely to contrast the numbers 24 against 7, it would be futile to follow out the botanical names of the various *Bo-trees;* but it may be remarked *en passant*, that No. 3 is a tree of the wet forests of Assam, Concan, Malabar, and Ceylon, while No. 11 is a palm-like plant which is entirely *maritime*, and abounds in the Sundarbands, wherein we have no record of Buddhist "sittings."

6 Vol. i. p. 263.

nation of all the extant Buddhist representations of their Bo-trees does not carry the extreme total beyond the legitimate "six or seven species altogether."[1]

Another indication which may prove of some import in this inquiry is to be gleaned from the Chinese text of the Travels of the Buddhist Pilgrim *Fah-Hian* (400—415 A.D.), which, in describing the town of Srávastí, proceeds to advert to "the ninety-six heretical sects of mid-India," who "build hospices" (*Puṇyasálás*) etc., concluding with the remark, "Devadatta also has a body of disciples still existing; they pay religious reverence to the three past Buddhas, but not to Sákya Muni."[2]

Again, an instructive passage is preserved in the Tibetan text of the Lalita-vistara, where, under the French version, "Le jeune Sarvárthasiddha,"[3] the baby Buddha, is represented as wearing in his hair the *Ṣrivatsa*, the *Swastika*, the *Nandyávarta* and the *Vardhamána*, the *three* symbols severally of the 10th, 7th and 18th Jaina Tírthankaras, and the *fourth* constituting the alternative designation of Mahávíra, and indicating his *mystic* device, which differed from his ordinary cognizance in the form of a lion.[4] Further on, the merits

[1] Tree and Serpent Worship, p. 116. Among the sculptures lately discovered at Barahát, are to be found "representations of five separate Bodhi-trees of as many different Buddhas, which are distinctly labelled as follows:—

(1). *Bhagavato Vipasino Bodhi*, that is, the Tree of *Vipasyin* or *Vipaswi*, the first of the seven Buddhas.

(2). *Bhagavato Kakusadhasa Bodhi.*

(3). *Bhagavato Konagamana Bodhi.*

(4). *Bhagavato Kasapasa Bodhi.*

(5). *Bhagavato Sakamunino Bodhi.*

These last are the four well-known Buddhists named *Krakuchhanda*, *Konágamani*, *Kásyapa*, and *Sákyamuni*." It is scarcely necessary for me to add, that I by no means concur in the early date attributed by General Cunningham to these sculptures.

[2] Rev. S. Beal, Travels of Fah-Hian, p. 82. *Foe koue ki*, cap. xx. Remusat's *Note* 35. Laidlay, pp. 168, 179. Spence Hardy, alluding to these sectaries, says, "they are called in general *Tírthakars*."—Manual of Buddhism, p. 290.

[3] "Grand roi, le jeune Sarvárthasiddha a au milieu de la chevelure un Çrívatsa, un Svastika, un Nandyávarta et un Vardhamâna. Grand roi, ce sont là les quatre-vingts marques secondaires du jeune Sarvárthasiddha." . . . Foucaux, p. 110. "Pendant qu'elle le préparait ces signes précurseurs apparurent: Au milieu de ce lait, un Çrivatsa, un Svastika, un Nandyávarta, un lotus, un Vardhamâna (Diagramme particulier dont la forme n'est pas indiquée), et d'autres signes de bénédiction se montrérent."—Cap. viii. p. 258 (see also pp. 305, 390).

[4] Colebrooke's Essays, vol. ii. p. 188. Asiatic Researches, vol. ix. p. 304. J.R.A.S. Vol. I. N.S. pp. 475-481. J.A.S. Bengal, vol. vii. p. 143. Burnouf, Lotus, pp. 624-645. Col. Low, Transactions R.A.S. Vol. III.

of the young Buddha are adverted to as, "qui est apparu par l'effet de la racine de la vertu des précédents Djinas."

The importance of these indications will be better appreciated, when it is understood that the twenty-four statues of the Jaina saints were all formed upon a single model, being indistinguishable, the one from the other, except by the *chinas* or subordinate marks on the pedestals, which constituted the discriminating *lakshanas* or *mudrás* of each individual Tírthankara. These crypto-devices were, in other cases, exhibited as frontal marks, or delegated to convenient positions on the breast and other parts of the nude statue. In this sense, Jainism may be said to have been a religion of signs and symbols, comprehending many simple objects furnished by nature and further associated with enigmatical and *Tantric* devices, the import of which is a mystery to modern intelligence.[1]

The following is a list of the twenty-four

Jaina Tírthankaras, with their Parentage and Discriminating Symbols.[2]

Names.	Symbols.
1. Ṛishabha, of the race of *Ikshwáku*, *Prathama Jina*, "the first Jina" .	a Bull
2. Ajita, son of *Jitaṣatru*	an Elephant
3. Sambhava, son of *Jitári*	a Horse
4. Abhinandana, son of *Sambara*	an Ape
5. Sumati, son of *Megha*	a Curlew
6. Padmaprabha, son of *Ṣrídhara* . . .	a Lotus
7. Supárṣwa, son of *Pratishṭha*	a *Swastika*
8. Chandraprabha, son of *Mahásena* . .	the Moon
9. Pushpadanta, or Suvidhi, son of *Supriya*	an Alligator
10. Ṣitala, son of *Dṛidharatha*	a *Ṣrivatsa*

[1] In modern times, Mr. Hodgson tells us, he was able to discriminate statues, which passed with the vulgar for any god their priests chose to name, by the crucial test of their "minute accompaniments" and "frontal appendages."—J.R.A.S. Vol. XVIII. p. 395. See, also, the Chinese-Buddhist inscription from Keu-Yung Kwan, with its *mudrás*, and Mr. Wylie's remarks upon *dháranis*.—J.R.A.S. Vol. V. N.S. p. 22.

[2] Colebrooke's Essays, vol. ii. p. 187; As. Res. vol. ix. p. 305. Mr. Burgess, Indian Antiquary, 1873, vol. i. p. 134.

	Names.	Symbols.
11.	Ṣreyán (or Ṣriyánsa), son of *Vishṇu* . .	a Rhinoceros
12.	Vásupújya, son of *Vasupújya*	a Buffalo
13.	Vimala, son of *Kṛitavarman*	a Boar
14.	Ananta (Anantajit), son of *Sinhasena* .	a Falcon
15.	Dharma, son of *Bhánu*	a Thunderbolt
16.	Ṣánti, son of *Viṣwasena*	an Antelope
17.	Kunthu, son of *Súra*	a Goat
18.	Ara, son of *Sudarṣana*	a *Nandyávarta*
19.	Malli, son of *Kumbha*	a Jar
20.	Munisuvrata (Suvrata), son of *Sumitra* .	a Tortoise
21.	Nimi, son of *Vijaya*	blue Water-lily
22.	Nemi (or Arishṭanemi), s. of *Samudrajaya*	a Conch
23.	Párṣwa (Párṣwanátha), son of *Aṣwasena*	a hooded Snake
24.	Vardhamána, also named *Vira*, *Mahávira*, etc., surnamed *Charama-tirthakṛit*, or "last of the Jinas," "emphatically called *Ṣramaṇa* or the saint," son of Siddhártha	a Lion.[1]

In addition to these discriminating symbols, the different Tírthankaras are distinguished by the tint of their complexions. No. 1 is described as of a yellow or golden complexion, which seems to have been the favourite colour,

[1] Dr. Stevenson has tabulated some further details of the Jaina symbolic devices in "Trisala's Dreams":

Elephant.	Bull.	Lion-Tiger.	Lakshmí.	A Garland.
Moon.	Sun.	Standard.	Jar.	Lotus Lake.
The Sea.	Heavenly Mansion.	Trisala.	Heap of Pearls.	Flameless Fire.

Lucky figures, [1]Srivatsa, [2]Satvika, [3]Throne, [4]Flower-pot, [5]couple of Fishes, [6]Mirror, [7]Nandiyávarta, [8]Vardhamána.—Kalpa Sutra, page i.

Dr. Stevenson has an instructive note upon Jaina emblems, which I append to his Table:—"In the prefixed scheme of the emblems of the different Tírthankaras, it may strike the reader that there is no vestige of anything like this Buddhist Chaitya in any of them. This arises from one remarkable feature of dissimilarity between the Jains and Buddhists. The Dagoba, or Buddhist

Nos. 6 and 12 rejoice in a "red" complexion, Nos. 8 and 9 are designated as "fair," No. 19 is described as "blue," and No. 20 as "black." Párṣwanátha is likewise "blue," while Mahávíra reverts to the typical "golden" hue, the सुवर्ण छवि *Suvarṇa chhavi*, "the golden form" claimed alike for Sákya Muni.[1]

In illustration of this tendency to faith in emblems among the Jainas, I quote the independent opinion of Captain J. Low regarding the origin of the celebrated *Phrabát*, or ornamental impress of the feet of Buddha,[2] and his demonstration of the inconsistent and inappropriate assimilation of the worship of symbols with the higher pretensions of the creed of Sákya Muni:—

"As the Phrabát is an object claiming from the Indo-Chinese nations a degree of veneration scarcely yielding to that which they pay to Buddha himself, we are naturally led to inquire why the emblems it exhibits are not all adored individually as well as in the aggregate. It seems to be one of those inconsistencies which mark the character of Buddhist schismatics; and it may enable us more readily to reach the real source of their religion, from which so many superstitions have ramified to cross our path in eastern research. To whatever country or people we may choose to assign

Chaitya, was a place originally appropriated to the preservation of relics, a practice as abhorrent to the feelings of the Jainas as it is to those of the Brahmans. The word Chaitya, when used by the Jainas, means any image or temple dedicated to the memory of a Tírthankara."—Kalpa Sutra, p. xxvi.

From quasi-Buddhist sources we derive independent Symbols of the Four Divisions of the *Vaibhdshika* School.

FOUR CLASSES.	SUBDIVISIONS.	DISTINCTIVE MARKS.
Rahula............... *Sakya's.*	4 sects, using the Sanskrit tongue	*Utpala padma* (water-lily) jewel, and tree-leaf put together in the form of a nosegay.
Kásyapa .... *Brahman's.*	6 sects, entitled "the great community," using a corrupt dialect............................	Shell or conch.
Upali .... *Súdra's.*	3 sects, styled "the class which is honored by many," using the language of the *Pisáchikas*	A *sortsika* flower.
Kátyáyana ..... *Vaisya's.*	3 sects, entitled "the class that have a fixed habitation," using the vulgar dialect.....	The figure of a wheel.

Csoma de Körös, J.A.S.B. vol. vii. p. 143.

[1] Asiatic Researches, vol. xv. p. 84.

[2] Examples of Jaina-Buddhist *Foot-prints* may be seen in Vol. III. N.S. of our Journal, p. 159.

the original invention of the *Phrabát*, it exhibits too many un doubted Hindu symbols to admit of our fixing its fabrication upon the worshippers of the latter Buddha; of whose positive dogmas it is rather subversive than otherwise, by encouraging polytheism. And further, the intent with which it was originally framed—namely, to embody in one grand symbol a complete system of theology and theogony—should seem to have been gradually forgotten, or perverted by succeeding ages to the purposes of a ridiculous superstition." —Capt. J. Low, "The Phrabát, or Divine Foot of Buddha from Bali and Siamese Books," Transactions R.A.S. Vol. II. p. 64.[1]

The existing traditions of the Jainas, on the other hand, consistently adhere to the reverence of nature's forms or the more elaborated diagrams and curious devices of their ancient creed,[2] which is here shown to have been incompatible with the advanced tenets of Buddhism. The Vaishṇavás, equally in their turn, had their *Vishṇu-pad*; but when we meet with the symbolical impression of the feet under their adaptative treatment, we find it decorated and adorned with a totally different series of minor emblems to those affected by the early Jainas.[3]

Dr. Stevenson, in editing the text of the leading Jaina authority, *the Kalpa Sútra*, in 1848,[4] arrived *independently* at

[1] A pertinent inquiry is made by R. Friederich in the last Number of our Journal (Vol. IX. N.S. p. 65): "Were the Buddhists of Java *Jainas*?"

[2] Col. W. Franklin, in his account of the Temple of Párswanátha at Samet-Ṣikhar, describes the statues as having the "head fashioned like a turban, with seven expanded heads of serpents, *Coluber Naga*, or hooded snake, the invariable symbol of Párswanátha." The summit of the hill, emphatically termed by the Jainas *Samet Ṣikhar*, comprises a table-land flanked by "twenty small Jaina temples. In them are to be found the *Vasu-Pádikas* or 'sacred feet,' similar to what are to be seen in the Jaina Temple at Châmpânagar. On the south side of the mountain is a very large and handsome flat-roofed temple, containing several figures of this deity, which exhibit the never-failing attributes of Párswanátha and the Jaina religion, viz. the crowned serpent and cross-legged figures of Jineṣwara or Jina, the ruler and guardian of mankind."—Asiatic Researches, vol. ix. pp. 528, 530. "In their temples, the Swetámbaras have images of all these persons (the twenty-four Jinas), which they worship; but their devotions are more usually addressed to what are called representations of their feet."—Dr. B. Hamilton, Mysore, p. 538.

[3] General Cunningham has published a fac-simile of the Gaya *Vishṇu-pad*, which, however, he designates in the Plate, "Buddha-pad," executed in A.D. 1308: in this, although many symbols of Indian origin and local currency are displayed, we miss the leading *Swastika*, and the other mystic diagrams more immediately associated with the Jaina and secondary Buddhist systems.—Arch. Rep., 1871, vol. i. p. 9, pl. vii.

[4] The extant MS. text of the Kalpa Sútra contains a record that "900 years after MAHÁVÍRA, and in the 80th year of the currency of the *tenth* hundred,

a similar conclusion with Colebrooke as to the relative positions of Jainism and Buddhism, in reference to their common source and the more recent innovations and arrogant assumptions of the latter creed. He sums up his remarks in the subjoined passage:

"There are, however, yet one or two other points in the accounts the Jains give us, which seem to have a historic bearing. The first is the relation said to have subsisted between the last Buddha and the last Tírthankara, the Jains making Mahávíra Gautama's preceptor, and him the favourite pupil of his master. . . . . In favour of the Jain theory (of priority), however, it may be noticed, that Buddha is said to have seen 24 of his predecessors (Mahávanso, I. c. i.), while in the present Kappo he had but four. The Jains, consistently with their theory, make Mahávíra to have seen 23 of his predecessors, all that existed before him in the present age. This part of Buddhism evidently implies the knowledge of the 24 Tírthankaras of the Jains. Gautama, however, by the force of natural genius, threw their system entirely into the shade, till the waning light of Buddhism permitted its fainter radiance to re-appear on the western horizon."[1]—Kalpa Sútra, London, 1848, p. xii.

Dr. Stevenson was peculiarly competent to express an opinion on this and collateral questions, as he had made the "ante-Brahmanical worship of the Hindus"[2] a subject of his especial study, during his lengthened career, as a missionary in the Dekhan, in direct association with the people of the land. Among other matters bearing upon Jainism, he gives an instructive account of the process of making a god, as traced in the instance of VIṬṬAL or VITHOBA, commencing with the "rough unhewn stone of a pyramidical or triangular shape,"[3] which formed the centre of the druidical

this Book was written and publicly read in the currency of the 93rd year." Hence, taking Mahávíra's period at 503 B.C., its date is fixed at "454 A.D. and its publication at 466 A.D."—Stevenson's Kalpa Sutra, p. 95. Colebrooke's Essays, vol. ii. p. 193.

[1] "After writing the above I found my conclusion anticipated by Mr. Colebrooke, and I am happy that it now goes abroad with the suffrage of so learned an Orientalist—Trans. R.A.S. Vol. I. p. 522."

[2] J.R.A.S. Vol. V. pp. 189, 264; Vol. VI. p. 239; Vol. VIII. p. 330. See also J.A.S. Bengal, articles on cognate subjects, vol. iii. (1834), p. 495; vol. vi. p. 498.

[3] J.R.A.S. (1839), Vol. V. p. 193 *et seq.* Among other questions adverted to, Dr. Stevenson remarks:—"Veṭṭal is generally, in the Dekhan, said to be an *Avatár* of

circle of similarly-shaped blocks—proceeding, in the second stage, to their adornment with red-ochre tipped with white, to imitate fire, the further development of the central block into "a human figure," "with two arms," and its coincident promotion to the shelter of a temple with more complicated rites and ceremonies; and, finally, in other cases, to the transformation of "the form of a man, but without arms or legs," into "a fierce and gigantic man, perfect in all his parts."[1]

Dr. Stevenson, in a subsequent article,[2] followed up his comparison of the later images of *Vithoba*[3] with the normal ideals of the Jaina *nude* statues. One of his grounds for these identifications is stated in the following terms: "The want of suitable costume in the images (of Vithoba and Rakhami), as originally carved, in this agreeing exactly with the images the Jainas at present worship, and disagreeing with all others adored by the Hindus"—who, "with all their faults, had always sense of propriety enough to carve their images so as to represent the gods to the eye arrayed in a way not to give offence to modesty."

The author then goes on to relate how the Brahmanists of

Ṣiva, and wonderful exploits performed by him are related in a book called the Veṭṭal Pachísi; but which composition has not had the good fortune to gain the voice of the Brahmans and be placed among the Máhátmyas. On the contrary, they look upon it merely as a parcel of fables, and dispute the claims of Veṭṭal to any divine honours whatever."—Dr. Stevenson, J.R.A.S. Vol. V. p. 192.

1 Dr. John Wilson, J.R.A.S. Vol. V. p. 197. "The temple of Vetál at Aráwalí, near Sáwant Wádí."

2 J.R.A.S. Vol. VII. p. 5.

3 The legend of the creation of Jaggannátha, accepted by his votaries, points to an equally simple origin, which, in this instance, took the form of a drift log of Nim-wood. This *dára* or "branch" having been pronounced on examination to be adorned with the emblems of the *Sanka*, *Gadá*, *Padma* and *Chakra*, was afterwards, by divine intervention, split "into the four-fold image of *Chatur Múrti*. A little colouring was necessary to complete them, and they then became recognized as Ṣri Krishna or Jagannáth, distinguished by its black hue, Báldeo, a form of Ṣiva, of a white colour, Subhadrá, the sister, . . of the colour of saffron."

In this case the Brahmans seem to have surpassed themselves in their theatrical adaptations, for they are said to have adopted a practice of dressing-up the figure of Ṣrí Jíú, in a costume appropriate to the occasion, to represent the principal deities of the ruling creeds. "Thus at the Rám Navamí, the great image assumes the dress and character of Ráma; at the Janam Ashtamí, that of Krishna; at the Kálí Pújá, that of Kálí," with two other alternative green-room transformations, which we need not reproduce.—Stirling's Orissa, Asiatic Researches, vol. xv. p. 318.

later days appropriated the sacred sites and adapted the very images of the local gods to their own purposes. His description is most graphic of the way in which the *nude* statues of Vithoba and *Rakhami*, at *Pandarpúr*, were clothed in appropriate Hindu garments and made to do duty for the Brahmanical *Krishna* and *Rukmini*. Not less caustic is the completion of the tale in the account of the "image-dresser's" appearance over night at feasts, in the borrowed habiliments of his patron god, to be restored for the benefit of the admiring multitude on the following morning.[1]

Among other suggestive inquiries, Dr. Stevenson has instituted a comparison between the equality of all men before their god—indicative of *pre-caste* periods—at the several shrines of Vithoba and Jaggannátha,[2] and the inferential claims of the Jainas to the origination of the ever-popular pilgrimage to the latter sanctuary. Incidentally, it may be mentioned that the title of "Jaggannátha is an appellation given by the modern Jainas to their *Tirthankara* Párswanátha in particular."[3] General Cunningham, in his work on the Bhílsa Topes,[4] long ago pointed out the absolute identity of the outline of the modern figures of Jagganátha with the *trisúl* or curved-trident ornament so frequent in the early Buddhist sculptures,[5] and, in like manner, Burnouf had detected the coincidence of the form of the *Vardhamánakya*, or mystic symbol of Mahávíra above adverted to, with the outline of the Bactro-Greek Monogram so common on the

[1] No less acute is Dr. Stevenson's analysis, in another volume of our Journal (Vol. VIII. p. 330), of the position traditionally held by Ṣiva in India—his absence "from the original Brahmanical theogony," his imperfect assimilation with the later forms of their ritual—and the conclusion "that the worship of Ṣiva is nothing more than a superstition of the aboriginal Indians, modified by the Brahmans, and adopted into their system," for their own ends. An opinion which has been fully confirmed by later investigations.

[2] Journal R.A.S. Vol. VII. p. 7, and Vol. VIII. p. 331. See also Col. Sykes, Vol. VI. p. 420, *note* 3.

[3] Journ. A.S., p. 423.

[4] "The triple emblem, represented in fig. 22, pl. xxxii., is one of the most valuable of the Sánchi sculptures, as it shows in the clearest and most unequivocal manner the absolute identity of the holy Brahmanical Jaggannáth with the ancient Buddhist triad."—Bhilsa Topes (London, 1854), p. 358. Fac-similes of these figures may be seen at p. 450, Journ. R.A.S., Vol. VI. o.s. See also Laidlay's translation of *Fo-kwe-ki*, pp. 21-26, 261.

[5] The symbol forms a distinct object of worship at Amravati.—Fergusson's "Tree and Serpent Worship," pl. lxx. etc.

local coins.[1] This last identification opens out a very wide field of speculation, inasmuch as this particular mark has now been found in all its integrity, on the person of a Jaina statue in the Indian Museum. Another coincidence which may prove to have some bearing upon the relative claims of Jainas and Buddhists to the Lion pillars,[2] and the frequent representations of that animal upon the sculptures on the Topes, etc., is that the Lion proves to have been a special emblem of *Mahávira,* as the mystic trident in its turn answered to his second title of *Vardhamána.*

Before taking leave of the question of the relations once existing between Mahávíra and Buddha, it remains for me to cite a most curious passage, furnishing a vivid outline of the intercourse between *Guru* and *Chela,* and foreshadowing the nascent doubts of the *disciple*—which occurs in the *Bhagavati,*[3] a work recently published by Prof. Weber, of the existence of which neither Colebrooke nor Wilson were cognizant. I may add in further support of the identity of *Gautama* and *Ṣakya Muni*—so freely admitted

[1] Burnouf, in noticing the 65 names of the figures traced on the supposed *Dharma pradipiká* or imprint of the foot of Buddha in Ceylon, remarks under the sixth or *Vardhamánakya* head: "C'est là encore une sorte de diagramme mystique également familier aux Bráhmanes et au Buddhistes; son nom signifie "le prospère."

"Quant à la figure suivante, on trouvera peut-être qu'elle doit être le Vardhamâna; je remarquerai seulement sur la seconde, , qu'elle est ancienne, et on la remarque fréquemment au revers des médailles de Kadphises et de quelques autres médailles indo-scythiques au type du roi cavalier et vainqueur (A.A. pl. x. 5, 9 *a*), et sur le troisième, qu'elle paraît n'être qu'une variante de la seconde."—Lotus, p. 627. "Waḍḍhamánañ kumárikañ." Mahávanso, I. c. xi. p. 70. Col. Sykes, J.R.A.S. VI. o.s. p. 456, No. 34, etc.

[2] The Kuhaon pillar is manifestly Jaina, though there is this to be said, that it is more fully wrought than the ordinary round monoliths, some of which Aṣoka may have found ready to his hand. It bears the inscription of Skanda Gupta (219 A.D.), but this need no more detract from its true age than the modern inscription of Vísala deva of A.D. 1164 would disturb the prior record of Aṣoka on the Dehli (Khizrábád) láṭ. "The bell (of the capital) itself is reeded, after the fashion of the Aṣoka pillars. Above this the capital is square, with a small niche on each side holding a naked standing figure, surmounted by a low circular band, in which is fixed the metal spike already described, as supporting a statue of a lion, or some other animal rampant. . . . . . On the western face of the square base there is a niche holding a naked standing figure, with very long arms reaching to his knees. Behind, there is a large snake folded in horizontal coils, one above the other, and with its seven heads forming a canopy over the idol."—General Cunningham, Arch. Rep. i. p. 93.

[3] Fragment der Bhagavatí. Ein beitrag zur kenntniss der heiligen litteratur und sprache der Jaina. Von A. Weber, Berlin, 1867, p. 315. The author, a Jaina writer named *Malayagiri*, flourished in the thirteenth century A.D.

in previous quotations[1]—that the Iranian texts equally designate him by the former epithet.[2] And it is to be remembered that Buddhism very early made its way in force over parts of Bactria—as the construction of the *Nau Bihár* at Balkh, lately identified by Sir H. Rawlinson,[3] suffices to prove. An edifice which Hiouen Thsang commemorates as "qui a été construit par le premier roi de ce royaume."[4]

"At that time, then, at that juncture, the holy Mahâvîra's eldest pupil, Indrabhûti,—houseless, of Gautama's Gotra, seven (cubits) high, of even and regular proportions, with joints as of diamond, bull and arrow, fair like the streak on a touchstone or like lotus pollen, of mighty, shining, burning, powerful penance, pre-eminent, mighty, of mighty qualities, a mighty ascetic, of mighty abstinence, of dried-up body, of compact mighty resplendency, possessed of the fourteen preliminary steps, endowed with the four kinds of knowledge, acquainted with all the ways of joining syllables, in moderate proximity to the holy Çramaṇa Mahâvîra, with knees erect and lowered head, endowed with a treasury of meditation,—lived edifying himself by asceticism and the bridling of his senses.

"Thereupon that holy Gautama, in whom faith, doubt, and curiosity arose, grew and increased, rose up. Having arisen he went to the place where the sacred Çramaṇa Mahâvîra was. After going there, he honours him by three pradakshiṇa circumambulations. After performing these, he praises him and bows to him. After so doing, not too close, not too distant, listening to him, bowing to him, with his face towards him, humbly waiting on him with folded hands, he thus spoke." . . . .

I have already adverted to Fah-Hian's mention of a sect, in India, who declined to accept Ṣákya Muni as their

[1] This has not, however, always been conceded. Prof. Wilson, in his remarks upon "Two Tracts from Nipál," says Dr. Buchanan "has only specified two names, Gautama and Ṣákya, of which the first does not occur in the Nipál list, whilst, in another place, he observes that Ṣákya is considered by the Burmese Buddhists as an impostor. . . The omission of the name of Gautama proves that he is not acknowledged as a distinct Buddha by the Nipálese, and he can be identified with no other in the list than Ṣákya Sinha."—Essays, vol. ii. p. 9. At p. 10 Prof. Wilson contests Buchanan's assertion, and adds that in the Pali version of the Amara Kosha GAUTAMA and ṢÁKYA SINHA and ADITYABANDHU are given as synonyms of the son of ṢUDDHODANA."

[2] Fravardin Yasht (*circa* "350-450 B.C."), quoted by Dr. Haug, Essay on the Sacred Language of the Parsees, Bombay, 1862, p. 188.

[3] *Quarterly Review*, 1866, and his "Central Asia," Murray, 1875, p. 246.

[4] Mémoires, vol. i. p. 30. "*Nava saṅghárāma.*" See also Voyages, p. 65.

prophet, but who avowedly confessed their faith in one or more of his predecessors.

Some very instructive passages in this direction have been collected by the Rev. S. Beal, in his revised edition of the Travels of Fah-Hian.[1] Among the rest, referring to the Chinese aspects of Buddhism, shortly after A.D. 458, he goes on to say:

"The rapid progress of Buddhism excited much opposition from the Literati and followers of Lao-tseu. The latter affirmed that Sakya Buddha was but an incarnation of their own master, who had died 517 B.C., shortly after which date (it was said) Buddha was born. This slander was resented by the Buddhists, and they put back the date of their founder's birth in consequence—first, to 687 B.C., and afterwards to still earlier periods."—p. xxvi.

A coincident assertion of priority of evolution seems to have been claimed, *in sitû*, at the period of the visit to India of the second representative Chinese pilgrim, *Hiouen Thsang* (A.D. 629-645).

His references to the Jainas, their practices, and their supposed appropriation of the leading theory, and consequent modification of portions of the Buddhist creed, are set forth, at length, in the following quotation:—

In describing the town of *Siñhapúra*, Hiouen Thsang proceeds: "A côté et à une petite distance du *Stoupa*, on voit l'endroit où le fondateur de la secte hérétique qui porte des vêtements blancs (*Çvêtavâsa*?), comprit les principes sublimes qu'il cherchait, et commença à expliquer la loi. Aujourd'hui, on y voit une inscription. A côté de cet endroit, on a construit un temple des dieux. Les sectaires qui le fréquentent se livrent à des dures austérités. . . La loi qu'a exposée le fondateur de cette secte, a été pillée en grande partie dans les livres du *Bouddha*, sur lesquels il s'est guidé pour établir ses préceptes et ses règles. . . Dans leurs observances et leurs exercices religieux, ils suivent presque entièrement la règle des *Çramaṇas*, seulement, ils conservent un peu de cheveux sur leur tête, et, de plus, ils vont nus. Si par hazard, ils portent des vêtements, ils se distinguent par la couleur blanche. Voila les différences, d'ailleurs fort légères, qui les séparent des autres. La statue de leur maître divin ressemble, par une sorte d'usurpation, à celle

[1] London, Trübner, 1869.

de *Jou-laï* (du Tathâgata); elle n'en diffère que par le costume; ses signes de beauté (mahápouroucha lakchaṇâni) sont absolument les mêmes."[1]—Mémoires sur les contrées occidentales, Paris, 1857, vol. i. p. 163.

In this conflict of periods, the pretensions of the Northern Buddhists may be reduced, by the internal testimony of their own books, to severely approximate proportions; and here Mr. Brian Hodgson's preliminary researches present themselves, with an authority hitherto denied them; perchance, because they were so definitively in advance of the ordinary knowledge of Buddhism, as derived from extra-national sources. In this case Mr. Hodgson was able to appeal to data, contributed from the very *nidus* of Buddhism in Magadhá—whose passage, into the ready refuge of the Valley of Nipál, would *prima facie* have secured an unadulterated version of the ancient formulæ, and have supplied a crucial test for the comparison of the southern developments, as contrasted with the northern expansions and assimilations of the Faith. Mr. Hodgson observes:—

"I can trace something *very like* Buddhism into far ages and realms: but I am sure that *that* Buddhism which has come down to us, in the Sanskrit, Pálí, and Tibetan books of the sect, and which only we do or can *know*, is neither old nor exotic."—J.A.S.B. 1837, p. 685.[2]

[1] One of Hiouen Thsang's contributions to the place and position of the Jainas in reference to the Buddhists *proper*, upon whom he has been supposed exclusively to rely, is exhibited in his faith in a native magician of the former creed, the truth of whose predictions he frankly acknowledges in the following terms:—"Avant l'arrivée du messager du roi *Kûmdra*, il y eut un hérétique nu (*Ni-kien-Nirgrantha*), nommé *Fa-che-lo* (*Vadjra*), qui entra tout à coup dans sa chambre. Le Maître de la loi, qui avait entendu dire, depuis longtemps, que les *Ni-kien* excellaient à tirer l'horoscope, le pria aussitôt de s'asseoir et l'interrogea ainsi, afin d'éclaircir ses doutes: 'Moi *Hiouen-Thsang*, religieux du royaume de *Tchi-na*, je suis venu dans ce pays, il y a bien des années, pour me livrer à l'étude et à de pieuses recherches. Maintenant, je désire m'en retourner dans ma patrie; j'ignore si j'y parviendrai ou non.'" He then goes on to relate: "Le *Ni-kien* prit un morceau de craie, traça des lignes sur la terre, tira les sorts et lui répondit en ces termes."—Hiouen-Thsang, vol. i. (Voyages), p. 228. See also vol. i. p. 224; and (Memoires) vol. i. (ii.), pp. 42, 93, 354; vol. ii. (iii.), p. 406.

[2] In the same sense, another distinguished writer on Buddhism remarks: "There is no life of Gotama Buddha, by any native author, yet discovered, that is free from the extravagant pretensions with which his history has been so largely invested; from which we may infer that the records now in existence were all prepared long after his appearance in the world."—Spence Hardy, J.R.A.S. Vol. XX. p. 135.

Col. Tod's observations were not designed to extend to the question of the relative age of the Jaina and Buddhist creeds, but they serve to show the permanence and immutability of the former faith in a portion of the continent of India, where the people, beyond all other sectional nationalities, have preserved their individuality and reverence for local traditions. They explain, moreover, how the leading tenet of Jainism—which was shared in a subdued form by Buddhism[1]—came under its exaggerated aspect to leave their best kings at the mercy of less humane adversaries.[2]

Col. Tod proceeds to speak of the Jainas in the following terms:—

"The Vedíaván (the man of secrets or knowledge, magician), or Magi of Rájasthán. The numbers and power of these sectarians are little known to Europeans, who take it for granted they

[1] "The practical part of the Jain religion consists in the performance of five duties and the avoidance of five sins.

"The duties are—1. Mercy to all animated beings; 2. Almsgiving; 3. Venerating the sages while living, and worshipping their images when deceased; 4. Confession of faults; 5. Religious fasting.

"The sins are—1. Killing; 2. Lying; 3. Stealing; 4. Adultery; 5. Worldly-mindedness."—Kalpa Sûtra, p. xxii.

The Jainas "believe that not to kill any sentient being is the greatest virtue." —The Chintâmaṇi, ed. Rev. H. Bower, Madras, 1868, p. xxi.

The leading contrast between the simple duties of the Jainas and the later developments introduced by the various schools of Buddhists may be traced in the following extracts:

"1. From the meanest insect up to man, thou shalt kill no animal whatever; 2. Thou shalt not steal; 3. Thou shalt not violate the wife or concubine of another."—Gützlaff, "China Opened," London, 1838, p. 216.

"There are three sins of the body: 1. The taking of life, Murder (1); 2. The taking that which is not given, Theft (2); 3. The holding of carnal intercourse with the female that belongs to another, Adultery (3)."—Spence Hardy, Manual of Buddhism, p. 461.

"The ten obligations" commence with "1. Not to kill; 2. Not to steal; 3. Not to marry; 4. Not to lie, etc."—The Rev. S. Beal, Fah-hian, p. 59. Mr. Beal goes on to expound the four principles involved in the existence of Buddhism, which are defined as these:—"1. That man may become superior to the Gods; 2. That *Nirvána* is the Supreme good; 3. That religion consists in a right preparation of heart (suppression of evil desire, practice of self-denial, active benevolence); 4. That men of all castes, and women, may enjoy the benefits of a religious life."—p. i.

[2] "To this leading feature in their religion (the prohibition of the shedding of blood) they owe their political debasement: for Komarpal, the last King of Anhulwara, of the Jain faith, would not march his armies in the rains, from the unavoidable sacrifice of animal life that must have ensued. The strict Jain does not even maintain a lamp during that season, lest it should attract moths to their destruction."—i. p. 519. The oil-mill and the potter's wheel are stopped for four months in the year, when insects most abound."—i. p. 521. At p. 520 Col. Tod enlarges upon the mines of knowledge (of the Jaina) books by the thousand, etc.

are few and dispersed. To prove the extent of their religious and political power, it will suffice to remark, that the pontiff of the *Khartra-gatcha* (true branch), one of the many branches of this faith, has 11,000 clerical disciples scattered over India; that a single community, the Ossi or Oswal (Ossa in Marwar), numbers 100,000 families; and that more than half the mercantile wealth of India passes through the hands of the Jain laity."—Tod, under Mewar, vol. i. p. 518.

Col. Tod's contemporary, and superior officer, Gen. Malcolm, gives us an equally striking insight into the active aggressiveness of the Brahmans and the helpless submissiveness of the Jainas in his current narrative :—

"Six years ago, the Jains built a handsome temple at Ujjain; a *Juttee*, or priest of high character, arrived from Guzerát to consecrate it, and to place within the shrine the image of their favourite deity (Parswanáth); but on the morning of the day fixed for this purpose, after the ceremony had commenced and the Jains had filled the temple expecting the arrival of their idol, a Brahman appeared conveying an oval stone from the river Seepra, which he proclaimed as the emblem of Mahádeva, (and his following) soon drove the unarmed bankers and shopkeepers from their temple, and proclaimed 'Mahádeva as the overthrower of Jains.'"—Malcolm, Central India, vol. ii. p. 160. See also Edward Conolly, in J.A.S.B., 1837, p. 834.

In addition to the personal experiences and graphic narratives of Col. Tod, as detailed in his "Rájasthán," a new class of testimony, from indigenous sources, has lately reached us, in the contributions of an independent visitor to the courts of the Chiefs of the Rájpút states, whose careful examination and reproduction of the monuments existing *in sitú* has been associated with the acquisition of an amount of ancient lore, as preserved among the people themselves, which has not always been accessible under the necessarily reserved attitude of English officials.

I cite M. Rousselet's own words regarding the nature of the documents in the possession of the Jainas, and the reiterated charges they advance against the heretical Buddhists :

"Les livres religieux des Jaïnas, dont la traduction jetterait un grand jour sur les âges reculés de l'histoire de l'Inde, ont été délaissés jusqu'à présent par nos savants orientalistes. Si l'on en croit les traditions conservées par les prêtres de cette secte, l'origine du jaïnisme remonterait à des centaines de siècles avant Jésus-Christ; il paraît, en tout cas, établi qu'il existait bien avant l'apparition de Çakya Mouni, et il est même possible que les doctrines de ce dernier ne soient qu'une transformation des doctrines jaïnas. Les Bouddhistes reconnaissent du reste Mahavira, le dernier Tirthankar jaïna, comme le précepteur de Çakya. Les Jaïnas considèrent, de leur côté, les Bouddhistes comme des hérétiques, et les ont poursuivis de tout temps de leur haine."—p. 373.

We could scarcely have expected any contributory evidence towards the antiquity of the Jaina creed from Brahmanical sources, and, yet, an undesigned item of testimony to that end is found to be embalmed in the "Padma Purāṇa," where, in adverting to the deeds of *Vrihaspati* and his antagonism to *Indra*, Jainism is freely admitted to a contemporaneous existence with the great *Gods* of the Brahmans, and though duly designated as "heretic," is confessed, in the terms of the text, to have been a potent competitor for royal and other converts, in very early times.[1] I am by no means desirous of claiming either high antiquity or undue authority for the *Hindu Purāṇas*, but their minor admissions are at times instructive, and this may chance to prove so.[2]

[1] "The *Asuras* are described as enjoying the ascendancy over the Devatas, when *Vrihaspati*, taking advantage of their leader *Sukra's* being enamoured of a nymph of heaven, sent by *Indra* to interrupt his penance, comes among the former as *Sukra*, and misleads them into irreligion by preaching heretical doctrines; the doctrines and practices he teaches are Jain, and in a preceding passage it is said that the sons of Raji embraced the Jina Dharmma."—Padma Purāna, Wilson, J.R.A.S. Vol. V. p. 282. See also pp. 287, 310–11.

[2] Professor Wilson, arguing upon the supposed priority of the Buddhists, attempted to account for the frequent allusions to the Jainas in the Brahmanical writings by concluding that "since the *Bauddhas* disappeared from India, and the *Jainas* only have been known, it will be found that the Hindu writers, whenever they speak of *Bauddhas*, show, by the phraseology and practices ascribed to them, that they really mean *Jainas*. The older writers do not make the same mistake, and the usages and expressions they give to *Bauddha* personages are not *Jaina*, *but Bauddha*."—Essays, vol. i. p. 329.

It is to be added, however, that Prof. Wilson, when he put this opinion on record in 1832, had to rely upon the limited knowledge of the day, which presupposed that the Jainas had nothing definite to show prior to the ninth century (p. 333). He was not then aware of the very early indications of their unobtrusive power in Southern India in Ṣaka 411 (A.D. 489), if not earlier, as proved by Sir W. Elliot's Inscriptions (J.R.A.S. 1837, Vol. IV. pp. 8, 9, 10, 17, 19): and still less could he have foreseen the new revelations from Mathurá, which, of course, would have materially modified his conclusions.

The *Pancha Tantra*—the Indian original of Æsop's Fables—which has preserved *intact* so many of the ancient traditions of the land—also retains among the network of its ordinary homespun tales and local stories, a very significant admission of the position once held by the Jaina sect amid the social relations of the people. The fable, in question, appears in the authorized Sanskrit text, which, under some circumstances, might have caught the eye of Brahmanical revisors; nevertheless we find in its context "the chief of the *(Jaina)* convent" expressing himself, "How now, son; what is it you say? Are we Brahmans, think you, to be at any one's beck and call? No, no; at the hour we go forth to gather alms, we enter the mansions of those votaries only who, we know, are of approved faith."[1]

That Chandra Gupta was a member of the Jaina community is taken by their writers as a matter of course, and treated as a known fact, which needed neither argument nor demonstration.[2] The documentary evidence to this effect is

[1] This is Prof. Wilson's *own* rendering of the text. As we have seen, his leading tendencies were altogether against the notion of the antiquity or ante-Buddhistical development of the Jaina creed (Essays, vol. iii. p. 227); and yet he was forced on many occasions, like the present, to admit that the *terms* were Buddhist, but the *tenor* was Jaina. In a note on the Pancha Tantra (p. 20, vol. ii.) he remarks, "From subsequent passages, however, it appears that the usual confusion of Bauddha and Jaina occurs in the Pancha Tantra; and that the latter alone is intended, whichever be named." And with regard to the quotation given above he goes on to say: "The chief peculiarity, however, of this story is its correct delineation of Jain customs; a thing very unusual in Brâhmanical books. The address of the barber, and the benediction of the Superior of the *Vihára*, are conformable to Jain usages. The whole is indeed a faithful picture. . . . The accuracy of the description is an argument for some antiquity; as the more modern any work is, the more incorrect the description of the Jainas and Bauddhas, and the confounding of one with the other."—1840, vol. ii. p. 76.

[2] Book No. 20. Countermark 774, Mackenzie MSS., J.A.S. Bengal, vol. vii. p. 411.

"Section 8. Chronological tables of Hindu râjas (termed Jaina kings of the Draviḍa country in the table of contents of book No. 20).

"In the 4th age a mixture of names, one or two of them being Jaina; Chandra Gupta is termed a Jaina. Chola râjas. Himasila a Jaina king."

The reporter, the Rev. William Taylor, adds the *remark*, "These lists, though imperfect, may have some use for occasional reference."

"The extinction of the *Brahman* and *Kshatriya* classes was predicted by Bhadra-Bahu Muni, in his interpretation of the 14 dreams of Chandra Gupta, whom they, the Sráwak Yatís, make out in the *Buddha-vilása*, a *Digambar* work, to have been the monarch of Ujjayani."—Trans. R.A.S. Vol. I. p. 413.

"And Chandra Gupta, the king of Pâtaliputra, on the night of the full moon

of comparatively early date, and, apparently, absolved from all suspicion, by the omission from their lists of the name of Aṣoka, a far more powerful monarch than his grandfather, and one whom they would reasonably have claimed as a potent upholder of their faith, had he not become a pervert.

The testimony of Megasthenes would likewise seem to imply that Chandra Gupta submitted to the devotional teaching of the *sermánas*, as opposed to the doctrines of the Brahmans. The passage in Strabo runs as follows:—*Τοῖς δὲ βασιλεῦσι συνεῖναι δι' ἀγγέλων πυνθανομένοις περὶ τῶν αἰτίων, καὶ δι' ἐκείνων θεραπεύουσι, καὶ λιτανεύουσι τὸ θεῖον.*—Strabo, xv. i. 60.

We must now turn to the authoritative account of the succession of the Mauryas, as presented by the Brahmanical texts, which had so many chances of revision, both in time and substance, in their antagonism to all ancient creeds, and less-freely elaborated delusions, than their own more modern system professed to teach the Indian world.

The most approved of their Puránas, under the chronological and genealogical aspects—*the Vishṇu Puráṇa*—introduces the succession of the Mauryas in the following terms:

"Upon the cessation of the race of Nanda, the Mauryas will possess the earth; for Kauṭilya will place Chandragupta on the throne. His son will be Bindusára; his son will be Aṣokavardhana; his son will be Suyaṣas; his son will be Daṣaratha; his son will be Sangata; his son will be Ṣáliṣúka; his son will be Somaṣarmaṇ;

in the month of Kártika, had 16 dreams. . . . ."—Mr. Lewis Rice, Indian Antiquary, 1874, p. 155.

Mr. Rice adds the "Chronology of the Rájávali Kathe," as given by Deva Chandrá, to the following effect: "After the death of Víra Varddhamána Gautama and other Kevalis, 62 years. Then Nandi Mitra and other Ṣruta Kevalis, 100 years. Then Viṣákha and other Daṣa purvis, 183. Then Nakshatra and other Ekadaṣángadhara, 233. Then was born Vikramáditya in Ujjayini; . . . . and he established his own era from the year of Rúdirodgári, the 605th year after the death of Varddhamána."

"Intepretation of the 16 dreams of Chandra Gupta.

"1. All knowledge will be darkened.

"2. The Jaina religion will decline, and your successors to the throne take *dikshe*.

"3. The heavenly beings will not henceforth visit the Bharata *Kshetra*.

"4. The Jainas will be split into sects.

"5. The clouds will not give seasonable rain, and the crops will be poor.

"6. True knowledge being lost, a few sparks will glimmer with a feeble light.

"7. Áryakhaṇḍa will be destitute of Jaina doctrine.

"8. The evil will prevail and goodness be hidden. . . . .

"16. Twelve years of dearth and famine will come upon this land."

his son will be Ṣatadhanwan; and his successor will be Bṛihadratha. These are the ten Mauryas, who will reign over the earth for 137 years."—Vishṇu Puráṇa, book iv. cap. xxiv.

The full list of the Kings of Magadhá, obtained from these sources, runs as follows:

i.	PRADYOTANA.	xv.	MAHÁNANDIN.[2]
ii.	PÁLAKA.	xvi.	NANDA, *Mahápadma*.[3]
iii.	VIṢÁKHAYÚPA.	xvii.	SUMÁLYA & 7 BROTHERS ("the Brahman Kauṭilya will root out the 9 Nandas").
iv.	JANAKA.		
v.	NANDIVARDHANA.[1]	xviii.	CHANDRA GUPTA.
vi.	ṢISUNÁGA.	xix.	BINDUSARA.
vii.	KÁKAVARṆA.	xx.	AṢOKAVARDHANA.
viii.	KSHEMADHARMAN.	xxi.	SUYAṢAS.
ix.	KSHATTRAUJAS.	xxii.	DAṢARATHA.
x.	VIDMISÁRA (BIMBISÁRA).	xxiii.	SANGATA.
xi.	AJÁTAṢATRU.	xxiv.	ṢÁLIṢÚKA.
xii.	DARBHAKA.	xxv.	ṢOMASARMAN.
xiii.	UDAYÁṢWA.	xxvi.	SATADHANWAN.
xiv.	NANDIVARDHANA.	xxvii.	BṚIHADRATHA.

The inquiry might here be reasonably raised, as to how a *Brahman*, like *Kautilya*, came to select, for sovereignty, a man of a supposedly adverse faith. But though our King-maker was a *Brahman*, he was not necessarily, in the modern acceptation of the term, a "*Bráhmanist*." The fact of the *Brahmanas* being bracketed in equal gradation with the *Sramanas* of the Jainas and Buddhists, in the formal versions of Aṣoka's edicts, clearly demonstrates that the first-named class had not, as yet, succeeded to the exclusive charge of kings' consciences, or attained the leading place in the hierarchy of the land which they subsequently claimed. Moreover, in the full development of their power, the Brahmans, as a rule, recognized their proper *métier* of guiding and governing from within the palace, and but seldom sought to become ostensibly reigning kings. Thus, supposing *Kautilya* to have been, as is affirmed in some passages, an hereditary minister,[4] he might well have sought to secure a submissive

[1] "5 Pradyota kings, 138 years." [2] "10 Ṣaiṣunága kings, 362 years."

[3] "He will be the annihilator of the Kshatrya race; for, after him, the kings of the earth will be *Ṣúdras*."

[4] Hindu Theatre, p. 145. "Vishṇu Gupta," son of Chaṇaka (hence Cháṇakya). He is described in the *Vṛihat-Kathá* as a "Bráhman of mean appearance, digging in a meadow."—H. T. p. 140, and Wilson's Works, vol. iii. p. 177; see also vol. iii. p. 354, and the Mahawanso, p. 21, with the full list of references, pp. lxxvi, *et seq.*

prince, without regard to his crude ideas of faith, and one unlikely to trench upon the growing pretensions of the Bráhmanical class. But, among other things, it is to be kept in view that, hitherto, there had been no overt antagonism of creeds, regarding which, as will be seen hereafter, Aṣoka so wisely counsels sufferance and consideration.

The leading question of caste, also, has a very important, though seemingly indirect, bearing upon the subject under discussion. It is clear that the whole theory of Indian *castes* originated in a simple natural division of labour associated with heredity of occupations, constituting, as civilization advanced, *ipso facto*, a system of social class discrimination; each section of the community having its defined rights and being subject to its corresponding responsibilities.[1] In the initiatory stage this simple distribution of duties clearly had no concern with creeds or forms of religious belief.

But beyond this, we have already seen (p. 3) that it was not incompatible with their obligations to their own faith, that Brahmans should officiate in Jaina temples—and, as almost a case in point, we find very early instances of Jaina Kings entertaining Brahman *Purohits*,[2] but it need not for a moment be supposed that these "spiritual guides" taught their sovereigns either the Vedic or Brahmanical system of religion.[3]

The conception of caste itself was obviously indigenous, and clearly an institution of home growth, which flourished and

[1] In the South and Central India the term *caste* seems still to represent *class*. "The Hindus, as in all parts of India, are divided into four great castes; but it will be preferable to speak of the inhabitants of this country as nations and classes; for it is in this manner they divide themselves and keep alive those attachments and prejudices which distinguish them from each other.—Malcolm's "Central India," vol. ii. p. 114.

[2] "While Padmapara was reigning in the city of Kotikapura. . . His Queen being Padmaṣri, and his *purohita* Soma Somarsi, a Brâhman."—Rajavali Kathe, Ind. Antiquary, 1874, p. 154.

[3] Govinda Râya makes a grant of land to a "Jaina Brahman."—Journal Royal Asiatic Society, Vol. VIII. p. 2; see also Colonel Sykes, J.R.A.S., Vol. VI. pp. 301, 305, and F. Buchanan, Mysore, vol. iii. p. 77.

It has elsewhere been remarked by other commentators:—"We see from the history of the Buddhist patriarchs, that the distinction of castes in no way interfered with the selection of the chiefs of religion. Sâkya Muni was a Kshatrya; Maha Kasyapa, his successor, was a Brâhman; *Shang nu ho sieou*, the third patriarch, was a Vaisya; and his successor, *Yeou pho Khieouto*, was a Sudra."—Remusat, note, cap xx. *Foe koi ki*, Laidlay's Translation, p. 178.

"Saugata books treating on the subject of caste never call in question the antique fact of a fourfold division of the Hindu people, but only give a more

engrafted itself more deeply as the nation progressed in its own independent self-development. In this sense we need not seek to discover any reference to its machinery in the authentic texts of the Vedas.[1] The Aryan pastoral races, who reached India from distant geographical centres, however intellectually endowed, were, in their very tribal communities and migratory habits, unfitted and unprepared for such matured social conditions.

The intrusion of a foreign race, in considerable numbers, would tend to fix the local distribution, and add a new division of its own to those already existing among people of the land. It might be suggested that the Vedic Aryans thus constituted, in their new home, the *fifth* of the "five classes of men" to whom they so frequently refer in the text of the *Rig Veda.*[2]

But there are decided objections to any such conclusion, as in one instance the five classes are distinctly alluded to as within the Aryan pale, in opposition to the local *Dasyus.*[3]

liberal interpretation to it than the current Bráhmanical one of their day."—B. H. Hodgson, J.R.A.S. Vol. II. p. 289.

And to conclude these references, I may point to the fact that Sâkya Muni, in one instance, is represented as having promised a "young *Brâhman* that he shall become a perfect *Buddha*."—Ksoma de Körös, Asiatic Researches, vol. xx. p. 453.

[1] Muir, J.R.A.S. N.S. Vol. I. p. 356; Sanskrit Texts, vol. i. pp. 7, 15, etc.; vol. v. p. 371. Colebrooke, As. Res. vol. vii. p. 251; Essays, vol. i. pp. 161, 309. Max Müller, Ancient Sanskrit Literature, p. 570. Wilson, Rig Veda, vol. i. p. xliv.

[2] "Over the five men, or classes of men" (*pancha kshitinám*).—Rig Veda, Wilson's translation, vol. i. pp. 20, 230, 314; ii. p. xv., "The five classes of beings," p. 170; iii. p. xxii., "The five races of men" (*pánchajanydsu kṛishṭishu*) 87; "The five classes of men," pp. 468, 506, etc. "The commentator explains this term to denote the four castes, *Brahman*, *Kshatriya*, *Vaiṣya*, and *Súdra*, and the barbarian or *Nishdda;* but *Sayaṇa*, of course, expresses the received opinions of his own age."—Wilson, Rig Veda, vol. i. p. xliii; also vol. ii. p. xv. See also Muir, vol. i. p. 176, *et seq.*

Pliny's detail of the castes or classes of India differs slightly from that of Megasthenes', and, like the Vedic tradition, estimates the number of divisions at *five*, excluding the lowest servile class. "The people of the more civilized nations of India are divided into several classes. One of these classes tills the earth, another attends to military affairs, others, again, are occupied in mercantile pursuits, while the wisest and most wealthy among them have the management of the affairs of State, act as judges, and give counsel to the King. The fifth class entirely devoting themselves to the pursuit of wisdom, which, in these countries, is *almost held in the same veneration as religion.*" . . . "In addition to these, there is a class in a half-savage state, and doomed to endless labour; by means of their exertions, all the classes previously mentioned are supported."—Pliny, vi. 22. 19, Bohn's edition, 1855.

[3] "The sage ATRI, who was venerated by the five classes of men, . . . and baffling, showerers (of benefits), the devices of the malignant *Dasyus.*"—Wilson, vol. i. p. 314 (R.V. i. viii.).

So that these references must be supposed either to apply to the Aryan tribes, as once distinguished from each other in their previous dwelling-places, or to refer to the independent waves of immigration of the clans across the Indus, which would establish a sufficiently marked subdivision of the parent race.

On the other hand, it is clear that if they had no birth-caste, they had very arrogant notions of *Varṇa* "colour," which, under modern interpretation, has come to have the primary meaning of *caste*. We find them speaking of the *A'ryam varṇam*, "the Aryan-colour;"[1] and our "white-complexioned friends" are contrasted with the black skins and imperfect language of the indigenous races.[2]

These utterances appear to belong to the period of the Aryan progress through the Punjáb. Whether after their prolonged wanderings, the surviving members of the community reached the sacred sites on the Saraswatí in diminished force, we have no means of determining; but they would, as far as we can judge, have here found themselves in more densely inhabited districts, in disproportionate numbers to the home population, and cut off from fresh accessions from the parent stock.

But, however few in numbers, they were able to place their mark upon the future of the land, to introduce the worship of their own gods, to make their hymns the ritual, and finally, as expositors of the new religion, to elevate themselves into a sanctity but little removed from that of the deity.[3]

We have now to inquire, what bearing this view of *caste*

[1] "He gave horses, he gave the Sun, and INDRA gave also the many-nourishing cow: he gave golden treasure, and having destroyed the *Dasyus*, he protected the Aryan tribe."—Wilson, R.V. vol. iii. p. 56. *A'ryam varṇam* "the Aryan colour."—Muir, vol. v. p. 114; and ii. 282, 360, 374. "INDRA . . . divided the fields with his white-complexioned friends."—Wilson, R.V. vol. i. p. 259.

[2] (Indra) "tore off the black skin." Vol. ii. p. 35 (ii. i. 8). (Indra) "scattered the black-sprung servile" (hosts). Vol. ii. p. 258 (ii. vi. 6). (Dasyus) "who are babblers defective in speech." Vol. iv. p. 42. "may we conquer in battle the ill-speaking man." Vol. iv. p. 60.

[3] "viii. 381. No greater crime is known on earth than slaying a Bráhman; and the King, therefore, must not even form in his mind an idea of killing a priest."

"ix. 317. A Bráhman, whether learned or ignorant, is a powerful divinity."

"ix. Thus, although Bráhmans employ themselves in all sorts of mean occupation, they must invariably be honoured; for they are something transcendently divine."—G. C. Haughton, "The Institutes of Manu" (1825).

has upon the pretensions of the Jainas to high antiquity. It is clear that the elaboration and gradual development of the subdivisions of caste must have been the work of ages; in early times limited to four classes of men, it has so grown that, in our day, in a single district in Upper India, the official statistical return gives no less than ninety-five classes of the population, as ranged under the heading of "Caste,"[1] and the full total for the entire government of the North-Western Provinces mounts up "to no less than 560 castes among the Hindus" alone.[2]

If this be taken as the rate of increase, to what primitive times must we assign the pre-caste period, and with it the indigenous population represented by those, who, with the simplest form of worship, avowedly lived a life of equality before their Maker; and so long resisted any recognition of caste, till the force of example and surrounding custom led them exceptionally, and in a clumsy way,[3] to subject the free worship of each independent votary to the control of a ministering priesthood.

We may conclude, for all present purposes, that Vindusára followed the faith of his father, and that, in the same belief—whatever it may prove to have been—his childhood's lessons were first learnt by Aṣoka.

The Ceylon authorities assert that Vindusára's creed was "Brahmanical," but, under any circumstances, their testimony would not carry much weight in the argument about other lands and other times, and it is, moreover, a critical question as to how much they knew about Brahmanism *itself*, and whether the use of the word *Brahman* does not merely imply, in their sense, a non-Buddhistic or any religion opposed to their own.[4]

[1] Report on Sahâranpur, Elliot's Glossary, vol. i. p. 296.

[2] Ibid, p. 283. Census Report for 1865.

[3] "VRISHABHANÁTHA was incarnate in this world . . . at the city of *Ayodhyá*. . . . He also arranged the various duties of mankind, and allotted to men the means of subsistence, viz. *Asi*, 'the sword;' *Masi*, 'letters' (*lit.* ink); *Krishi*, 'agriculture;' *Vánijya*, 'commerce;' *Paṣupála*, 'attendance on cattle.' . . . Thus Vrishabhanâtha established the religion of the Jains, in its four classes or castes, of *Bráhmans*, *Kshatris*, *Vaisyas*, and *Sudras*."—C. Mackenzie, Asiatic Researches, vol. ix. p. 259.

[4] "The father (of Aṣoka) being of the Brahmanical faith, maintained (bestowing daily alms) 60,000 Brahmans. He himself in like manner bestowed them for 3 years."—Mahawanso, p. 23.

I now arrive at the primary object, which, in nominal terms, heads this paper, regarding the relative precedence of Jainism and Buddhism, as tried and tested by the ultimate determination of "the early faith of Aṣoka."

In the preliminary inquiry, I have often had to rely upon casual and inconsecutive evidence, which my readers may estimate after their own ideas and predilections. I have at length to face what might previously have been regarded as the crucial difficulty of my argument; but all doubts and obscurities in that direction may now be dissipated before Aṣoka's *own* words, which he or his advisers took such infinite pains to perpetuate—under the triple phases of his tardy religious progress—on rocks and big stones, and more elaborately-prepared Indian *Láṭs* or monoliths.

It is fully ascertained, that the knowledge of the characters of this *Láṭ* alphabet, together with the power of interpreting the meaning of these edicts, had been altogether lost and obscured in the land, where these very monuments stood undefaced, up to the fourteenth century A.D.; when Fírúz Sháh, on the occasion of the removal of two of the northern monoliths to his new city on the Jumna, ineffectually summoned the learned of all and every class and creed, from far and near, to explain the writing on their surfaces.[1] It is therefore satisfactory to find that, so to say, *Jaina* records had preserved *intact* a tradition of what the once again legible purport of the inscriptions reveals, as coincident with the subdued and elsewhere disregarded pretensions of the sect.

Abúl Fazl, the accomplished minister of Akbar, is known to have been largely indebted to the Jaina priests and their carefully preserved chronicles, for much of his knowledge of the past, or *Hindú*, period of the empire he had to describe statistically, under the various aspects of its soils, its revenues, its ancient legends, its conflicting creeds, etc. In his *A'ín-i-Akbarí* he has retained, in his notice of the kingdom of Kashmír, *three* very important entries, exhibited in the

[1] My Pathán Kings of Dehli, p. 292. General Cunningham, Arch. Rep. vol. i. pp. 155, 161. Elliot's Historians, vol. iii. p. 352.

original Persian version quoted below,[1] which establish: (1) that Aṣoka himself first introduced "JAINISM," *eo nomine*, into the kingdom of Kashmír; (2) that "Buddhism" was dominant there during the reign of Jaloka; and (3) that Brahmanism superseded Buddhism under Rája *Sachinara*.[2]

[1] وچون فرماندهي باشوك پسرِ عمّ راجه جنك باز گرديد كيشِ برهمن انداخته آئينِ جَئِين برگرفت.—Dr. Blochmann's revised text, p. ٥٧٩. During the reign of Jaloka Buddhism is stated to have been prevalent. (وآئينِ بودّه دران زمان روائي يافت). Under Raja Sachinara the Brahmans again asserted their supremacy در زمانِ راجه نر برهمان بر بودّه چيره دست امدند و پرستش جاى آنان خاك توده گشت p. 580.

[2] KINGS OF KASHMÍR AFTER 35 PRINCES "WHOSE NAMES ARE FORGOTTEN."

PERSIAN NAMES.	SANSKRIT NAMES (As. Res. xv.).
لوه	(*Lava*).
كشن پورِ او	*Kuseṣaya*.
كپگهندر پورِ او (variant تپجينير)	*Khagendra*.
شرندر پورِ او	*Surendra*.
گودهر از قومِ ديگر	*Godhara*.
سورن پسرِ او	*Suvarna*.
جنك پسرِ او	*Janaka*.
شچي نر پسرِ او	*Sachinara*.
اشوك پسرِ عمِّ جنك	*Aṣoka*, descended from the paternal great-uncle of Khagendra.)
جلوك پسرِ او	*Jaloka*.
دامودر از اولاد اشوك	*Dámodara*.
هشك, زشك, (var. پيشك) كنشك هرسه برادر آئينِ بودّه داشتند	*Hushka, Jushka, Kanishka*.
ابهمن	*Abhimanyu*.

Calcutta Text, p. ٥٧٤. Gladwin, vol. ii. p. 171. Prinsep's Essays, Useful Tables, p. 243.

In brief, this extraneous evidence, from possibly secondary Jaina sources, is fully consistent with what Aṣoka has still to disclose in the texts of his own inscriptions; but it conveys, indirectly, even more than those formal and largely-distributed official documents—which merely allow us to infer that Aṣoka's conversion to Buddhism occurred late in his life or reign. But the annals of Kashmír, on the other hand, more emphatically imply that either he did not seek to spread, or had not the chance or opportunity of propagating his new faith in the outlying sections of his dominions; and that, in this valley of Kashmír, at least, Buddhism came after him, as a consequence of his southern surrender rather than as a deliberate promulgation of a well-matured belief on his part.

The leading fact of Aṣoka's introduction or recognition of the Jaina creed in Kashmír, above stated, does not, however, rest upon the sole testimony of the Muhammadan author, but is freely acknowledged in the Brahmanical pages of the *Rája Taranginí*—a work which, though finally compiled and put together only in 1148 A.D., relies, in this section of its history, upon the more archaic writings of *Padma Mihira* and *Srí Chhavillákára*. Professor Wilson's recapitulation of the context of this passage is somewhat obscure, as, while hesitating to admit that Aṣoka "introduced" into Kashmír "the *Jina Sásana*," he, inconsistently, affirms that "he invented or originated" it. If so, we must suppose that *Jainism* had its germ and infantile birth in an outlying valley of the Himálaya in 250 B.C.—a conclusion which is beyond measure improbable.[1]

[1] Professor Wilson's paraphrase runs: "The last of these princes being childless, the crown of Kashmír reverted to the family of its former rulers, and devolved on AṢOKA, who was descended from the paternal great uncle of KHAGENDRA. This prince, it is said in the *Aín i-Akbari*, abolished the Brahmanical rites, and substituted those of *Jina*: from the original (text of the Raja Taranġini), however, it appears that he by no means attempted the former of these heinous acts, and that, on the contrary, he was a pious worshipper of Ṣiva, an ancient temple of whom in the character of Vijayeṣa he repaired. With respect to the second charge, there is better foundation for it, although it appears that this prince did not introduce, but invented or originated the *Jina Sásana*."—As. Res. vol. xv. p. 19.

The text and purport of the original are subjoined; the latter runs: "Then the prince Aṣoka, the lover of truth, obtained the earth; who sinning in subdued affections produced the *Jina Sásana*. Jaloka, the son and successor of Aṣoka,

I had outlined and transcribed the subjoined sketch of the contrasted stages of Aṣoka's edicts, before the *Indian Antiquary* containing Dr. Kern's revision of the translations of his predecessors came under my notice.

As I understand the position of the inquiry at this moment, Dr. Kern is aided by no novel data or materials beyond the reach of those who came to the front before him, and it may chance to prove that he has been precipitate in closing his case, while a new and very perfect version of the same series of inscriptions, at Khalsi, is still awaiting General Cunningham's final *imprimatur*—a counterpart engrossed in more fully-defined characters, which Dr. Kern does not appear to have heard of. Dr. Kern's method of dealing with his materials might not commend itself to some interpreters. He confesses that *the* original, or *Palace* copy, forming the basis of all other variants, was cast in the dialect of Magadhá, and he then goes through the curious process of reducing the Girnár text—which he takes as *his* representative *test*—into classical or Brahmanic Sanskrit, on which he relies for his competitive translation. At the same time he admits, without reserve, that the geographically distributed versions of the guiding *scripture* were systematically adapted to the various dialects of "Gujarátí

was a prince of great prowess; he overcame the assertors of the *Bauddha* heresies, and quickly expelled the Mlechhas from the country. . . . .

"The conquest of Kanauj by this prince is connected with an event not improbable in itself, and which possibly marks the introduction of the Brahmanical creed, in its more perfect form, into this kingdom, and Jaloka is said to have adopted thence the distinction of castes, and the practices which were at that time established in the neighbouring kingdoms. . . . He forbore in the latter part of his reign from molesting the followers of the Bauddha schism, and even bestowed on them some endowments."—As. Res. vol. xv. p. 21.

Troyer's translation of 102 runs:

"Ce monarque (Aṣoka) ayant éteint *en lui* tout penchant vicieux, embrassa la religion de Djina, et étendit *sa domination* par des enclos d'élévations sacrées de terre dans *le pays* de Çuchkala, *où est située* la montagne de Vitastá.

103. La Vitastá passait dans la ville au milieu des bois sacrés et des Viháras; c'était là où s'élevait, bâti par lui, un sanctuaire de Buddha, d'une hauteur dont l'œil ne pouvait atteindre les limites."—vol. ii. p. 12.

A notice which may have some bearing upon these events is to be found in the *Dulva*. It purports to declare: "100 years after the disappearance of Sakya, his religion is carried into Kashmír. 110 years after the same event, in the reign of Aṣoka, King of Pátaliputra, a new compilation of the laws . . . was prepared at Alláhábád."—J.A.S. Bengal, vol. i. p. 6.

or Maráthí—Mágadhí, and Gándhárí" [the Semitic version of Kapurdigiri].

I should have had more confidence in this rectification of the translations of all previous masters of the craft, if the modern critic had proceeded upon diametrically opposite principles, and had recognized the confessed necessity of the variation and distribution of dialects, site by site, as a fact making against the pretended supremacy of classical Sanskrit at this early date.[1]

Singular to say, with all these reservations, I am fully prepared to accept so much of Dr. Kern's general conclusions as, without concert, chances opportunely to support and confirm my leading argument, with regard to the predominance of Jainism in the first and second series of Aṣoka's Inscriptions. Dr. Kern, elsewhere, relies on a short indorsement of, or supplementary addition to, the framework of the Girnár Inscription, as satisfactorily proving, to his perception, the Buddhistical import of the whole set of Edicts which precede it on the same rock.[2]

I am under the impression that this incised scroll is of later date than the body of the epigraph. It is larger in size, does not range with the rest of the writing, and does not, in terms, fit-in with the previous context. Of course should it prove to be authentic and synchronous in execution with the other chiselled letters, and, at the same time, of *exclusively* Buddhist tendency, I might regard its tenor as

[1] The pretence of the universality of the Sanskrit language in India at this period has often been contested in respect to the method of reconstruction of these ancient monuments. Mr. Turnour was the first to protest against James Prinsep's submission to the *Sanskritic* tendencies of his Pandits. Mr. B. Hodgson, in like manner, consistently upheld the local claims and prior currency of the various forms of the vernaculars, and, most unquestionably, Professor Wilson's own perception and faculty of interpreting this class of inter-provincial records was damaged and obscured by his obstinate demands for good dictionary Sanskrit.

[2] "In one place only—I mean the signature of the Girnár inscription—the following words have reference to Buddha. Of this signature there remains,

. . . *va sveto hasti savalokasukháharo náma*.

What has to be supplied at the beginning I leave to the ingenuity of others to determine, but what is left means 'the white elephant' whose name is 'Bringer of

of more importance; but, even accepting all Dr. Kern's arguments in favour of "*White* Elephants," which I distrust altogether, how are we to reconcile the repeated arrays of elephants, (the special symbol of the second *Jina*), upon acknowledged Jaina sculptures, with anything but the general identity of symbols of both sects, and a possible derivation on the part of the Buddhists?

Dr. Kern thus concludes his final *résumé*:—

"The Edicts give an idea of what the King did for his subjects in his wide empire, which extended from Behár to Gándhára, from the Himáláya to the coast of Coromandel and Páṇḍya. They are not unimportant for the criticism of the Buddhistic traditions, though they give us exceedingly little concerning the condition of the doctrine and its adherents. . . .

"At fitting time and place, [Aṣoka] makes mention, in a modest and becoming manner, of the doctrine he had embraced; but nothing of a Buddhist spirit can be discovered in his State policy. From the very beginning of his reign he was a good prince. His ordinances concerning the sparing of animal life agree much more closely with the ideas of the heretical Jainas than those of the Buddhists." (p. 275.)

THE EDICTS OF AṢOKA.

Prof. Wilson, when revising the scattered texts of Aṣoka's Edicts within the reach of the commentators of 1849, declared, and, as we may now see, rightly maintained, that there was nothing *demonstrably* "Buddhist" in any of the preliminary or Rock Inscriptions of that monarch, though, then and since, he has been so prominently put

happiness to the whole world.' That by this term Ṣâkya is implied, there can be no doubt (he entered his mother's womb as a white elephant,—Lalita Vistara, p. 63). . . . . Even if the signature is not to be attributed to the scribe, the custom evidently even then prevalent, and still in use at the present day, of naming at the end of the inscription the divinity worshipped by the writer or scribe, can offer no serious difficulty."—I. A. p. 258. [If Sakya Muni was the seed of the white elephant, how came he to be so disrespectful to his deceased relatives as to speak of his dead friend "*the white elephant*" Devadatta killed, as "cet être qui a un grand corps, en se décomposant, remplirait toute la ville d'une mauvaise odeur"?]

forward as the special patron and promoter of *the Creed* of Sakya Muni.[1]

In the single-handed contest between Buddhism and Brahmanism, Prof. Wilson made no pretence to discover any *status* —throughout the whole range of these formal records—for the latter religion; except in the vague way of a notice of the Brahmans and Sramans mentioned in the corresponding palæographic texts, which were, in a measure, associated with the coeval references of the Greek authors to these identical designations. But no suggestion seems to have presented itself to him, as an alternative, of old-world *Jainism* progressing into a facile introduction to philosophic Buddhism.

We have now to compare the divergencies exhibited between the incidental records of the tenth, twelfth, and possibly following years, with the advanced declarations of the twenty-seventh year of Aṣoka's reign. We find the earlier proclamations advocating *Dharma*,[2] which certainly does not come up to our ideal of "religion," represented in its simplest phase of duty to others, which, among these untutored peoples,

[1] "In the first place, then, with respect to the supposed main purport of the inscription, proselytism to the Buddhist religion, it may not unreasonably be doubted if they were made public with any such design, and whether they have any connexion with Buddhism at all."—J.R.A.S. Vol. XII. p. 236. "There is nothing in the injunctions promulgated or sentiments expressed in the inscriptions, in the sense in which I have suggested their interpretation, that is decidedly and exclusively characteristic of Buddhism. The main object of the first appears, it is true, to be a prohibition of destroying animal life, but it is a mistake to ascribe the doctrine to the Buddhists alone." p. 238. "From these considerations, I have been compelled to withhold my unqualified assent to the confident opinions that have been entertained respecting the object and origin of the inscriptions. Without denying the possibility of their being intended to disseminate Buddhism, . . . there are difficulties in the way, . . . which, to say the least, render any such an attribution extremely uncertain." p. 250.

[2] The four *Dharmas*, in their simplicity, are defined by the Northern Jainas as "merits," as consequent upon the five *Mahávratas* or "great *duties*."—Wilson's Essays, vol. i. p. 317. This idea progressed, in aftertimes, into a classification of the separate duties of each rank in life, or the "prescribed course of duty." Thus "giving alms," etc., is the *dharma* of the householder, "administering justice" of a king, "piety" of a Brahman, "courage" of a Kshatriya.—M. Williams, *sub voce*. "Later Jaina interpretations of the term *Dharma* in Southern India extend to 'virtue, duty, justice, righteousness, rectitude, religion.' It is said to be the quality of the individual self which arises from action, and leads to happiness and final beatitude. It also means Law, and has for its object *Dharma*, things to be done, and *Adharma*, things 'to be avoided.' This *Dharma* is said by the Jainas to be eternal. *Dharma*, as well as *Veda*, if they are true Virtue and Law, are attributes or perfections of the Divine Being, and as such are eternal."—Chintamani, Rev. H. Bower, p. xl. See also Max Müller's "Sanskrit Literature," p. 101: "In our Sútra *Dharma* means Law," etc. The intuitive

assumed the leading form of futile mercy to the lower animals, extending into the devices of "Hospitals" for the suffering members of the brute creation, and ultimately, in after-times, progressing into the absurdity of the wearing of respirators and the perpetual waving of fans, to avoid the destruction of minute insect life. An infatuation, which eventually led to the surrendering thrones and kingdoms, to avoid a chance step which should crush a worm, or anything that crept upon the face of the earth; and more detrimental still, a regal interference with the every-day life of the people at large, and the subjecting of human labour to an enforced three months' cessation in the year, in order that a moth should not approach a lighted lamp, and the revolving wheel should not crush a living atom in the mill.

I have arranged, in the subjoined full *résumé* of the three phases or gradations "of Aṣoka's faith," as much of a contrast as the original texts, under their modern reproductions, admit of; exhibiting, in the first period, his feelings and inspirations from the tenth to the twelfth year after his inauguration; following on to the second, or advanced phase of thought, which pervades the manifestos of his twenty-seventh year; and exhibiting, as a climax of the whole series of utterances, his free and outspoken profession of faith in the hitherto unrecognized "*Buddha.*"

The difference between the first and second series of declarations or definitions of *Dharma* is not so striking as the interval in point of time, and the opportunities of fifteen years of quasi-religious meditation, might have led us to expect; but still, there is palpable change in the scope of thought—"a marked advance in faith"; only the faith is indefinite, and the morals still continue supreme. Happily, for the present inquiry, there is nothing in these authentic documents which has any pretence to be either Vedic or

feeling that "laborare est orare" seems to have prevailed largely in the land, and would undoubtedly have been fostered and encouraged under the gradual development of caste. The great Akbar appears to have participated in the impressions of his Hindu subjects; for we find him, in the words of his modern biographer, described as one "who looks upon the performance of his duties as an act of divine worship."—Dr. Blochmann's translation of the *Áín-i-Akbari*, p. iii.

Brahmanical, and therefore we can pass by, for the moment, all needless comparisons between the terms "Brahmans and Sramans"—the latter of whom equally represented Jainas and Buddhists—a controversy to which undue emphasis and importance has been hitherto assigned, and confine ourselves to Aṣoka's aims in departing from the silence of the past, and covering the continent of India with his written proclamations. His ideas and aspirations, as exhibited in his early declarations, are tentative and modest in the extreme: in fact, he confesses, in his later summaries, that these inscribed edicts represent occasional thoughts and suggestive inspirations; indeed, that they were put forth, from time to time, and often, we must conclude, ostentatiously *dated*, without reference to their period of acceptance or their ultimate place on the very stones on which we find them.

When closely examined, the two sets of edicts, contrasted by their positions as Rock and Pillar Inscriptions, covering, more or less, a national movement of fifteen years, resolve themselves into a change in the *Dharma* or religious law advocated by the ruling power of very limited and natural extent. The second series of manifestos are marked, on the one hand, by a deliberate rejection of some of the minor delusions of the earlier documents, and show an advance to a distinction and discrimination between good and evil animals, a more definite scale of apportionment of crimes and their appropriate punishments, completed by an outline of the ruling moral polity, reading like a passage from Megasthenes,[1] in regard to the duties of inspectors, and forming a consistent advance upon Chandra Gupta's moral code.

[1] Arrian xii.; Strabo xv. 48; Diod. Sic. ii. 3. There are several points in the Greek accounts of Indian creeds which have hitherto been misunderstood, and which have tended to complicate and involve the true state of things existing in the land at the periods referred to. Among the rest is *the* grand question, in the present inquiry, of Jaina *versus* Buddhist, of which the following is an illustration:—Fah Hian, chap. xxx. "*The honourable of the age* (Buddha) has established a law that no one should destroy his own life."

Mr. Laidlay adds, as a commentary upon this passage:—"The law here alluded to is mentioned in the Dulva (p. 162 to 239); where, in consequence of several instances of suicide among the monks, . . . Sâkya prohibits discourses upon that subject. So that the practice of self-immolation ascribed by the Greek historians to the Buddhists was, like that of going naked, a departure from orthodox principles."—p. 278.

The Rev. S. Beal, in his revised translation of Fah Hian, in confirming this

All these indications, and many more significant items, may, perchance, be traced by those, who care to follow the divergencies presented in the subjoined extracts; but no ingenuity can shake the import of the fact, that, up to the twenty-seventh year of his reign, Aṣoka had no definite idea of or leaning towards Buddhism, as represented in its after-development. His final confession and free and frank recognition of the name and teaching of Buddha in the Babhra proclamation, form a crucial contrast to all he had so elaborately advocated and indorsed upon stone, throughout his dominions, during the nearly full generation of his fellow-men, amid whom he had occupied the supreme throne of India.

As my readers may be curious to see the absolute form in which this remarkable series of Palæographic monuments were presented to the intelligent public of India, or to their authorized interpreters, in the third century B.C., I have, at at the last moment,[1] taken advantage of Mr. Burgess's very successful paper-impressions, or *squeezes*, of the counterpart inscription on the Girnár rock, to secure an autotype reproduction of the opening tablets of that version of the closely parallel texts of Aṣoka's Edicts. Those who are not conversant with ancient palæographies may also be glad of

conclusion of Mr. Laidlay, emphatically declares, "I doubt very much whether there is any reference to Buddhists in the Greek accounts."—pp. xlii, 119. See also J.R.A.S. Vol. XIX. p. 420, and Vol. VIII. N.S. p. 100.

"A long series of the rock inscriptions at Ṣravaṇa Beḷgoḷa, in the same old characters, consist of what may be termed epitaphs to Jaina saints and ascetics, both male and female, or memorials of their emancipation from the body. . . . It is painful to imagine the pangs of slow starvation, by which these pitiable beings gave themselves up to death and put an end to their own existence, that by virtue of such extreme penance they might acquire merit for the life to come. . . . The irony is complete when we remember that avoidance of the destruction of life in whatever form is a fundamental doctrine of the sect." . . . The inscriptions before us are in the oldest dialect of the Kanarese. The expression *muḍippidar*, with which most of them terminate, is one which seems peculiar to the Jainas." —Mr. Lewis Rice, Indian Antiquary, 1873, p. 322.

The passages regarding *suicidal* philosophers will be found in Megasthenes (Strabo xv. i. 64, 73); Q. Curtius viii. ix. sec. 33; Pliny, vi. c. 22, sec. 19; Arrian xi.

The *naked* saints figure in Megasthenes (Strabo xv. 60), Cleitarchus (Strabo xv. 70), Q. Curtius, viii. ix. 33.

[1] Mr. Burgess's Report for 1874–5 reached me on the 15th February, 1877, a few days only before the Meeting of the Royal Asiatic Society at which this paper was read. These paper-impressions are now deposited in the Library of the India Office.

the opportunity of examining the nature of the alphabetical system here in force—which constituted, in effect, the *Alphabet Mère* of India at large. These inscriptions, of about 250 B.C., contribute the earliest specimens of indigenous writing we are able to cite, their preservation and multiplication being apparently due to a newly-awakened royal inspiration of engraving edicts and moral admonitions on stone. This alphabetical system must clearly have passed through long ages of minority before it could have attained the full maturity in which it, so to say, suddenly presents itself over the whole face of the land. And which from that moment, unimproved to this day, asserts its claim to the title of the most perfect alphabet extant.

The Sanskrit-speaking Aryans discarded, in its favour, the old Phœnician character they had learnt, laboriously transformed, and finally adapted to the requirements of their own tongue, during their passage through the narrow valleys of the Himalaya, and their subsequent residence on the southern slopes of the range, in the Sapta Sindhu or Punjab, which scheme of writing would appear to have answered to the term of the *Yavanáni lipi* of Pánini and the earlier Indian grammarians.

In this second process of adaptation, the Aryans had to repudiate the normal ethnographic sequence of the short and long vowels, to add two consonants of their own (ज्ञ, ष) utterly foreign to the local alphabet, and to accept from that alphabet a class of letters, *unneeded* for the definition of Aryan tongues; an inference which is tested and proved by the fact that accomplished linguists of our age and nationality are seldom competent to pronounce or orally define the current Indian cerebrals.[1]

[1] Prinsep's Essays (Murray, 1858), pp. ii. 43, 144, 151, etc. Burnouf, Yasna, p. cxlv. Bopp's Grammar (Eastwick), i. 14. Lassen, "Essai sur le Pali," p. 15. J.R.A.S., o.s. X. 63; XII. 236; XIII. 108; XV. 19; N.S. I. 467; V. 423. J.A.S. Beng., 1863, p. 158; 1867, p. 33. Journ. Bom. Branch R.A.S., 1858, p. 41. Ancient Indian Weights (Numismata Orientalia, Part i. Trübner, 1874), pp. 3, 6, 21, 48. Numismatic Chronicle, 1863, p. 226. Caldwell, Dravidian Grammar (edit. 1875), pp. 13, 45, 64, 69, 82, 92, etc. Muir, Sanskrit Texts, ii. xxiv, and 34*n*, 440*n*, 468, 488, etc. Weber, "Greek and Indian Letters," Ind. Ant. 1873, p. 143. "On the Dravidian Element in Sanskrit

Plate I. exhibits a facsimile of Tablets 1, 2, of the Girnár rock. Of the former I have merely transliterated the first sentence. But as I have had occasion to extract the full translation of Tablet 2, I have now added the type-text, in the old character, together with an interlineation in Roman letters,[1] which will admit alike of preliminary readings, and suggest further crucial comparisons by more advanced students.

THE CONTRASTED TENOR OF THE THREE PERIODS OF AṢOKA'S EDICTS.—PERIOD I., 10TH AND 12TH YEARS AFTER HIS *abhishek* OR ANOINTMENT.

The first sentence of the Rock-cut Edicts, of the twelfth year of Aṣoka's reign, commences textually:[2]

𑀇𑀬𑀁 𑀥𑀁𑀫𑀮𑀺𑀧𑀻 𑀤𑁂𑀯𑀸𑀦𑀁 𑀧𑀺𑀬𑁂𑀦 𑀧𑀺𑀬𑀤𑀲𑀺𑀦𑀸 𑀭𑀸𑀜𑀸 𑀮𑁂𑀧𑀺𑀢𑀸

Iyam dammalipi Devánam piyena piyadasiná rádñá lepitá.

"This is the edict of the beloved of the gods, Raja Priyadasi—the putting to death of animals is to be entirely discontinued." . . . . .

The second tablet, after referring to the subject races of India and to "Antiochus by name, the Yona (or Yavana) Raja," goes on to say: "(two designs have been cherished

Dictionaries," by the Rev. F. Kittel, Mercara, Indian Antiquary, 1872, p. 235. F. Muller, "Academy," 1872, p. 319.

[1] This type was originally cut under James Prinsep's own supervision. I am indebted to the Asiatic Society of Bengal for the *font* now employed, which is in the possession of Messrs. Austin. Some slight modifications of the original will be noticed, especially in regard to the attachment of the vowels; but otherwise the type reproduces the normal letters in close facsimile. The most marked departure from the old model is to be seen in the vowel *o*, which in the original scheme was formed out of the a ¯ and ¯e, thus 𑀫𑁄; whereas, in the type, for simplicity of junction, the *e* and the *a* have been ranged on one level, in this form 𑀫𑁄. It will be seen that the Sanskrit श *ṣ* has not yet put in an appearance, the local स *s* having to do duty for its coming associate. A full table of the alphabet itself will be found in Vol. V. N.S. of our Journal, p. 422.

[2] I quote as my leading authority Professor Wilson's revised translation of the combined texts embodied in the Journ. R.A.S. Vol. XII. p. 164, et seq., as his materials were necessarily more ample and exact than Prinsep's original transcripts, which were unaided by the highly important counterpart and most efficient corrective in Semitic letters from Kapurdigiri, the decipherment of which was only achieved by Mr. Norris in 1845.

by Priyadasi: one design) regarding men, and one relating to animals."

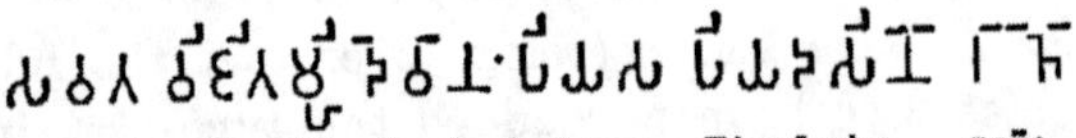

Savata vijitamhi Devánaṁpiyasa Piyadasino raño

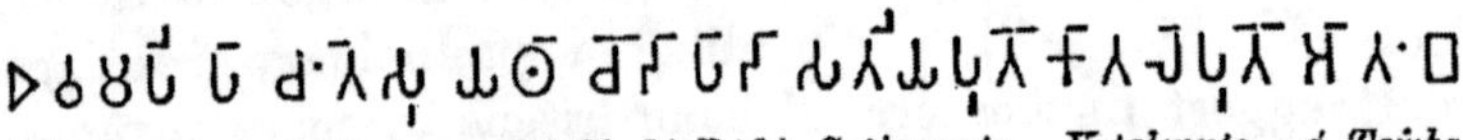

evamapi pá chaṁtesu yathá Choḍá Páḍá Satiyaputo Ketaleputo á Taṁba-

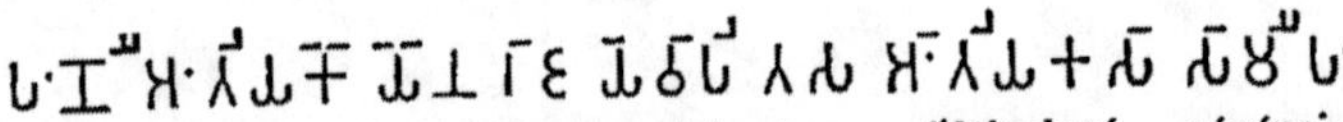

paṁṇi, Antiyako Yonarája yevápi tasa Aṁtiyakasá sámípaṁ

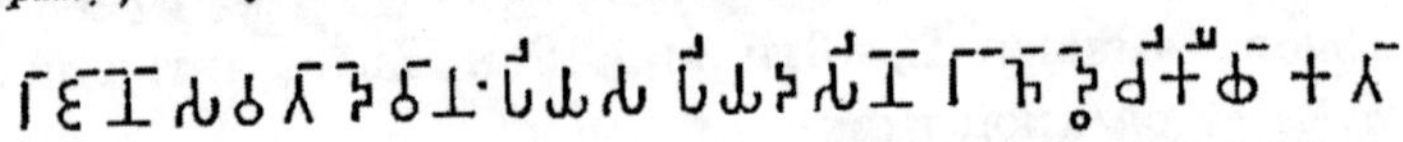

rájáno savatá Devánaṁpiyasa Piyadasino ráño dve chikichhá katá

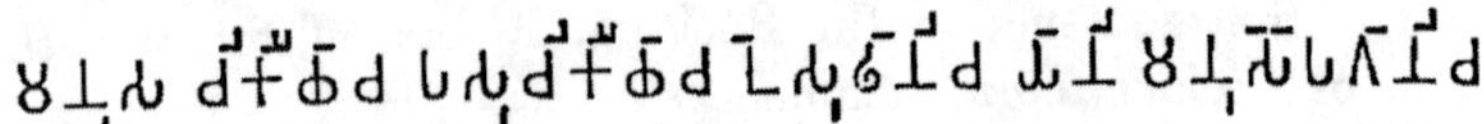

manusa chikichhácha pasuchikichhácha osuḍhánicha yáni manusopagánicha

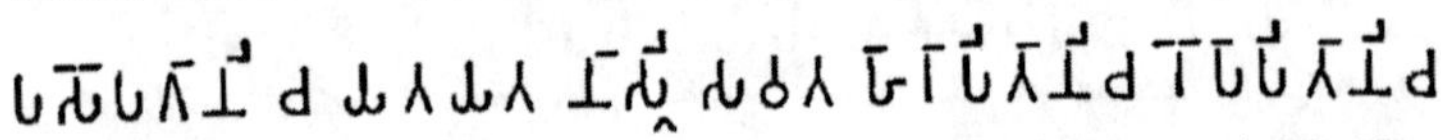

pasopagáni cha yata-yata násti savata hárápitánicha ropápitánicha

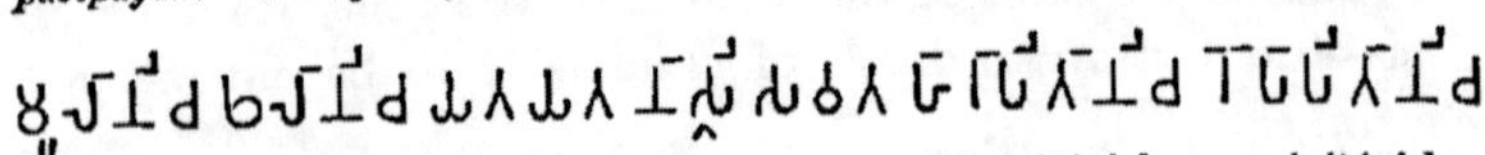

múlánicha phalánicha yata-yata násti savata hárápitánicha ropápitánicha

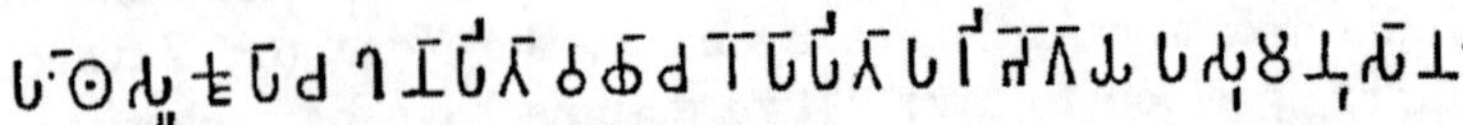

paṁthesú kúpacha khanápitá vachhácha ropápitá paribhogáya pasumanusánaṁ.

I give Dr. Kern's later translation of this passage entire, on account of its historical interest; there does not seem to be any material conflict in his rendering of the religious sense:

"In the whole dominion of King Devánámpriya Priyadarṣin, as also in the adjacent countries, as Chola, Paṇḍya, Satyaputra, Keralaputra, as far as Támraparṇí, the kingdom of Antiochus the Grecian king and of his neighbour kings, the system of caring for the sick, both of men and of cattle, followed by King Devánámapriya Priyadarṣin, has been everywhere brought into practice; and at all places where useful healing herbs for men and cattle were wanting he has caused them to be brought and planted; and at all

ASOKA'S INSCRIPTION AT GIRNÁR.

places where roots and fruits were wanting he has caused them to be brought and planted; also he has caused wells to be dug and trees to be planted, on the roads for the benefit of cattle."—Indian Antiquary, p. 272; Arch. Rep. 1874–5, p. 99.

The 3rd section adverts to "expiation," and the 4th continues: "During a past period of many centuries, there have prevailed, destruction of life, injury to living beings, disrespect towards kindred, and irreverence towards Sramans and Brahmans."[1]

The 5th edict, after a suitable preamble, proceeds:

"Therefore in the tenth year of the inauguration have ministers of morality been made,[2] who are appointed for the purpose of presiding over morals among persons of all the religions, for the sake of the augmentation of virtue and for the happiness of the virtuous among the people of Kamboja, Gandhara, Naristaka and Pitenika. They shall also be spread among the warriors, the Brahmans, the mendicants, the destitute and others." . . .

The 6th edict declares:—"An unprecedently long time has passed since it has been the custom at all times and in all affairs, to submit representations. Now it is established by me that . . the officers appointed to make reports shall convey to me the objects of the people"—and goes on to define the duties of supervisors of morals, and explain their duties as "informers," etc., continuing:— .

"There is nothing more essential to the good of the world, for which I am always labouring. On the many beings over whom

[1] Dr. Kern's elaborate criticism of Burnouf's revision of Prof. Wilson's translation of this passage (Lotus de la Bonne Loi, p. 731) scarcely alters the material sense quoted above. His version runs:

"In past times, during many centuries, attacking animal life and inflicting suffering on the creatures, want of respect for Bráhmans and monks."

Dr. Kern, in the course of his remarks upon his new rendering, observes, "Apart from the style, there is so little exclusively Buddhistic in this document, that we might equally well conclude from it that the King, satiated with war, had become the president of a peace society and an association for the protection of the lower animals, as that he had embraced the doctrine of Ṣâkya Muni."—I. A., p. 262.

[2] The Cuttack version of the Edicts differs from the associate texts, saying, "who shall be intermingled with all the hundred grades of unbelievers for the establishment among them of the faith, for the increase of religion . . . in Kambocha and Gandhára, in Surâstrika and Pitenika, . . . and even to the furthest (limits) of the barbarian (countries). Who shall mix with the *Brahmans* and *Bhikshus*, with the poor and with the rich."—p. 190; Prinsep, J.A S. Bengal.

I rule I confer happiness in this world,—in the next they may obtain *Swarga* (heaven)."[1]

Tablet 7 does not seem to call for any remark. Tablet 8 refers to some change that came over the royal mind in the tenth year of his reign. "Piyadasi, the beloved of the gods, having been ten years inaugurated, by him easily awakened, that moral festival is adopted (which consists) in seeing and bestowing gifts on Brahmanas and Ṣramanas, . . . overseeing the country and the people; the institution of moral laws," etc.

Burnouf's amended translation differs from this materially. He writes:

"[*Mais*] Piyadasi, le roi chéri des Dêvas, parvenu à la dixième année depuis son sacre, obtient la science parfaite que donne la Buddha. C'est pourquoi la promenade de la roi est cette qu'il faut faire, ce sont la visite et l'aumône faites aux Brâhmaṇes et aux Samaṇas." . . .

I see that Dr. Kern now proposes to interpret this contested passage as,

"But King Devánámpriya Priyadarṣin, ten years after his inauguration, came to the true insight. Therefore he began a walk of righteousness, which consists in this, that he sees at his house and bestows gifts upon Bráhmaṇs and monks. . . . Since then this is the greatest pleasure of King Devánámpriya Priyadarṣin in the period after his conversion" [to what?].—I. A. p. 263.

In his remarks upon the tenor of this brief tablet Dr. Kern continues,

"It is distinguished by a certain simplicity and sentiment of tone, which makes it touch a chord in the human breast. There is a tenderness in it, so vividly different from the insensibility of the later monkish literature of Buddhism, of which Th. Pavie observes, with so much justice, 'Tout reste donc glacé dans ce monde bouddhique.'"

Tablet 9, speaking of festivities in general, declares:

"Such festivities are fruitless and vain, but the festivity that bears great fruit is the festival of duty, such as the respect of the servant to his master; reverence for holy teachers is good, tender-

[1] Lassen renders this, "my whole endeavour is to be blameless towards all creatures, to make them happy here below and enable them hereafter to obtain *Svarga*."—Indian Antiquary, p. 270.

ness for living creatures is good, liberality to Brahmans and Sramanas is good. These and other such acts constitute verily the festival of duty. . . With these means let a man seek *Swarga*."[1]

Tablet 10 contrasts the emptiness of earthly fame as compared with the "observance of moral duty," and section 11 equally discourses on "virtue," which is defined as "the cherishing of slaves and dependents, pious devotion to mother and father, generous gifts to friends and kinsmen, Brahmanas and Sramanas, and the non-injury of living beings."

Tablet 12 commences: "The beloved of the gods, King Priyadasi, honours all forms of religious faith,"[2] . . . and enjoins "reverence for one's own faith, and no reviling nor injury of that of others. Let the reverence be shown in such and such a manner, as is suited to the difference of belief,"[3] . . "for he who in some way honours his own religion and reviles that of others, saying, having extended to all our own belief, let us make it famous, he, who does this, throws difficulties in the way of his own religion: this, his conduct cannot be right." . . . . The Edict goes on to say, "And as this is the object of all religions, with a view to its dissemination, superintendents of moral duty, as well as over women, and officers of compassion, as well as other officers" (are appointed).[4]

The 13th Tablet, which Professor Wilson declined to translate, as the Kapur di Giri text afforded no trustworthy corrective, seems, from Mr. Prinsep's version, to recapitulate much that has been said before, with a reiterated "injunction for the non-injury of animals and content of living creatures," sentiments in which he appears to seek the sympathy of the "Greek King Antiochus," together (as we now know[5]) with that of the "*four* kings Ptolemy, Antigonus, Magas and

[1] Dr. Kern's conclusion of Tablet 9 runs as follows, "By doing all this, a man can merit heaven; therefore let him who wishes to gain heaven for himself fulfil, above all things, these his duties."—I. A., p. 271.

[2] Dr. Kern's rendering says "honour all sects and orders of monks."

[3] "so that no man may praise his own sect or contemn another sect."

[4] "For this end, sheriffs over legal proceedings, magistrates entrusted with the superintendence of the women, hospice-masters (?) and other bodies have been appointed."—I. A., p. 268.

[5] Gen. Cunningham, Arch. Report, vol. i. p. 247, and vol. v. p. 20. See also my "Dynasty of the Guptas in India," p. 34. I append the tentative trans-

Alexander." The postscript in larger letters outside the square of this tablet adds, according to Prinsep, "And this place is named the WHITE ELEPHANT, conferring pleasure on all the world."

Prof. Wilson, in conclusion of his review of the purport of these palæographic documents, adverts to the Tablet numbered 14 in the original list, but he does not seem to have had sufficient confidence in his materials to have ventured upon a continuous translation.[1]

PERIOD II. THE ADVANCED STAGE.

The contrasted Láṭ or Monolithic Inscriptions,[2] as opposed

literation of the several versions of this tablet, which I had prepared for the latter work.

My learned friends are unwilling as yet to compromise themselves by a translation of the still imperfect text.

TRANSLITERATIONS OF TABLET XIII. OF THE AṢOKA INSCRIPTIONS AT (1) KAPUR-DI-GIRI, (2) KHALSI, AND (3) GIRNÁR.

1. *Ka.* Antiyoka namá Yona raja paran cha tenan Antiyokena chatura |||| rajanọ
2. *Kh.* Antiyoga náma Yona . . lan chá tena Antiyo . ná chatali + lajane
3. *Gir.* . . . . . Yona raja paran cha tena . . . . chapṭena[*sic*]rajano

1. *Ka.* Traramaye namá Antikina namá Máka namá Alikasandaro namá
2. *Kh.* Tulamaye náma Antekina náma Máká náma Alikyasadale náma
3. *Gir.* Turamáyo cha Antakana cha Magá cha . . . .

1. *Ka.* nicham Choḍa, Panḍa, Avam Tambupanniya hevammevamhena raja
2. *Kh.* nicham Choḍa, Panḍiya, Avam Tambapaniyá hevameváhevamevá . . lájá
3. *Gir.* . . . .

1. *Ka.* Vishatidi Yonam Kamboyeshu Nibha Kanabhatina Bhojam Piti
2. *Kh.* Vishmavasi Yona Kambojasu Nubha Kánábha Pantisa Bhoja Piti
3. *Gir.* . . . .

1. *Ka.* Nikeshu, Andrapulideshu savatam . . . .
2. *Kh.* Nikesa Adhapiladesa savatá . . . .
3. *Gir.* . . ndhepirandesu savata . . . .

Under the Elephant at Khalsi, *Gajatemre?* At Girnár, *Sveto hasti*, as above, p. 34.

[1] The 14th Edict at Girnár is more curious, in respect to the preparation of the Edicts, than instructive in the religious sense. Dr. Kern's revision produces, "King Devánámpriya Priyadarṣin has caused this righteousness edict to be written, here concisely, there in a moderate compass, and in a third place again at full length, so that it is not found altogether everywhere worked out; (?) for the kingdom is great, and what I have caused to be written much. Repetitions occur also, in a certain measure, on account of the sweetness of certain points, in order that the people should in that way (the more willingly) receive it. If sometimes the one or other is written incompletely or not in order, it is because care has not been taken to make a good transcript (*chhdyá*) or by the fault of the copyist (*i.e.* the stone-cutter)."—I. A., p. 275.

[2] J. As. Soc. Bengal, vol. vi. 1837, p. 566. The text on the Dehli láṭ has been taken as the standard; these edicts are repeated verbatim on the three other láṭs of Allahábád, Betiah and Radhia.

to the ROCK edicts already examined, open, in the text of the Tablet on the northern face of the Dehli pillar, with these words:

A

"In the 27th year of my anointment, I have caused this religious edict to be published in writing.[1] I acknowledge and confess the faults that have been cherished in my heart. From the love of virtue, by the side of which all other things are as sins—from the strict scrutiny of sin, etc., . . . by these may my eyes be strengthened and confirmed (in rectitude)." . . .

In the 10th line the King continues:

"In religion (*dhamma*) is the chief excellence: but religion consists in good works:—in the non-omission of many acts: mercy and charity, purity and chastity;—(these are) to me the anointment of consecration. Towards the poor and the afflicted, towards bipeds and quadrupeds, towards the fowls of the air and things that move on the waters, manifold have been the benevolent acts performed by me." . . . .

The concluding section of this tablet is devoted to a definition of the "nine minor transgressions," of which the following five alone are specified: "mischief, hard-heartedness, anger, pride, envy."

B

The text of the western compartment of the Dehli láṭ begins:

"In the 27th year of my anointment, I have caused to be promulgated the following religious edict. My devotees in very many hundred thousand souls, having (now) attained unto knowledge;[2] I have ordained (the following) fines and punishments for their transgressions.

Prinsep's half-admitted impression, that these inscriptions

[1] Burnouf renders this opening, "La 26ième année depuis mon sacre j'ai fait écrire cet édit de la loi. Le bonheur dans ce monde et dans l'autre est difficile à obtenir sans un amour extrême pour la loi, sans une extrême attention, sans une extrême obéissance," etc.—Lotus, p. 655.

[2] Dr. Kern's translation departs from this meaning in a striking manner, and substitutes: "I have appointed sheriffs over many hundred thousands of souls in the land, I have granted them free power of instituting legal prosecution and inflicting punishment."

were necessarily of a Buddhist tendency, led him into the awkward mistake of interpreting धात्री *dhátri* as "the myrobalan tree," instead of "a nurse," and the associate *aswattha* as "the holy fig-tree," in which he was followed by Lassen (Ind. Alt. vol. ii. p. 256), instead of the *asvatha abhitá* "consolés et sans crainte" of Burnouf, who corrected the translation in the following words: "De même qu'un homme, ayant confié son enfant à une nourrice expérimentée, est sans inquiétude [et se dit:] une nourrice expérimentée garde mon enfant, ainsi ai-je institué des officiers royaux pour le bien et le bonheur du pays."—Lotus de la bonne Loi, p. 741.

Prinsep's text here resumes the subject of transgressions, and "according to the measure of the offence shall be the measure of punishment, but (the offender) shall not be put to death by me."[1] "Banishment (shall be) the punishment of those malefactors deserving of imprisonment and execution."

The text proceeds with a very remarkable passage: "Of those who commit murder on the high road, even none, whether of the poor or of the rich, shall be injured on my three especial days."[2]

If we could rely upon the finality of this translation, we might cite, in favour of the Jaina tendency of the edict, the curious parallel of *the Jainas* under Akbar, who obtained a *Firmán* to a somewhat similar tenor in favour of the life

[1] It is curious to trace the extent to which these Jaina ideas developed themselves in after-times, and to learn from official sources how the simple tenets of mercy, in the abstract, progressed into the demands and rights of *sanctuary* claimed by and conceded to the sect.

"Maharana Srí Ráj Sing, commanding. To the Nobles, Ministers, Patels, etc., of Mewar. From remote times, the temples and dwellings of the Jainas have been authorized; let none therefore within their boundaries carry animals to slaughter. This is their ancient privilege.

"2. Whatever life, whether man or animal, passes their abode for the purpose of being killed, is saved (*amra*).

"3. Traitors to the state, robbers, felons escaped confinement, who may fly for sanctuary (*sirna*) to the dwellings (*upasrá*) of the Yatis, shall not be seized by the servants of the court. . . By command, Sáh Dyal, Minister. Samvat 1749 (A.D. 1693)."—Tod. vol. i. p. 553.

[2] Singular to say, with all this excellent mercy to animals, there is a reference to injuring (*torturing?*), and later even to "*mutilation*" of the human offender! —J.A.S.B. vol. vi. p. 588. See also Foe-koue-ki, cap. xvi.

of animals, and their exemption from slaughter on certain days peculiarly sacred in their *Rubric.*[1]

C

The tablet, on the southern compartment, gives a list of the "animals which shall not be put to death," enumerating many species of birds, the specific object of whose immunity it is difficult to comprehend—and especially exempting the females of the goat, sheep, and pig, . . . concluding with the declaration that "animals that prey on life shall not be cherished."

The Edict goes on to specify the days of fasts and ceremonies, closing with the words,

"Furthermore, in the twenty-seventh year of my reign, at this present time, twenty-five prisoners are set at liberty."

D

The Monolithic Inscriptions are continued in the eastern compartment, the text of which Prinsep translated in the following terms:

"Thus spake King DEVÁNAMPIYA PIYADASI: In the twelfth year of my anointment, a religious edict (was) published for the pleasure and profit of the world; having destroyed that (document) and regarding my former religion as sin, I now for the benefit of the world proclaim the fact. And this . . . I therefore cause to be destroyed; and I proclaim the same in all the congregations; while I pray with every variety of prayer for those who differ from me in creed, that they following after my proper example may with me attain unto eternal salvation: wherefore the present

[1] *Firmán* of Akbar. "Be it known to the Muttasuddies of Malwa, that the whole of our desires consists in the performance of good actions, and our virtuous intentions are constantly directed to one object, that of delighting and gaining the hearts of our subjects.

"We, on hearing mention made of persons of any religious faith whatever, who pass their lives in sanctity, etc., . . . shut our eyes on the external forms of their worship, and considering only the intention of their hearts, we feel a powerful inclination to admit them to our association, from a wish to do what may be acceptable to the Deity."

The prayer of the petitioners was: "That the Padishah should issue orders that during the twelve days of the month of Bhadra called Putchoossur (which are held by the Jainas to be particularly holy), no cattle should be slaughtered in the cities where their tribe reside."—Ordered accordingly, 7th Jumád-us-Sáni, 992 Hij. Era.—Malcolm, Central India.

edict of religion is promulgated in this twenty-seventh year of my anointment."

"Thus spake King Devánampiya Piyadasi. Kings of the olden time have gone to heaven under these very desires. How then among mankind may religion (or growth in grace) be increased, yea through the conversion of the humbly-born shall religion increase. . . . Through the conversion of the lowly-born if religion thus increaseth, by how much (more) through the conviction of the high-born and their conversion shall religion increase."

Prinsep concludes his version of this division of the Inscription:—

"Thus spake King Devánampiya Piyadasi:—Wherefore from this very hour I have caused religious discourses to be preached, I have appointed religious observances—that mankind having listened thereto shall be brought to follow in the right path and give glory unto God."

If Dr Kern's amended reading of the opening paragraphs of this tablet is to be accepted as final, we must abandon any arguments based upon a supposed cancelment of previous manifestos.[1] But the reconstruction in question—whether right or wrong—will not in the least degree affect my main argument of the pervading *Jaina* tendencies of the Monolithic edicts.

Dr. Kern's translation runs as follows:

"King Devánámpiya Priyadarṣin speaks thus:—12 years after my coronation, I caused a righteousness-edict to be written for the benefit and happiness of the public. Every one who leaves that unassailed shall obtain increase of merit in more than one respect. I direct attention to what is useful and pleasant for the public, and take such measures as I think will further happiness, while I provide satisfaction to my nearest relatives and to (my subjects) who are near as well as to them who dwell far off."

[1] Prof. Wilson, while criticizing and correcting much of Prinsep's work upon these documents, remarked, "If the translation (of the text of the eastern compartment) is correct, and in substance it seems to be so, there are two sets of opposing doctrines in the inscriptions, and of course both cannot be Buddhist. Mr. Prinsep comes to the conclusion that the Buddhist account of the date of Aṣoka's conversion, the fourth year of his reign, is erroneous, and that he could not have changed his creed until after his twelfth year. Then it follows that most, if not all the Rock inscriptions are not Buddhist, for the only dates specified are the tenth and twelfth years. Those on the Láṭs appear to be all of the twenty-seventh year. If, however, those of the earlier dates are not Buddhist, neither are those of the later, for there is no essential difference in their purport. They all enforce the preference of moral to ceremonial observances" (J.R.A.S. vol. xii. p. 250).

II. a. The Aim and Purpose of the Inscriptions.

The Dehli pillar, in addition to the four edicts inclosed within square tablets, has a supplementary inscription encircling the base of the column. In this proclamation Aṣoka, after enumerating his own efforts for the good of his people after the truly Indian ideal of planting trees and excavating wells along the high roads, goes on to arrange for the missionary spread of his religion, in these terms:

"Let the priests deeply versed in the faith (or let my doctrines?) penetrate among the multitudes of the rich capable of granting favours, and let them penetrate alike among all the unbelievers whether of ascetics or of householders. . . . Moreover let them for my sake find their way among the bráhmans (*bábhaneshu*) and the most destitute." . . .

The text proceeds:

"Let these (priests) and others most skilful in the sacred offices penetrate among" . . . "my Queens, and among all my secluded women," . . . "acting on the heart and on the eyes of the children, . . . for the purpose (of imparting) religious enthusiasm and thorough religious instruction."

After much more of similar import, the Edict concludes:

"Let stone pillars be prepared, and let this edict of religion be engraven thereon, that it may endure unto the remotest ages."

The separate Edicts of the Aswastama Inscription at Dhauli[1] continue these exhortations in the subjoined terms:

"My desire is that in this very manner, these (ordinances) shall be pronounced aloud by the person appointed to the *stupa*; and adverting to nothing else but precisely according to the commandment of Devánampiya, let him (further) declare and explain them."[2] . . . . "And this edict is to be read at (the time of) the

[1] "The Aswastama is situated on a rocky eminence forming one of a cluster of hills, three in number, on the south bank of the Dyah river near to the village of Dhauli. The hills alluded to rise abruptly from the plains, . . . and have a singular appearance, no other hills being nearer than eight or ten miles." —Major Kittoe, J.A.S.B. vol. vii. p. 435.

[2] Burnouf revised this translation, with his usual critical acumen, in 1852. The following quotation gives his varied version:—"Aussi est-ce là ce qui doit être proclamé par le gardien du *stûpa* qui ne regardera rien autre chose, (ou *bien*, aussi cet édit a dû être exprimé au moyen du *Prâkrita* et non dans un autre idiome). Et ainsi veut ici le commandement du roi Chéri des Devas. J'eu confié l'exécution au grand ministre. . . .

"Et cet édit doit être entendu au *Nakhata Tisa* (Nakchatra Tichya) et à la fin

lunar mansion Tisa, at the end of the month of *Bhátun*: it is to be made heard (even if) by a single listener. And thus (has been founded) the Kálanta *stupa* for the spiritual instruction of the congregation.[1] For this reason is this edict here inscribed, whereby the inhabitants of the town may be guided in their devotions for ages to come."—J.A.S. Bengal, May, 1837, pp. 444–5.

Period III. Positive Buddhism.

The Bhabra Edict.[2]

Professor Wilson's translation of the Bhabra Edict—unlike his previous renderings of Aṣoka's rock inscriptions, where he was at the mercy of succeeding commentators—was undertaken at a time when he, in his turn, had the advantage of the revised interpretations of Lassen and Burnouf. It may be taken, therefore, as a crucial trial of strength on his part.

But the most curious coincidence in connexion with the present inquiry is that, in default of critical Sanskrit aids, he was obliged to have recourse to the vulgar tongue of the *Jaina* Scriptures for an explanation of the obscure opening terms, in the word *bhante* "I declare, confess," etc., etc., which proved, to his surprise, to constitute the ordinary *Jaina* preliminary form of prayer or conventional declaration of faith.[3]

I prefix Burnouf's translation, as exhibiting the inevitable divergences in the individual treatment of these obscure writings:

du mois Tisa (4 letters) au *Nakhata*, même par un seule personne il doit être entendu. Et c'est ainsi que ce *stûpa* doit être honoré jusqu'à la fin des temps, pour le bien de l'assemblée."—Burnouf, B. L. 673.

See also my article in the J.R.A.S. Vol. I. N.S. p. 466; and the Kalpa Sútra, pp. 16, 17.

[1] As a possible commentary upon this, the avowedly Buddhist *Lalita-Vistara* says: "The rehearsal of religious discourse satiateth not the godly."—Preface, p. 24, Sanskrit Version, Rajendralála.

[2] At Bairath, three marches N.E. of Jaipúr.

[3] "But in turning over the leaves of a Jaina work (the Parikramanavidhi), which, according to Dr. Stevenson, means the Rules of Confession to a Guru, I found the word *Bhante* . . . repeated fourteen times, and in every instance with the pronoun *aham*—*aham bhante*—preceding apparently some promise or admission; 'I declare, I promise, or acknowledge.' The book is written in the Mágadhi of the Jainas, mixed with provincial Hindi, and is full of technicalities, which it would require a learned *Yati* to expound."—J.R.A.S., Vol. XVI. p. 361.

"Le roi Piyadasa, à l'Assemblée du Magadha qu'il fait saluer, a souhaité et peu de peines et une existence agréable. Il est bien connu, seigneurs, jusqu'où vont et mon respect et ma foi pour le Buddha, pour la Loi, pour l'Assemblée. Tout ce qui, seigneurs, a été dit par le bienheureux Buddha, tout cela seulement est bien dit. Il faut donc montrer, seigneurs, quelles [en] sont les autorités; de cette manière, la bonne loi sera de longue durée: voilà ce que moi je crois nécessaire. En attendant, voici, seigneurs, les sujets qu'embrasse la loi: les bornes marquées par la *Vinaya* (ou la discipline), les facultés surnaturelles des Ariyas, les dangers de l'avenir, les stances du solitaire, le *Sûta* (*sûtra*) du solitaire, la spéculation d'Upatisa (Çariputtra) seulement, l'instruction de Lâgula (Ráhula), en rejetant les doctrines fausses: [voilà] ce qui a été dit par le bienheureux (Buddha). Ces sujets qu'embrasse la loi, seigneurs, je désire, et c'est la gloire à laquelle je tiens le plus, que les Religieux et les Religieuses les écoutent et les méditent constamment, aussi bien que les fidèles des deux sexes. C'est pour cela, seigneurs, que je [vous] fais écrire ceci; telle est ma volunté et ma déclaration."—Lotus, p. 725.

Prof. Wilson's translation is as follows:

"Piyadasi, the King, to the general Assembly of Mágadha, commands the infliction of little pain and indulgence to animals.

"It is verily known, I proclaim, to what extent my respect and favour (are placed) in Buddha, and in the Law, and in the Assembly.

"Whatsoever (words) have been spoken by the divine Buddha, they have all been well said, and in them, verily I declare that capability of proof is to be discerned: so that the pure law (which they teach) will be of long duration, as far as I am worthy (of being obeyed). For these, I declare, are the principal discipline (Vinaya), having overcome the oppressions of the Aryas, and future perils, (and refuted) the songs of the Munis, the sútras of the Munis, (the practices) of inferior ascetics, the censure of a light world, and (all) false doctrines. These things, as declared by the divine Buddha, I proclaim, and I desire them to be regarded as the precepts of the Law. . . . These things I affirm, and have caused to be written (to make known to you) that such will be my intention."—Journ. R.A.S. Vol. XVI. (1851), p. 357. See also Translation, Journ. A.S. Bengal, vol. ix.

I subjoin Dr. Kern's newly-published translation, for the double purpose of comparison with the redactions of his predecessors, and to satisfy the modern world, that whatever diversities may have existed in the spirit or method of interpretation of the difficult passages of the 1st and 2nd series of Aṣoka's Edicts, our international savants are fully in accord as to the first appearance *in monumental writing* of the name of *Buddha*, that is, some time in or after the 27th year of Aṣoka.

"King Priyadarṣin (that is, the Humane) of Magadha greets the Assembly (of Clerics) and wishes them welfare and happiness. Ye know, sirs, how great is our reverence and affection for the triad which is called Buddha (the master), Faith, and Assembly. All that our Lord Buddha has spoken, my Lords, is well spoken: wherefore, Sirs, it must indeed be regarded as having indisputable authority; so the true Faith shall last long. Thus, my Lords, I honour (?) in the first place these religious works . . . [seven in number] uttered by our Lord Buddha . . . For this end, my Lords, I cause this to be written, and have made my wish evident."—*Indian Antiquary*, Sept. 1876, p. 257.

In concluding this section of the inquiry, I am anxious to advert to a point of considerable importance, the true bearing of which has, hitherto, scarcely been recognized. Under the old view of the necessary Buddhistic aim and tendency of both the Rock and Pillar Edicts, a subdued anomaly might have been detected in Aṣoka's designating himself as *Devánampiya*, "the beloved of the gods." We have seen at page 41 in what terms the rock inscriptions are phrased; the pillar edicts, in like manner, commence with the same title of *Devánampiye* Piyadasi lája,[1] while the Bhabra Inscription unconditionally rejects the *Devánampiya*, which we may infer would have been inconsistent with Aṣoka's sudden profession of Buddhism, and opens with the restricted entry of 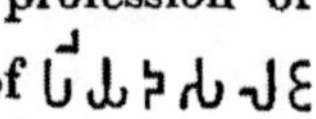 *Piyadasa laja.*

Now, it involves a more than remarkable coincidence, that this same term of *Devánampiya*, or "Beloved of the gods," should prove to have been an established and conventional title among the Jainas,[2] equally, as, in a less important sense, was

[1] J.A.S. Bengal, vol. vi. p. 577.

[2] In Stevenson's translation of the Kalpa Sútra *Rishabha datta* is thus addressed by *Devanandi*, the mother of Mahávíra (pp. 26, 30), and he, in return, salutes her as "O beloved of the gods" (pp. 27, 29, etc.). At p. 54 King Sidd-

the associate *Piyadasaṇe*, "lovely to behold." "Siddhártha" is represented in the text of the Kalpa Sútra, as "issued forth the king and lord of men, the bull and lion among men, lovely to behold," etc. Dr. Stevenson adds, in a note: "This is the famous epithet पियदसणे *Piyadasaṇe* that occurs so frequently in the ancient inscriptions, and which we have met with several times before." Piyadassi is further given as the name of one of the 24 (*Jaina ?*) Buddhos in the opening passage of the Mahávanso.[1] Mr. Turnour contributes the following additional quotation from the Páli annals: "Hereafter the prince Piyadáso, having raised the *chhatta*, will assume the title of AṢOKO the Dhanma Rája, or righteous monarch."[2]

Thus, while we can comprehend that the retention of the simple title of "Pyadasi," by an avowed Buddhist, was harmless enough, the rejection of the designation of "Beloved of the gods" became a clear necessity for any convert to a religion which *ipso facto* repudiated all gods.

The title of Devánampiya does not seem to have been admitted into the scriptures of the Northern Buddhists,[3] who were deferred converts; but it was carried down with the earliest spread of the faith to Ceylon, in B.C. 246, by "Devánampiya Tissá,"[4] together with, as we have seen, many of the other elements and symbols of the Jaina creed.

Amid the varied indirect sources of information bearing upon the "faith of the Mauryas," now available, we should scarcely have looked for any contributions from the formal

hártha, in explaining Trisalá's dream, commences, "O beloved of the gods." At pp. 56, 61, speaking to the royal messengers, he addresses them as "O beloved of the gods," and at p. 64 the "interpreters of dreams" are received with the same complimentary greeting.

[1] Mahavanso, vol. i. p. 75.

[2] J.A.S. Bengal, vol. vi. p. 1056. See also Wilson, J.R.A.S. Vol. XII. p. 244.

[3] The objection to the term *Devánampiya* of course does not extend to the inevitable *Devaputra* of the Lalita-vistara—the "heaven-born" need not have been compromised by his later apostacy.—See Rajendra Lála's (Sanskrit text), *Preface*, pp. 14, 15, 21, etc.

[4] Maháwanso, pp. 4, 68, 62, etc. Indian Antiquary, 1872, p. 139. Rhys Davids, Inscription of Gamini Tissa, son of Devánampiya Tissa, at Dambula, Ceylon.

pages of dictionaries or grammars. Nevertheless, amid the odd words cited, for other purposes, we discover, in Patanjali's commentary on the *Sútras* of Páṇini, a most suggestive record by the annotator, who is supposed to date somewhere about B.C. 160–60,[1] regarding the gods of the Mauryas. Prof. Goldstücker's translation of Páṇini's leading text, with the illustration added by Patanjali, is subjoined:

"'If a thing,' says *Páṇini*, 'serves for a livelihood, but is not for sale' (it has the affix *ka*). This rule *Patanjali* illustrates with the words 'Ṣiva, Skanda, Viṣákha,' meaning the idols that represent these divinities, and at the same time give a living to the men who possess them—while they are not for sale. And 'why?' he asks. 'The *Mauryas* wanted gold, and therefore established religious festivities.' Good; (Páṇini's rule) may apply to such (idols as *they* sold); but as to idols, which are hawked about (by common people) for the sake of such worship as brings an immediate profit, their names will have the affix *ka*."[2]

That there are many difficulties in the translation, and still more in the practical interpretation of this passage, need not be reiterated.[3] The first impression the context conveys

[1] This is Prof. Weber's date; Prof. Goldstücker assigned Patanjali to 140–120 B.C.; and Prof. Bhandarkar fixes the date of his chapter iii. at 144–142 B.C.—Ind. Ant. 1872, p. 302.

[2] Goldstücker's Páṇini, p. 228. Prof. Goldstücker goes on to add: "Whether or not this interesting bit of history was given by Patanjali ironically, to show that even affixes are the obedient servants of kings, and must vanish before the idols which *they* sell, because they do not take the money at the same time that the bargain is made—as poor people do—I know not. . . . I believe, too, if we are to give a natural interpretation to his (Patanjali's) words, . . . that he lived *after the last king* of this (Maurya) dynasty."—p. 229.

Prof. Weber's critical commentary upon Goldstücker's rendering of this passage, amid other argumentative questions as to the period of Páṇini himself, proceeds:

"Patanjali, in commenting on rule v. 3, 99, of Páṇini, . . . in the case of a life sustenance-serving (object, which is an image, the affix ka is *not* used), except when the object is valuable. . . . . In the case of a saleable, *e.g.* Ṣiva, Skanda, Viṣákha, the rule does not apply." . . .

"The gold-coveting *Maurya* had caused images of the gods to be prepared. To these the rule does not apply, but only to such as serve for immediate worship (*i.e.* with which their possessors go about from house to house) [in order to exhibit them for immediate worship, and thereby to earn money]."—Indian Antiquary, 1873, p. 61.

[3] Prof. Weber's opinion on the bearing of this passage is to the following effect: "In the passage about the Mauryas I must leave it to others to decide if Patañjali's words do really imply it as his opinion that Pâṇini himself, in referring to images that were saleable, had in his eye such as those that had come down from the Mauryas. I never said more than this. And Bhâṇḍârkar goes too far when he says: 'Prof. Weber *infers* that Pâṇini in making his rule *had* in his eye,' etc. My words are: 'According to the view of Patañjali;' 'Patañjali is undoubtedly of

seems to refer to the multitudinous images of the *Jaina* Mauryas, which were so easily reproduced in their absolute repetitive identity, and so largely distributed as part and parcel of the creed itself, of which we have had so many practical exemplifications in the preceding pages.[1] But Patanjali's direct reference to the Maurya gods of his day—that is to say, during the reign of that staunch adherent of the Brahmans, the *Suṅga Pushpamitra*[2]—under the definite names of *Ṣiva*, *Skanda*, *Viṣákha*, opens out a new line of inquiry as to the concurrent state and progress of Brahmanism, and his evidence undoubtedly indicates that their branch of the local religion was in a very crude and inchoate stage at the period referred to—an inference which is more fully confirmed by the testimony of numismatic remains.[3]

Among the extant examples of the mintages of Hushka, Jushka, and Kanishka, we meet with the self-same designations of the three Brahmanical gods, under the counterpart Greek transcription of OKPO, ΣKANΔO, and BIZAΓO. The only

opinion;' 'Be this as it may, the notice is in itself an exceedingly curious one.' Now with regard to this very curious and odd statement itself, I venture to throw it out as a mere suggestion, whether it may not perhaps refer to a *first* attempt at gold coinage made by the Mauryas (in imitation of the Greek coins). It is true no Maurya coin has been discovered as yet, so far as I know, but this may be mere chance: the real difficulty is how to bring Patañjali's words into harmony with such an interpretation, the more so as in *his* time no doubt gold coins were already rather common."—Indian Antiquary, July, 1873, pp. 208, 209.

[1] "As these twenty-four Tírthankaras are incarnations of wisdom, and are divine personages who appeared in the world and attained the enjoyment of heavenly bliss, the Jainas consider them to be *Swámis*, equal to the divine-natured *Arugan*. . . . And accordingly they build temples in honour of these Tírthankaras, and make images like them, of stone, wood, gold, and precious gems, and considering these idols as the god Arugan himself, they perform daily and special *pujas*, and observe fasts and celebrate festivals in their honour."—p. xix. Notice on Jainism, by Sástram Aiyar, from "The Chintámaṇi," edited by the Rev. H. Bower, Madras, 1868.

[2] Pushpamitra is the king who offered 100 *dinárs* for the head of every *Ṣramana*, and hence obtained the title of *Munihata*, "Muni-killer."—Burnouf, vol. i. p. 431.

[3] I must add that in other portions of the "Mahábháshya" reference is made to "the Brahmanical deities of the Epic period, Ṣiva, Vishṇu, etc.; to Vásudeva or Kṛishṇa as a god or demi-god, and to his having slain Kansa and bound Bali." Mr. Muir, from whose analysis of Prof. Weber's Indische Studien (1873) I take this information, adds: "The genuineness of the whole of Patanjali's work itself, as we now have it, is not, Prof. Weber considers, beyond the reach of doubt, as some grounds exist for supposing that the work, after having been mutilated or corrupted, was subsequently reconstructed, and at the same time perhaps received various additions from the pen of the compiler." See also *Academy*, 8th August, 1874, p. 156.

other Brahmanical gods that apparently attained any prominence, at the epoch of these three Indo-Scythian kings, which, for the moment, we may accept as at or about the commencement of our era, would seem to have been Ṣiva's supposed consort, ΑΡΔΟΧΡΟ, and *Mahásená*, which latter embodiment is elsewhere understood as a mere counterpart of Ṣiva.[1] In the same manner, *Skanda* constitutes the title of a "son of Ṣiva," and *Viṣákha* is the conventional name of *Kárttikeya* or *Skanda*, "the god of war," and finally, *Kumára* is simply a synonym of *Skanda*. In fact we have here nothing but the multiform *Ṣiva* personally, or the various members of his family. So that the combined testimony of the grammarian and the material proofs exhibited by the coins would almost necessitate the conclusion that, at the commencement of our era, *Brahmanism* had not yet emerged from *Ṣaivism*, whose Indian origin is now freely admitted by the leading authorities.

In testing the position of Saivism, at approximate periods, we are able to appeal to the independent testimony of the coins of a collateral division of the Indo-Scythic race, whose leading designation follows the term of ΟΟΗΜΟ ΚΑΔΦΙϹΗϹ.

It has hitherto been usual to place this branch of the Scythic intruders considerably earlier, in point of time, than their fellow and more permanently-domiciled brotherhood; but the question as it is presented, under later lights, seems to resolve itself into a geographical rather than an epochal severance. The Kadphises *horde* settled themselves in lands where the Bactrian Páli alphabet and quasi-Aryan speech were still current. The Kanerki group, wherever their first Indian location may have been, clearly followed Iránian traditions in the classification and designations of their adopted gods, in the regions of their abundant mintages.

The Kadphises forms of Saivism may be followed in detail in Plate X. of Prof. Wilson's Ariana Antiqua. The

[1] *Mahá-sená*, "a great army," an epithet of *Kárttikeya* or *Skanda*; of *Ṣiva*. So also *Senápati*, "army chief," name of *Kárttikeya*; of *Ṣiva*, etc.—M. Williams, in vocibus.

conjoint legends appertaining to which are couched in the following terms:

Latin-Greek—BACIΛΕΥC ΟΟΗΜΟ ΚΑΔΦΙCIC.

Bactrian-Pali—

Maharajasa Rajadhirajasa Sarva-loga-iṣwarasa Mahiṣwarasa Kapiṣasa.
Of the Great King, King of Kings, ruler of the whole world, the Great Lord (of) Kapisa.[1]

We have here, again, *Ṣiva* very much under the guise of a God of War (Nos. 9, 13), though the trident is suggestive of Neptune and the ill-defined drooping garment, in the left hand, is reminiscent of the lion's skin of Hercules. But the Saivism is complete in No. 5, even to the spiral shell-shaped hair[2] (less apparent in No. 13), with the conventional VÁHANA or Bull, which now becomes constant and immutable; following on in Nos. 12–21 the leading type exhibits various gradations of the gross hermaphrodite outline of half man, half woman, with "the necklace of skulls," possibly disclosing the first definite introduction to *caste* threads, out of which so many religious conflicts grew in later days.

Under any circumstances, the present coincidences must be accepted as beyond measure, critical, when we find Patanjali, a native of Oudh, speaking of things on the banks of the Soane, at Patna, and Scythian intruders on the Kábul river, responding in practical terms, as to the ruling *Ṣaivism* which covered, with so little change, a range of country represented in the divergent paths of a continuous highway, starting from the extreme geographical points here named.

For the purposes of the illustration of the international associations, and the accepted religions of the period, we are beyond measure indebted to the recent numismatic contributions of the Peshâwar find. These coins, comprising the large total of 360 gold pieces, all belong to the combined Kanishka brotherhood, or tribal communities, to which reference has been made in my previous article in the Journal,[3] and in

[1] Prinsep's Essays, vol. ii. p. 213. Ariana Antiqua, p. 354. J.R.A.S. Vol. XX. p. 239. Solinus tells us: Quidam libri Caphusam. In alii: Caphisam. Plinius Capissam vocat. cap. liv. p. 827.

[2] Rudra and Pushan are said to wear their hair wound or braided spirally upwards into the form of a shell called "Kapardin."—Muir, vol. v. p. 462.

[3] Journal Royal Asiatic Society, Vol. IX. p. 8 *et seq.*

the earlier pages of this paper. The triple series of *obverse* legends are restricted to the following repetitive Greek transcriptions:

GREEK LEGENDS ON THE KANERKI COINS.

1. PAO NANO PAO KANHPKI KOPANO.
2. PAO NANO PAO OOHPKI KOPANO.
3. PAO NANO PAO BAZOΔHO KOPANO.

These titles seem to have been more or less sectional and eventually to have become hereditary, like Arsaces, Cæsar, etc., and though probably applicable in the first instance severally to the three brothers, they appear, in process of time, to have become dynastic as the conventional titular designation of the head of the family or tribe, for the time being, and to have continued in imitative use, especially in the instance of BAZOΔHO,[1] for many centuries. Until, indeed, as I have previously remarked, the Greek characters become altogether unintelligible,[2] though the mint types are still mechanically reproduced.

I have now to describe, as briefly as the subject will admit of, the coins I have selected for insertion in the accompanying Plate II., which were primarily arranged to illustrate the objects of worship admitted into the Indo-Scythian Pantheon; but, which, under subsequent discoveries, have assumed a more important mission in the general range of inquiry.

CONTENTS OF PLATE II.

KANERKI.

No. 1. (*Obverse.* King standing to the front, in the conventional form represented in Ariana Antiqua, pl. xi. fig. 16, *worn die.*

Legend. Constant. PAO NANO PAO KANHPKI KOPANO.)

Reverse. Figure as in the Plate. *Legend* NANA PAO, *Nanaia.*

[1] The identity of Bazdeo as one of the three brothers, and as the person alluded to in the Mathurá inscriptions under the title of *Vásudeva*, in conjunction with *Kanishka* and *Huvishka*, seems to be now placed beyond doubt; but the new coins teach us to discriminate Bazdeo as the third king, in opposition to my suggestion (Vol. IX. p. 11, *suprà*) that *Vásudeva* might have been "the titular designation of Kanishka."

[2] Prinsep's Essays, pl. xxii. 4, 5, 6–11, 13. J.R.A.S. o.s. Vol. XII. Pl. IV. the same figures. Ariana Antiqua, pl. xiv. figs. 12, 13, 16, 17.

INDO-SCYTHIAN COINS.

OOERKI.

No. 2. (*Obverse.* King seated cross-legged, wearing a close-fitting helmet, with bossed cheek-plates and flowing fillets, ornamental coat fastened by two brooches or link-buttons in front, flames issue from both shoulders. He holds a small mace in the right hand, and a spear in the left.)

Reverse. Figure as in Plate. *Legend.* ΗΡΑΚΙΛΟ, *Hercules.*

No. 3. (Bust of the King, as in the ordinary Kadphises types (A.A. xiv. 2). Quilted coat, flame issuing from the right shoulder, close cap, double feather frontlet, half moon, spiked mace, etc.)

Reverse. Figures as in Plate. *Legend.* ΜΑΟ *Moon*, ΜΙΙΡΟ *Sun.*

No. 4. (*Obverse.* Ooerki, old form (A.A. xiv. 6), die much worn.)

Reverse. Figure as in Plate. *Legend.* ΡΙΑΗ (or ριρη or ριδη), *Pallas.* This type was first introduced at Rome by Domitian, A.D. 80, who affected to be the son of Pallas Capitolina.—Trésor de Numismatique, p. 42.

No. 5. (*Obverse.* ΟΟΗΡΚΙ, (A.A. xiv. 6), worn-out die.)

Reverse. Figure as in Plate. *Legend.* ΩΡΟΗ or ωρον. *Varuna.*

No. 6. (*Obverse.* Well-executed bust of King, with close-fitting cap, eagle feather frontlet, and flowing *Sassanian* fillets at the back; silken dress, with large necklace. He holds a small mace, and an *ankus* (elephant goad).

Reverse. Figure as in Plate. *Legend.* ϹΑΡΑΠΟ, *Sarapis.*

No. 7. (*Obverse.* King seated, the general outline of the device is similar to that of No. 2; but the crossed legs are merged in rising clouds. The helmet has a prominent frontlet in the form of the sun, no cheek-plates, the ear and beard are visible, flames on shoulders, spear and mace, the coat is more than usually open in front and displays an embroidered under-garment.)

Reverse. Figure as in the Plate. *Legend.* ΖΕΡΟ (Ceres), *Diana.* Device imitated from a coin of Augustus, A.U.C. 744, B.C. 10. —Trésor de Numismatique, vii. 12.

No. 8. (Bust of King, similar to No. 2; Sun frontlet, in this instance the helmet has a cheek bar only, and shows the ear, traces of Sassanian fillets, etc. Armlets, link-brooch, mace, spear, etc. In one example of the Mars *reverse*, the *obverse* head is similar to No. 16 *infrà*, but the King wears a pallium.)

Reverse. Figure of a Roman warrior, as in the Plate. There are five varieties of this reverse. In one instance the figure of Mars holds what is described, in the Trésor de Numismatique, as "un bouclier rond," a type which occurs on the money of Germanicus, A.U.C. 801, A.D. 47 (Pl. xix. 7, 8).

Legend. PAO PHΘPO (Rao-rethro), *Mars.*

No. 9. (*Obverse.* Bust of King, as in No. 7.)

Reverse. Figure as in the Plate.

Legend. OANINΔA (Oaninda), *Anandates.*

No. 10. (*Obverse.* Bust as in No. 3. No flame on shoulder, *Sassanian* fillets.)

Reverse. As in the Plate. *Legend.* MAAΣHNO (Mahásená), an Indian form of *Mars* ? *Siva* ?

No. 11. (*Obverse.* Bust as in No. 3.)

Reverse. Device as in the Plate. *Legends.* ΣKANΔO, KOMAPO, BIZAΓO; *Skanda, Kumára, Viṣákha.*

No. 12. (*Obverse.* Bust of King, with ornamental jacket, armlets, mace, spear, flames on shoulders, etc. Peaked cap as in A.A. xiv. 5, but with bossed cheek-plates.)

Reverse. Device as in the Plate. *Legend.* AΘPO, Zend *A'tars* (the Roman Vulcan).

No. 13. (*Obverse.* Bust of King as in No. 8.)

Reverse. Device as in the Plate; exhibiting a three-faced Indian form of Ṣiva wearing short drawers *(jánghiyá)*, in front of which appears, for the first time, a marked definition of the Priapus, which however has nothing in common with the local *Linga.* The left hands hold the trident and an Indian thunderbolt. The one right hand grasps the wheel or *chakra* (the symbol of universal dominion), the other is extended to the small goat.

Legend. OKPO. *Ugra* the "fierce" (a title of Ṣiva).

No. 14. *Obverse.* As exhibited in the Plate. The King wears a Roman *pallium*; ornamental cap with cheek-plates and well-defined *Sassanian* fillets; in the right hand the small iron-bound mace,[1] in the left a standard, surmounted by Ṣiva's *Váhana* or the bull *Nandi*, in the conventional recumbent position.

[1] General Cunningham was under the impression that this object was a Buddhist praying-wheel. I prefer to look upon it as an iron-bound mace, a counterpart of the modern club, so effective in strong hands, known by the name of *lohd-band láthi.* The *gurz* of Feridún was an historical weapon. The use of which was affected by the great Mahmúd of Ghazni and his successors after him. The Kadphises Scythians also were demonstrative about maces, but theirs took the form of a bulky wooden club. See also Tabari (O.T.F.), vol. ii. p. 228.

Legend, legible. ρAO NANO PAO Oηρκι κοραvo.

Reverse. Ṣiva, three-faced, four-armed, to the front, holding the trident, a club, a western form of the thunderbolt and a *gourd*, water-vessel ?

Legend. OKPA, Zend *ugra*, उग्र *Ugra*, the "fierce," "terrible."

No. 15. (*Obverse.* King's bust as in No. 8.)

Reverse. Roman figure, as in the plate, holding a brazier with ascending flames. *Legend.* ΦAPPO, Pharos. There are several varieties of this type: in one instance the figure holds a *simpulum*, such as is seen on the coins of Antonia Augusta, A.D. 37.—Trésor de Numismatique, pl. x. fig. 14.

No. 16. *Obverse.* King's bust as in the Plate. Ornamental jacket, armlets, mace and spear; with a curious peaked helmet having buffalo horns diverging upwards from below the frontlet, as is seen in certain Indo-Sassanian coins of a later age;[1] flowing fillets at the back, with *Sassanian* fillets distributed over each shoulder.

Reverse. A Roman type of abundance. *Legend.* APΔOXPO. The cornucopiæ and the style of dress belong to the period of Julius Cæsar and the early days of Augustus, A.U.C. 711, 33 B.C.—Trésor de Numismatique, pl. iii. fig. 1.

No. 17. (*Obverse.* Kadphises type of King's bust, with mace and *ankus*, Sassanian fillets.)

Reverse. Four-armed figure, as in the Plate. *Legend.* MANAO BAΓO, the *Moon-god.*

No. 18. (*Obverse.* Kadphises bust; silken garment, mace, *ankus*, etc., flame on right shoulder, ordinary fillets.)

Reverse. Male figure, as in the Plate. *Legend.* MAO, *Mao*, the Moon.

No. 19. (*Obverse.* King's bust as in A.A. xiv. 3; highly ornamental robe and collar, Sassanian fillets, etc.)

Reverse. Figure as in the Plate, with sword and staff, holding out a chaplet. *Legend.* MAO, the Moon.

No. 20. (*Obverse.* King's bust, with Roman pallium, peaked cap, and Sassanian fillets.)

Reverse. Female figure with Caduceus, as in the Plate.

Legend. NANO, *Nanaia.*

[1] See Prinsep, Essays, vol. ii. p. 115; Ariana Antiqua, pl. xvii. 5, etc.; Herodotus, vii. c. lxxvi.

No. 21. (*Obverse.* Juvenile bust of the King, with silken garment, mace, *ankus*, with a close-fitting compact helmet and Sassanian fillets.)

Reverse. Rayed figure, with flowing garments, as in the Plate. *Legend.* ΜΙΘΡΟ, *Mithra.*

No. 22. (*Obverse.* Old form of bust of the King, Kadphises style.)

Reverse. Figure as in the Plate. *Legend.* ΜΙΙΡΟ, *Mihira.*

No. 23. (*Obverse.* Well-executed profile, but less-finished bust, of the King; wearing the Roman *pallium*, with mace, spear, peaked cap, prominent frontlet, bold *halo*, bossed cheek-plates with flowing fillets of the ordinary character, associated with the Sassanian drooping falls on the back of the left shoulder, flame on the right shoulder.)

Reverse. Figure, also clothed in the pallium, as seen in the Plate. The type of the reverse follows, in a measure, the earlier examples of ΗΛΙΟϹ (A. A. xi. 16) and ΜΙΙΡΟ (A. A. xii. 15), and it has something in common with the beautiful reverse of No. 21 of our Plate II. Legend of "undetermined" import ΑΡΑΕΙΧΡΟ.

BAZΔHO.

No. 24. (*Obverse.* King *standing* to the front, in full Scythian cap-à-pied armour, with sword, spear, high pointed cap, reduced halo, falling fillets, with large Mithraic altar, into which the right hand of the King seems to be casting votive incense, as in A.A. xiv. 18.

Legend, constant. ΡΑΟ ΝΑΝΟ ΡΑΟ ΒΑΖΟΔΗΟ ΚΟΡΑΝΟ.)

Reverse. Figure as exhibited in the Plate. *Ṣiva trimukhi*, to the front, with top-knot, holding trident and noose (*paṣu*), clad in the Indian *dhoti*, naked above the waist.

Legend. Reversed-Greek ? ΟΚΡΟ.

No. 25. (*Obverse.* Full-length figure of the King, in bossed and armour fished skirt (as in A.A. xiv. 14).

Reverse. Figure as shown in the Plate. *Ṣiva*, single-faced, with top-knot, and bushy hair, clothed in the Indian *dhoti*, bold muscular development of the chest, trident, noose (*paṣu*), well-defined Bráhmaní bull, monogram, etc. *Legend.* ΟΚΡΟ.

No. 26. (*Obverse.* Standing figure of the King, the bosses of the body-armour appear in full detail, the fish-scale skirt is also given, as are the greaves and the rings, or serpent-like protection of the arms. The spear is here a subdued trident, with a bold central point and reduced side spikes; but the peculiarity of the whole device, in this instance, consists in the tall Kuzzalbásh-like cap, which is surmounted by the head of a bird.

Reverse. Ṣiva *trimukhi*, as reproduced in the Plate, with his bull in a varied position. The god, in addition to ordinary trident and noose, reveals a subdued but fully defined priapus in front of the folds of the *dhoti*, together with the first determinate representation of a Brahmanical or *caste* thread, which replaces the early necklace of skulls adverted to at p. 59.

One of the most important revelations of the Pesháwar *find* is the large amount of Roman influence to be detected amid the types of these Indo-Scythian coinages.

The earliest archæological trace of commercial or other intercourse between India and Rome is represented by the celebrated deposit in a tumulus at Manikyála, discovered by M. A. Court in 1833.

M. Court's description of the position and condition of the crypt is as follows:

"At ten feet from the level of the ground, we met with a cell in the form of a rectangular parallelogram, built in a solid manner, with well-dressed stones, firmly united with mortar. The four sides of the cell corresponded with the four cardinal points, and it was covered with a single massive stone. Having turned this over, I perceived that it was covered with inscriptions. In the centre of the cell stood a copper urn, encircling which were placed symmetrically eight medals of the same metal. . . . The urn itself was carefully enveloped in a wrapper of white linen tightly adhering to its surface. . . . The copper urn enclosed a smaller one of silver; the space between them being filled in with a paste of the colour of raw umber. . . Within the silver urn was found one much smaller of gold, immersed in the same brown paste, in which were also contained seven silver medals, with Latin characters.[1] The gold vessel

[1] 1. No. 19. pl. xxxiv. J.A.S. Bengal, vol. iii. A silver denarius of Mark Antony, struck while he was a member of the celebrated triumvirate; M. ANTONIUS. iii. VIR. R.P.C.—Vaillant, ii. p. 9. Riccio, pl. iv. 25. J. des Sav. 1836, p. 72 (A.U.C. 711).

2. No. 20. Julius Cæsar. Julia family, Riccio, xxiii. 31. R. Rochette. A.U.C. 694-704, "si connu et si commun."

3. No. 21. Cordia family. Ric. xiv. 1. R.R. A.U.C. 705. "Un denier d'Auguste, avec les têtes accouplées de Caïus et de Lucius Cæsars."

4. No. 22. Minucia family. Riccio, xxxiii. 7. Q. THERM. M.F. about A.U.C. 680.

enclosed four small coins of gold of the Græco-Scythic type[1] . .; also two precious stones and four pearls."

With a view to determine the age of the monument itself from external evidence, M. Raoul Rochette critically examined the Roman coins found in the inner coating of the main deposit. The result of his exhaustive study is subjoined in his own words:

"Maintenant, ce qui résulte de la réunion de ces sept monnaies de familles romaines, six desquelles sont reconnues avec certitude, et qui furent toutes frappées dans le cours des années 680 à 720 de Rome; ce qui résulte, non-seulement de la présence de ces sept monnaies, appartenant toutes aux derniers temps de la république, et de l'absence de monnaies consulaires ou impériales, c'est que le monument où on les avait déposées à dessein, appartient lui-même à la période de temps qui est celle de l'émission et de la circulation de ces monnaies; car le fait qu'on n'y a trouvé mêlé parmi elles ni un seul denier consulaire, ni un seul denier impérial, est certainement très-significatif; et ce ne peut être, à mon avis, une circonstance purement fortuite ou accidentelle qui ait réuni ainsi, dans un monument considérable, sept monnaies choisies entre toutes celles que le commerce avait portées dans l'Inde, et toutes frappées dans la période républicaine des guerres civiles, qui eurent principalement l'Orient pour théâtre."—*Journ. des Savants*, 1836, p. 74.

At one time it was fondly hoped that this monument might prove to have been the last resting-place of the ashes of Kanishka himself, but the inscription on the inverted slab effectually disposed of any such notion.[2] The covering stone of the crypt mentions *Samvat* 18, and the Mathurá inscriptions extend his reign to *Samvat* 33. The discovery, however, is of the highest importance under other aspects. It has been usual to associate Kanishka's name with Buddhism, and in

5. No. 23. Accoleia family. LARISCOLVS, i. 1. A.U.C. 710-720.
6. No. 24. Julia family. Ric. xxii. 4.
7. No. 25. Furia family. R. xxi. 8. R.R. A.U.C. 686. The latest authorities, therefore, limit the date of the most recent of these coins to B.C. 34. Prinsep's Essays, vol. i. p. 149.

[1] Four "gold coins found in the gold cylinder." Pl. xxxiv. vol. iii. J.A.S. Bengal.
1 and 2. Kanerki *bust* and peaked cap. *Rev.* Ṣiva, four-armed and OKPO.
3. Kanerki standing figure. *Rev.* Ṣiva, four-armed and OKPO.
4. Kanerki standing figure. *Rev.* Standing figure. AΘPO.

[2] Prof. Dowson, J.R.A.S. Vol. XX. O.S. p. 250.

his reign a new convocation of the Buddhists was convened, once again to revise and determine the authorized faith. If Kanishka ever was a Buddhist, he, like Aṣoka, must have become so late in life. His coins, as we have seen, are eminently Saiva, and this monument, erected during his reign, contained, within the gold cylinder in the innermost recess of its undisturbed chamber, no less than three coins bearing the image of Ṣiva, out of the four, selected for inhumation with the ashes of the person, in whose honour it was built. Moreover, so distinctly was the ruling Ṣaivism accepted in India, that we find the coins of NANA PAO conventionally denominated *Nánakas* (and elsewhere defined as bearing the mark of *Ṣiva*) in the authoritative text of Yajnavalkya's Hindu Law.[1] On the other hand, Indo-Scythic Buddhism is undemonstrative in the extreme, and one of the coins most relied upon to prove devotion to that faith[2] turns out, under the legends of the better specimens of the Peshâwar find, to bear the name of ΑΡΔΕΙΧΡΟ (No. 23, Pl. II.), whereas those coins which bear the unmistakable figure of Ṣákya Muni—as I shall show hereafter—clearly belong to a later period of the Kanerki series.

Under the system in vogue, in more advanced Buddhistic days, of the gradual enlargement of Topes and the concurrent exhibition of relics, which for convenience sake were placed near the summit of the mound, we find a later deposit three feet only from the top of this smaller Manikyâla *tope*, which consisted of three coins bearing the form and name of Ṣiva, and one coin only with the image and superscription of ΟΑΔΟ, the Wind.[3]

[1] Yajnavalkya's date is uncertain. Some commentators place him before Vikramâditya, others so late as the second century A.D. See my Ancient Indian Weights, p. 20. Prof. Wilson remarks that the name of णाणक *ṇáṇaka* occurs in the play of the *Mrichchhakati* (act i. scene 1), and the commentary explains the *ṇáṇaka* as शिवाङ्कटङ्क *Ṣiváṅka-taṅka*, or "coin with the mark of Ṣiva."

[2] General Cunningham, J.A.S. Bengal, 1845, p. 435, pl. ii. fig. 3.

[3] The four copper coins found above the stone cover of the tumulus, pl. xxxiv. vol. iii. J.A.S. Bengal, are identified with—

1. Kadphises, the King, standing. *Rev.* Ṣiva and Nandi, with Bactrian-Páli legends similar to A.A. Plate x. figs. 15, etc.
2. Coin of Kanerki, with *Rev.* ΟΑΔΟ.
3 and 4. Coin of Kanerki, with *Rev.* Ṣiva four-armed, ΟΚΡΟ.

We have now to seek to discover, from the numismatic remains,—which constitute the only positive data left us,—how it came to pass, that so many of the elements of Western forms of worship and classic Roman devices found their way into such a specially-dissevered section of the earth, as that which bowed to Indo-Scythian sway at and shortly before the commencement of our era.

The first and most obvious suggestion would point to ordinary commercial intercourse, the superior value of Indian produce, and the consequent import of Roman gold for the requisite balance of trade, about which Pliny was so eloquent. But in this case we are forced to admit some more direct and abiding influence. If the Roman gold had been suffered to remain intact in the shape it was received, as mere bullion, which sufficed for the traffic of the Western coast, we should have gained no aid or instruction in the explanation of the present difficulty.

But, fortunately, the recoinage of the original Roman aurei *in situ*, at whatever exact point it may ultimately be placed, must clearly be limited to a region, far removed from the inspiring centre, and separated by some natural belt of desert or hostile territory from free intercourse with old associations, or home relations.

In the Parthian dominions, which intervened between the extreme points indicated, there existed precisely such barriers: and excepting the perseverance with which their kings retained the eagles of Crassus, there was no notion of recognition or adoption of Roman devices by the Parthian monarchs till the Italian slave Mousa got her image placed on the Arsacidan mintages.

Whereas, among the distant communities in the far East, we discover consecutive imitations of Roman types, extending over a considerable space of time, and following irregularly the latest novelties and innovations of the Imperial mints; but always appearing in independent forms, as reproductions, with newly-engraved dies of inferior execution, but with Latin-Greek legends embodying Zend denominations; and, more distinctive still, uniformly accepting either the already-prepared *obverses* of the Indo-Scythian kings, or reviving their semblance from time to time in apparent recognition of the suzerain power.

The enigma above outlined seems to me to be susceptible of but one solution, which singularly accords with the given circumstances of time and place—that is, that the 10,000 captives of the army of Crassus,[1] who were transported to Merv-ul-rúd, on the extreme border of the Parthian dominions,[2] a site intentionally most remote from their ancestral homes, finding even that fertile valley, that pleasant Siberia, unprepared to accommodate so large and so sudden an influx of population, spread and extended themselves into the proximate dominions of the Indo-Scythians,[3] and freely ac-

[1] Plutarch in Crassus xxxi.—*Λέγονται δ' οἱ πάντες δισμύριοι μὲν ἀποθανεῖν, μύριοι δὲ ἁλῶναι ζῶντες.* Repeated in Appian Parth., p. 66.

[2] Pliny, N. H. vi. xvi. 18.—"Sequitur regio Margiane, apricitalis inclytæ, sola in eo tractu vitifera, undique inclusa montibus amœnis . . . et ipsa contra Parthiæ tractum sita: in qua Alexander Alexandriam condiderat. Qua diruta a barbaris, Antiochus Seleuci filius, eodem loco restituit Syriam; nam interfluente Margo, qui corrivatur in Zotale, is maluerat illam Antiochiam appellari. Urbis amplitudo circumitur circuitu stadiis lxx; in hanc Orodes Romanos Crassiana clade captos deduxit."

The references in Vell. Paterculus ii. 82, and Florus iv. 10, only go to show how mercifully the captives were treated, inasmuch as they were freely allowed to serve in the Parthian ranks. Justin, xlii. cap. v. affirms that the prisoners of both the armies of Crassus and Antony were collected and restored, with the standards, in B.C. 20, but this statement probably refers only to those who were within easy call; and the thirty-three years' residence in the distant valleys of the Indian Caucasus may well have reconciled the then surviving remnant of Crassus's force to their foreign home and new domestic ties. See also Suetonius, in Augusto, c. xxi., in Tiberio, c. ix.

[3] Ἀντιόχεια ἡ καλουμένη Ἔνυδρος, or *Antiochia irrigua*, was distant 537 *schœni*, by the Parthian royal road, from *Ctesiphon*, or Madain, on the Tigris: in continuation of the same highway, it was 30 *schœni* N.N.E. of Ἀλεξάνδρεια ἡ ἐν Ἀρείοις or *Alexandria Ariana*, the modern "Herát," from whence the route proceeded by Farrah and the Lake of Zaranj to *Sikohah*, the Σακαστανὴ Σακῶν Σκυθῶν or *Sacastana Sacarum Scytharum*, and hence to Bust and Ἀλεξανδρόπολις, μητρόπολις Ἀραχωσίας, or the modern Kandahár.—C. Müller, Geographi Græci Minores (Paris, pp. xci. 252, and Map No. x.).

Merv-ul-rúd 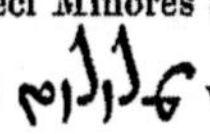 was selected as the seat of government of Khorasán on the Arab conquest, in preference to the more northern Merv 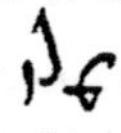 or *Merv Sháhjahán*—both which names are to be found on the initial Arabico-Pahlavi coins of Selim bin Ziád and Abdullah Hazim, in 63 A.H. (J.R.A.S. Vol. XII. p. 293, and XIII. p. 404). The early Arabian geographers, who officially mapped-out every strategic and commercial highway, tell us that important routes conducted the merchant or traveller from Merv-ul-rúd eastwards, by Túlikán, Farayáb and Maimana, to Balkh, whence roads branched-off to the southward, to Bamián, and by other lines to Andarábah, Parwán, and Kábul.

While Herát once reached, by the direct main line to the south, offered endless

cepting their established supremacy, settled themselves down as good citizens, taking in marriage the women of the country,[1] and forming new republics,[2] without objecting to the recognition of a nominal Suzerain—a political supremacy their fellow-countrymen so soon submitted to in its closer and more direct form of Imperator—at the same time that they retained their old manners and customs, and with them the religion of the Roman pantheon, with the due allowance of Antistes and possibly a Pontifex Maximus, in partibus infidelium.

To judge from the changes and gradations in the onward course of these mintages, it would seem as if the new settlers had either directly copied the *obverses* of the Indo-Scythians with their normal Greek legends, or possibly they may have been supplied with official mint-dies, which they used to destruction, and when, in turn, they had to renew these *obverse* dies, they imparted to the ideal bust of the suzerain many of their own conventional details of dress, etc. But in the process of imitation, they appear to have adhered as far as possible to a mechanical reproduction of the old quasi-Greek letters of the Indo-Scythian legend, while on their new and independent *reverses* they took licence in the Latin forms of the Greek alphabet, frequently embodying the current Zend terms in their own hybrid characters, and in some cases becoming converts to, or at least accepting the symbols of the local creeds. Their influence, on the other hand, upon local thought and Indian science, may perchance be traced in the pages of the *Pauliṣa-Siddhánta* and *Romaka-Siddhánta*, wherein their adopted Greek astronomy was insured a shorter passage to the East than the hitherto-recognized devious routes from Alexandria to the Western coast and other points

facilities for the dispersion of the new settlers in the six or seven roads which focussed in the centre formed by that ancient city. (See Sprenger's Post- und Reiserouten des Orients, maps 4, 5; M. N. Khanikof, "Asie centrale," Paris, 1861, map; Ferrier's Caravan Journeys, London, 1857, map.)

[1] Milesne Crassi conjuge barbara, etc.—Horace, Od. iii. 5. 5.

[2] A very suggestive indication has been preserved, in later authors, about the white-blood claimed by the ruling races of Badakhshán, Darwáz, Kuláb, Shighnán, Wakhán, Chitrál, Gilgit, Swát, and Bálti.—Burnes, J.A.S.B. vol. ii. p. 305; J.R.A.S. Vol. VI. p. 99; Marco Polo, cap. xxix. Yule's edit. i. p. 152. See also, for Kanishka's power in these parts, Hiouen Thsang, Mémoires, i. pp. 42, 104, 172, 199.

of contact could have afforded.[1] And, in another direction, these new suggestions may lead us to re-examine, with more authority, the later amplifications of the Zend alphabet,[2] and to expose the needless introduction of foreign vowels and diphthongs—the assimilation of the anomalous Latin ء *q* and the reception of the ڤ *f*, which was only dubiously represented in the Sanskrit alphabet by फ *ph*.

Prof. Max Müller has remarked that the mention of the word *dînár* is, in a measure, the test of the date of a Sanskrit MS.,[3] and so the use of the re-converted Roman *aurei* may serve to check and define the epoch of distant dynastic changes.

Pliny has told us of the "crime," as he calls it, of him who was the first to coin a *denarius* of gold,[4] which took place sixty-two years after the first issue of silver money, or in B.C. 207. Under Julius Cæsar the weight of the *aureus* was revised and fixed at the rate of forty to the *libra*, after which period the rate gradually fell, till, under Nero, forty-five *aurei* were coined to the *libra*.

The average weight of extant specimens of Julius Cæsar's *denarii* of gold is stated to run at about 125·66 grains, while similar pieces of Nero fall to a rate of 115·39 grains.

The Persian Daric seems to have been fixed at 130 grains.[5] The Greek gold pieces of Diodotus of Bactria weigh as much as 132·3 grains.[6]

The Indo-Scythian gold coins reach as high as 125,[7] but this is an exceptionally heavy return. The Kadphises' group of coins range up to 122·5, and support an average of 122·4; an average which is confirmed by the double piece, no. 5, pl. x. Ariana Antiqua, which weighs 245 grains.[8] The

[1] Colebrooke, Essays, vol. ii. p. 340. Wilford, Asiatic Researches, vol. x. pp. 55, 101, etc. Reinaud, Mem. sur l'Inde, pp. 332, etc. Whitney, Lunar Zodiac, 1874, p. 371. Kern, Preface to "Brihat Sanhitâ," p. 40, etc.

[2] J.R.A.S. Vol. XII. O.S. p. 272, and Vol. III. N.S. p. 266. Prinsep's Essays, vol. ii. p. 171.

[3] Sanskrit Literature, p. 245.

[4] xxxiii. 13.

[5] International Numis. Orient., Mr. Head, p. 30.

[6] Journ. Roy. As. Soc. Vol. XX. p. 122.

[7] Gen. Cunningham, J.A.S.B., 1845, p. 435. Coin of *Arasikro* (No. 23, Pl. II.).

[8] Coin in British Museum.

Kanerki series present a slightly lower average, but sustain, in numerous instances, a full measure of 122 grains. So that, allowing for wear or depreciation in recoinage, the official imitative mint-rate would not be far removed from the fall following close upon Julius Cæsar's full average, which progressively reached the lower figures above quoted under Nero. While the coin weights, on the one hand, serve to determine the initial date of the serial issues, the devices above described will suffice, on their part, to indicate the periods of inter-communion with the Imperial history as seen in the periodical introduction of copies of the new Roman types of Mint reverses.

To enable my readers to judge of the state of the religious beliefs of Upper India and the adjoining countries to the northward and westward, I have taken advantage of the very important discovery of the gold coins of the Scythic period above described, to compile, or rather to enlarge a previous Table,[1] exhibiting the names of the multitudinous gods recognized amid the various nationalities who, at this time, bowed to the Indo-Scythian sway.[2]

[1] Numismatic Chronicle, N.S. vol. xii. 1872, p. 113. My "Sassanians in Persia" (Trübner, 1873), p. 43.

[2] The faith or dominant creed of the three brothers, Kanerki, Ooerki, and Vasudeva (*Hushka*, *Jushka*, *Kanishka*), or that of their subjects, may be tested by the devices of the Peshâwar hoard of their coins.

KANERKI, Κανηρκι.	OOERKI, Οοηρκι.		BAZDEO, Βαζοδηο.
1. Μιιρο	1. Ριαη	10. Μαναο βαγο	1. Νανα
2. Μειρο	2. Ηρακιλο	11. Αθρο	2. Οκρο, under numerous forms
3. Μαο	3. Ωροη	11a. Ραο ρηθρο	
4. Αθρο	4. Σαραπο	12. Αραειχρο	
5. Νανα ραο	5. Ζερο	13. Φαρρο	
	6. Οανινδο	14. Νανα	
	7. Μιθρα (Μιιρο, Μιορο, Μορο, etc.)	15. Οκρο 16. Αρδοχρο 17. Μαασηνο	
	8. Μαο 9. Μαο with Μιιρο	18. { Σκανδο, Κομαρο, Βιζαγο }	

This table is confined to the list of 93 specimens, selected from the total Peshâwar *find* of 524 coins, as numismatic examples for deposit in the British Museum. The 60 coins brought home by Sir Bartle Frere from the same *trouvaille*, for the Indian Government, do not add any varieties to these lists.

VEDIC GODS.	IRÁNIAN GODS.	PERSIAN.	GREEK AND GRÆCO-ROMAN.	BRAHMANICAL.	BUDDHIST.
1. ΩΡΟΗ *Varuṇa*	1. ΟΑΔΟ *Vayu*	1. ΜΙΘΡΟ *Mithra*	1. ΗΛΙΟΣ *ἥλιος*	1. ΟΚΡΟ *Ṣiva*	1. ΒΟΔΑ ΣΑΜΑΝΑ *Boda Sramana*
2. ΟΡΔΑΓΝΟ *Agni*	2. ΜΙΙΡΟ *Mihira*	2. ΝΑΝΑ *Nana*	2. ΗΡΑΚΙΛΟ *Hercules*	2. ΑΡΔΟΧΡΟ *Parvati?*	
	3. ΑΡΔΕΙΧΡΟ	3. ΝΑΝΑ ΡΑΟ *Nana-rao*	3. ΡΙΑΗ *Rhea?* (Pallas Capitolina)	3. ΜΑΑΣΗΝΟ *Mahâsêna*	
	4. ΜΑΟ *Mao*	4. ΝΑΝΑΙΑ *Nanaia*	4. ΣΑΡΑΠΟ *Sarapis*	4. ΣΚΑΝΔΟ *Skanda*	
	5. ΜΑΟ and ΜΙΙΡΟ *Mao* and *Mihira*	5. ΟΑΝΙΝΔΟ *Anandates*	5. ΖΕΡΟ *Ceres?* (Diana)	5. ΚΟΜΑΡΟ *Kumâra*	
	6. ΜΑΝΑΟ ΒΑΓΟ *Maonh Bago*		6. ΡΑΟ ΡΗΘΡΟ *Raorêthro* (Mars)	6. ΒΙΖΑΓΟ *Viṣâkha*	
	7. ΑΘΡΟ *Atars*				
	8. ΦΑΡΟ *Pharo*, fire-*bearer*				

I have reduced both the description of Plate II., as well as the above Table, to the narrowest possible outlines, for two reasons: firstly, because I do not desire to anticipate or interfere with Mr. Vaux's more comprehensive description of Sir B. Frere's selections from the great Pesháwar *find*—which we may hope shortly to see in the pages of our Journal; and secondly, because I wish to await General Cunningham's mature report upon the same *trouvaille*, which is designed to form an article in the Numismata Orientalia, a work in which I am much interested. The only portions of the full number of 524 coins that I have examined are confined to the 93 specimens Sir E. C. Bayley has forwarded to me for the purpose of study and for *eventual* deposit in the British Museum, and the 60 coins from the same source brought home by Sir Bartle Frere, now in the Library at the India Office.

Nevertheless, there are some suggestive identifications embodied in the Table for which I may be held more immediately responsible, and which I must, as far as may be, endeavour to substantiate.

I. Vedic Gods.

The first, and most venturesome of these, is the association of the *ωροη* on the coins with the Vedic *Varuṇa*; but the process of reasoning involved becomes more simple, when we have to admit that *Οὐρανός* and *Varuṇa* are identical under independent developments from one and the same Aryan conception—and that, even if exception should be taken to the elected transcription of *Ωροη*, the manifestly imperfect rendering of the letters of the Greek legend freely admits of the alternative *Ωρου*.

Some difficulty has been felt, throughout the arrangement of the Table, as to under which of the first four headings certain names should be placed; in this instance, I have been led to put *Varuṇa* in the Vedic column, on account of the absence of the final Zend *o*—which would have associated the name more directly with the Iranian branch of worship.[1]

A similar reason might properly be urged for removing

[1] Muir, Sanskrit Texts, vol. v. pp. 58, 72, 76, 120, etc.; Haug, Sacred Writings of the Parsees, pp. 226, 230.

ΟΡΔΑΓΝΟ from column i. to column ii.; but in this case the "*Agni*" is preferentially Vedic,[1] and the Iranian branch has its own representative of "Fire," in the technical ΑΘΡΟ. There is also another objection to be met, in the matter of the prefix. It has been usual to follow Lassen's identification of ΑΡΔΟΧΡΟ, as meaning "half-Siva," *i.e.* the female form of that hermaphrodite god;[2] but these new legends suggest, if they do not prove, that the prefix ΑΡΔ corresponds to the Sanskrit ऋत *ṛita*, "worshipped," great, etc., instead of to the assumed अर्द्धं *arddhan*, "half." And as, in the present instance, the figure to which the designation is attached is clearly a male, with spear and crested helmet,[3] there can be no pretence of making a half-female out of this device.

II. Iranian Gods.

The opening ΟΑΔΟ of this list might well have claimed a place in column i., in virtue of its approximation to the Vedic *Váyu*—a term under which "the wind" is equally addressed in the Zend-Avesta: *Vâyus uparôkairyo*, "the wind whose business is above the sky."[4] But the term ΟΑΔΟ is certainly closer in orthography to the Persian باد *bád*,[5] and the class of coins upon which it is found pertain more definitely to the Iranian section of the Aryan race, and refer to days when the main body of the Vedic Aryans had long since passed on to the banks of the Jumna.

The ΜΙΙΡΟ has been committed to column ii. on simply

[1] "Agni is the god of fire, the Ignis of the Latins, the Ogni of the Slavonians. He is one of the most prominent deities of the Rig-Veda. . . Agni is not, like the Greek Hephaitos, or the Latin Vulcan, the artificer of the gods."—Muir, vol. v. p. 199.

[2] Journ. A.S. Bengal, 1840, p. 455; Ind. Alt. (new edition), vol. ii. p. 839; Wilson, Ariana Antiqua, p. 366.

[3] Ar. An. pl. xii. fig. 3; Journ. A.S. Bengal, 1836, pl. xxxvi. 1; Prinsep's Essays, pl. xxii. fig. 1; Journ. R.A.S. Vol. XII. o.s. Pl. VI. Fig. 1. I must add that the best specimens of the coins extant give the orthography of ΟΡΛΑΓΝΟ, which, however, has hitherto been universally accepted as ΟΡΔΑΓΝΟ;—a rectification which the parallel frequency of the prefix to other names largely encourages.

[4] Haug, p. 194; see also pp. 193–232.

[5] Lassen, J.A.S.B., 1840, p. 454; Wilson, Ariana Antiqua, p. 369; Muir, S. Texts, vol. v. p. 143, "Váyu does not occupy a very prominent place in the Rig-Veda."

orthographical grounds; and the MAO and MIIPO follow the same law. Among the many outward forms of the Moon-god, MANAO BAGO would almost seem to be a superfluous variant, were it not that the word *Mâonh* may assign it to a more definitely Zend-speaking locality.[1] Then, there are complications about male and female Moons,[2] which seem to be indicated in the varieties of outlines given to the figures of MAO, and it is clear that the ruling religious systems fully recognized both male and female Mithras.[3]

It is with much reserve that I venture to suggest any interpretation of the title of APAEIXPO. The opening letters may possibly be referred to the Sanskrit अर *ara* "swift,"[4] and, considering the mixed complications of letters and languages to be seen in parallel transcriptions, the EIXPO might be dubiously associated with *equus, ἴκκος, ἵππος, ἰκϜος*, the "coursier rapide," *i.e.* the Sun.[5]

AΘPO, as the type of Fire, the Roman Vulcan, sufficiently declares itself in the artistic rendering of his personal form.

[1] Haug, p. 180; Khurshîd and Mah Yashts.
"The first yasht is devoted to the sun, which is called in Zend *hvare kkshaêta* = (خورشيد) 'sun the King,' the second to the moon called *mâonh* = ماه."

"Je célèbre, j'invoque Ahura et Mithra, élevés, immortels, purs; et les astres, créations saintes et célestes; et l'astre Taschter (Tistrya), lumineux, resplendissant; et la lune, qui garde le germe du taureau; et le soleil, souverain, coursier rapide, œil d'Ahura Mazda; Mithra, chef des provinces."—Burnouf, Yasna, p. 375.

[2] Creutzer, p. xxiv, fig. 330, etc.; Maury, Hist. des Religions, Paris, 1859, vol. iii. p. 127, "*Sin* ou Lune des Assyriens . . avait une caractère hermaphrodite. Cette première explication nous donne deux divinités, placées, pour le dire en passant, dans l'ordre hiérarchique, Ahura et Mithra. Mais la séparation même de ces deux mots, *ahuraêibya* et *mithraêibya*, pourrait faire soupçonner qu'il est question en cet endroit de deux Mithras, et que *ahura* doit être regardé comme un titre: 'j'invoque, je célèbre les deux seigneurs Mithras.' Ces deux Mithras seraient sans doute Mithra mâle et Mithra femelle, dont le culte était, selon les Grecs, anciennement célèbre dans la Perse."—Burnouf, Yaçna, p. 351; Zend-Avesta, vol. i. p. 87.

[3] Muir, Sanskrit Texts, vol. v. p. 155, "The two sun gods celebrated in the hymns of the Rig Veda," "*Sûrya* and *Savitṛi*."

[4] "Thou, Súrya, outstrippest all in speed."—Wilson, Rig-Veda, vol. i. p. 131.

[5] As in note 1, Mr. Muir also considers that some passages in the Rig-Veda symbolize the Sun under the form of a horse.—Texts, vol. v. p. 158. Prof. Göldstucker has further traced the derivation of the name of the Aswins from "*aswa*, meaning literally the pervader, then the quick; then the horse, which becomes the symbol of the sun"—J.R.A.S. Vol. II. N.S. p. 14; Mrs. Manning, Ancient India, vol. i. p. 9. I am fully aware that a coin is extant bearing the letters APOOACΠO (Αρθοασπο?), but the use of the *aspa* "horse" in this case is not necessarily conclusive against the interpretation of the independent transcript above suggested.

The ΦΑΡΟ or ΦΑΡΡΟ is equally obvious in its intention and in the pictured outline given to the central figure. The name, of course, is derived from the Latin *fero*, as embodied in Lucifer and Diana Lucifera. The early Greeks only knew the designation as that of a light-house, without being able to supply a root for the word, or, indeed, to interpret it otherwise than as "an island in the bay of Alexandria." The term is constant in ancient Persian combinations, as Atraphernes, etc.,—which eventually settled into the *Atúrparn* or Fire Priest of the Sassanian period.[1]

III. Persian Gods.

I have repeated the name of ΜΙΘΡΟ in the Persian column, more out of regard to the early Persian worship of the god, than because I can trace the direct descent of the Mithra of Cyrus to the same Iranian deity in his Eastern home.

The simple enumeration of the various forms of the worship of *Nanaia* would fill volumes. Under its Persian aspect it may be sufficient to refer to Artaxerxes Mnemon's inscription at Susa, which specifies "Ormazd, Tanaitis, and Mithra,"[2] as the gods who "help" him. The thirty chapters of the Aban Yasht are devoted to *Ardvi Súra Anáhita*, "sublime, excellent, spotless," whom "Ahuramazda himself is said to have worshipped."[3] And, for the traditions of her worship in the lands with which these coins are indirectly associated, we may cite the many sacred places that still bear her name.[4]

The Oanindo, Anandates, is a new discovery; but I conclude there will be no difficulty in admitting her identity with the Anandates of Strabo.[5]

1 See J.R.A.S. Vol. XIII. o.s. p. 415, etc. We have now new and clear examples of the true [Pahlavi] *Atúrparn*. See also Haug, p. 250. "Soshyantos and Aṅgiras = *Atharvans*."

2 J.R.A.S. Vol. XV. p. 159.

3 Haug, pp. 178, 179.

4 J.A.S. Bengal, vol. iii. 449; v. 266. Masson, "Travels in Balúchistán." London, 1844, vol. iv. p. 391. Ariana Antiqua, p. 362.

5 Strabo xi. viii. 4: "They (the Persians) erected there a temple to Anaïtis, and the gods Omanus ('Ωμανοῦ καὶ 'Αναδάτου) and Anandatus, Persian deities who have a common altar." xv. iii. 15: "The same customs are observed in the

IV. Roman Gods.

In the identification of the whole list of the Roman and Græco-Roman gods, I have been guided more by the forms and figures stamped on the coins than by the legends which are supposed to define the names and attributes of each divinity, which must often be accepted as simply independent versions of the original nomenclature. I am uncertain about the decipherment of PIAH, but there can be little doubt for whom the figure is intended. In the same way the type of Mars is manifest; his title of PHΘPO may be referred to the Zend [Zend script] *eretha* ऋत "great," etc.,[1] and though ἐρυθρίας might find some advocates, Anquetil's *Verethre* "victorious" seems to be conclusive as to the derivation. It will be remembered that the nearly similar term of ΟΡΔΗΘΡΟΥ is to be found on the coins of *Kodes.*[2]

V. Brahmanical Gods.

These several deities, their nomenclatures and attributes, have already been fully adverted to, under their Saivic aspect, in the preceding pages.

I have only to add, in addition to what has already been said about ΑΡΔΟΧΡΟ, a reference to the fact which seems to have been hitherto lost sight of, that the second portion of this name does not coincide with the legitimate orthography of the ΟΚΡΟ of Ṣiva. Indeed, as far as direct numismatic evidence may furnish a test, Ṣiva is more directly associated with *Nana,* the *Párvati* of later belief,[3] than with the *Ardokro,* or the Roman definition of "abundance" on coin No. 16, Plate II.

temples of Anaïtis and of Omanus. Belonging to these temples are shrines, and a wooden statue of Omanus is carried in procession. These we have seen ourselves."

[1] Burnouf, Yasna, pp. 323, 377, 473.

[2] J.R.A.S. Vol. IV. N.S. p. 518. ΤΡΚΩΔΟΥ, ΟΡΔΗΘΡΟΥ, ΜΑΚΑΡΟΥ. See also Num. Chron. N.S. vol. xiii. p. 229.

[3] See coin No. 7, J.R.A.S. Vol. XII. O.S. Plate IV., and J.A.S. Bengal, vol. iv. fig. 7, pl. xxxviii., and Prinsep's Essays, vol. ii. pl. xxii. fig. 7, wherein ΟΚΡΟ *Ṣiva* appears upon the reverse in company with *Nana.*

VI. Buddhist.

Although I have felt bound to insert the words ΒΟΔΑ ΣΑΜΑΝΑ in my Table, on the authority of Gen. Cunningham, I have only been induced to admit any such possible reading by the coincident appearance of definite figures of Buddha, under the double aspect of the conventional standing and seated statues of the saint.

I am not myself prepared to follow the present interpretation of the legends, though better examples may modify my views.[1] But the point I have now more especially to insist upon is, that the appearance of these Buddhist figures is confined to inferior copper pieces of very imperfect execution, whose legends are absolutely chaotic in the forms and arrangement of the Greek letters. So that I should be disposed to assign the limited group of these *Buddha-device* coins to a comparatively late date in the general series of imitations: which, though still bearing the name and typical devices of *Kanerki*, would seem to consist of mere reproductions of old types by later occupants of the localities in which the earlier coins were struck.

The Mathurá Archæological Remains.

I adverted, at the commencement of this article, to the importance of the late archæological discoveries in and around the ancient city of Mathurá[2]—which so definitely

[1] The coin most relied on to prove the intention of the terms "ΟΜ ΒΟΔ or perhaps ΟΔΙ ΒΟΔ; either *Aum Buddha* or *Adi Buddha*," published by General Cunningham in 1845 (J.A.S. Bengal, p. 435, plate 2, fig. 3), presents a central figure on the reverse exactly like the outline of the ΑΡΔΕΙΧΡΟ of the present plate. His Nos. 6 and 7, as I have remarked, though clear in the definition of the figures of Buddha, are of coarse fabric, of far later date than the associate ΟΑΔΟ of the same plate, and finally, the letters of the legends are so badly formed and so straggling as to be utterly untrustworthy in establishing any definite reading. The other limited examples of this class of coins will be found in Ariana Antiqua, pl. xiii. figs. 1, 2, 3. Here, again, the figures are incontestable, but Prof. Wilson did not pretend to interpret the broken legends. Prinsep figured a coin of this description in fig. 11, pl. xxv. J.A.S. Bengal, vol. iii.; Prinsep's Essays, pl. vii. This coin was noticed, but left uninterpreted by Lassen in his paper in the J.A.S. Bengal, 1840, p. 456.

[2] Amid the cities which were supposed to have claims to the honour of becoming the birthplace of Ṣâkya Muni, Mathurâ is rejected because its kings had hereditary ideas inconsistent with the new faith, *i.e.* adhered to the old,

establish the prominence of the Jaina religion, in the full developments of its sacred statues and associate inscriptions, at or about the commencement of our era.[1]

The Mathurá sculptured monuments have preserved for modern examination the *nude* images of the saints of the Jainas,[2] with the devotional dedications of the votaries of the faith appended in all contemporary formality.

Jainism? "D'autres dirent: La ville de Mathoura, riche, éntendue, florissante, et animée par une population nombreuse, toute remplie d'hommes; ce palais du roi Soubâhou. . . D'autres dirent: Elle ne convient pas non plus; pourquoi? Parce que ce roi est né dans une famille où les vues fausses sont héréditaires, et qu'il règne sur des hommes pareils aux barbares."—Lalita Vistara, Foucaux, p. 25.

[1] General Cunningham was fully aware of the value of these discoveries, in their bearing upon the associate creeds of Jainism and Buddhism. That he should have ventured so far independently in the direction of the leading argument of this paper is highly encouraging. His remarks are to the following effect:

"This is perhaps one of the most startling and important revelations that has been made by recent researches in India. It is true that, according to Jaina books, their faith had continuously flourished, under a succession of teachers, from the death of Mahávíra in B.C. 527 down to the present time. Hitherto, however, there was no tangible evidence to vouch for the truth of this statement. But the Kankâli mound at Mathurá has now given us the most complete and satisfactory testimony that the Jaina religion, even before the beginning of the Christian era, must have been in a condition almost as rich and flourishing as that of Buddha.

"The Kankâli mound is a very extensive one, and the number of statues of all sizes, from the colossal downwards, which it has yielded, has scarcely been surpassed by the prolific returns of Buddhist sculpture from the Jail mound. But, as not more than one-third of the Kankâli mound has yet been thoroughly searched, it may be confidently expected that its complete exploration will amply repay all the cost and trouble of the experiment."—General Cunningham, Arch. Rep. vol. iii. p. 46.

[2] Albírúní (A.D. 1030) has furnished us with a description of the forms of many of the Indian idols, derived from the text of Varáha-Mihira (sixth cent. A.D.). He defines the contrast between the statues of Buddha and those of the *Arhats* or Jaina saints in the following terms: "Si tu fais la statue de Djina, c'est-à-dire Bouddha, tâche de lui donner une figure agréable et des membres bien faits. Il doit avoir les paumes de la main et le dessous des pieds en forme de nénufar. Tu le représenteras assis, ayant des cheveux gris, et respirant un air de bonté, comme s'il était le père des créatures. S'il s'agit de donner à Bouddha la figure d'un arhanta, il faut en faire un jeune homme nu, beau de figure, et d'une physionomie agréable. It aura les deux mains appuyées sur les genoux," etc.—Reinaud, Memoires sur l'Inde, p. 121. Dr. Kern's translation, direct from the original Sanskrit text, gives: "The god of the Jainas is figured naked, young, handsome, with a calm countenance, and arms reaching down to the knees; his breast is marked with the Çrivatsa figure."—J.R.A.S. Vol. VI. N.S. p. 328. See also Wilson, J.A.S. Bengal, vol. i. p. 4; Burnouf, vol. i. p. 312. I omitted to notice in my previous references to nude statues (pp. 14, 18, 19, etc.), the remarkable expressions made use of by Calanus to Onesicritus; after "bidding him to strip himself naked, if he desired to hear any of his doctrine," he adds, "you should not hear me on any other condition though you came from Jupiter himself." Plutarch in Alexander. The exaction of these conditions seems to point to the tenets of Jainism.

While on the subject of discriminating points, I add to the information, outlined

These *nude* statues of the Jaina Tírthankaras teach us, like so many other subordinate indications of the remote antiquity of the creed, in its normal form, to look for parallels amid other forms of worship in their initiatory stage—and here we are inevitably reminded of the time when men made idols after their own images,[1] and while those men, in the simplicity of nature, stood up, without shame, as the Creator had fashioned them.

The value of the dedicatory inscriptions towards the elucidation of my leading question is, however, still more precise and irrecusable, in respect to the age of the monuments themselves, in the conjoint record of the name of the great Saint *Mahávíra* and that of *Vásudeva*,—the ΒΑΖΟΔΗΟ of the Indo-Scythian coins above described,—the third brother, or, as the case may be, the nominal head of the third tribe of the "*Hushka*, *Jushka*, and *Kanishka*" once nomad community.

Of the twenty-four dated inscriptions given by General Cunningham in his Archæological Report for 1871–2, no less than seven refer either directly, or indirectly, in the forms of the pedestals and the statues to which they are attached, to the Jaina creed.

Nos. 2 and 3, dated *Sam.* 5; 4, dated *Samvat* 9, bear the name of Kanishka. No. 6, dated *Sam.* 20, is remarkable, as it specifies "the gift of one statue of *Vardhamana*" or *Mahávíra*.

at p. 9, a curious account of the modern Jaina reverence for the Footprints of their saints: "Shading the temple (of Vásinghji—one of the five snake brethren, at Thán) is a large *Ráyaṇa* tree—the close foliage of small dark green oval leaves, which makes the shade so grateful, apparently having had to do with its being consecrated as a sacred tree in Western India, where it is specially dedicated by the Jainas to their first Tírthankara—Rishabhanátha—the patron saint of Ṣatruñjaya—no shrine to him being complete without a Ráyaṇa tree overshadowing his *charana* or footprints."—Mr. Burgess, Arch. Rep. 1875, p. 5.

[1] Xenophanes, Colophonii Carminum Reliquiæ, by Simon Karsten (Brussels, 1830), p. vi. His interpretation of one of the leading passages of the Greek text runs:—"v. At mortales opinantur natos esse Deos, mortalique habitu et forma et figura præditos." And vi. continues: "Si vero manus haberent boves vel leones, aut pingere manibus et fabricari eadem quæ homines possent, ipsi quoque Deorum formas pingerent figurasque formarent tales, quali ipsorum quisque præditus sit, equi equis, boves autem bobus similes."—p. 41. Pliny, xxxiv. p. 9, under *iconicæ*, adds the Greek practice is, not to cover any part of the "body" of their statues. Max Müller, Sanskrit Literature, vol. ii. p. 388.

No. 16, with the date of *Sam.* 83, and the name of Mahárája Vásu-deva, records, on the pedestal of a naked statue, "the gift of an image." No. 18, in like manner, preserves, at the foot of "a naked figure," the entry of *Sam.* 87, and the titles of Mahárája *Rájatirája Sháhi Vásu-deva.*

No. 20, which is, perhaps, the most important of the whole series of inscriptions, is appended to a "Naked standing figure," and commences with the following words:

"*Siddham Aum? Namo Arahate Mahávirasya Devanásasya Rájnya Vásu Devasya Samvatsare* 98, *Varsha Máse,* 4 *divase,* 11 *etasya.*"

"Glory to the Arhat Mahávíra, the destroyer of the Devas! (In the reign) of King Vásu-deva, in the Samvat year 98, in Varsha (the rainy season), the 4th month, the 11th day," etc.

Without doubt this list might be largely extended from concurrent palæolithic documents, which do not so definitely declare themselves as of Jaina import; but enough has been adduced to establish the fact of the full and free usage of the Jaina religion in Mathurá so early as the epoch of the Indo-Scythian *Kanerkis.*

LINGUISTIC PUBLICATIONS

OF

TRÜBNER & CO.,

57 AND 59, LUDGATE HILL, LONDON, E.C.

Ahlwardt.—THE DIVÁNS OF THE SIX ANCIENT ARABIC POETS, Ennábiga, 'Antara, Tarafa, Zuhair, 'Algama, and Imruolgais; chiefly according to the MSS. of Paris, Gotha, and Leyden, and the collection of their Fragments: with a complete list of the various readings of the Text. Edited by W. AHLWARDT, 8vo. pp. xxx. 340, sewed. 1870. 12*s*.

Aitareya Brahmanam of the Rig Veda. 2 vols. See under HAUG.

Alabaster.—THE WHEEL OF THE LAW: Buddhism illustrated from Siamese Sources by the Modern Buddhist, a Life of Buddha, and an account of H.M. Consulate-General in Siam; M.R.A.S. Demy 8vo. pp. lviii. and 324. 1871. 14*s*.

Alif Laîlat wa Laîlat.—THE ARABIAN NIGHTS. 4 vols. 4to. pp. 495, 493, 442, 434. Cairo, A.H. 1279 (1862). £3 3*s*.

This celebrated Edition of the Arabian Nights is now, for the first time, offered at a price which makes it accessible to Scholars of limited means.

Andrews.—A DICTIONARY OF THE HAWAIIAN LANGUAGE, to which is appended an English-Hawaiian Vocabulary, and a Chronological Table of Remarkable Events. By LORRIN ANDREWS. 8vo. pp. 560, cloth. £1 11*s*. 6*d*.

Anthropological Institute of Great Britain and Ireland (The Journal of the). Published Quarterly.

Vol I., No. 1. January–July, 1871. 8vo. pp. 120–clix, sewed. Illustrated with 11 full page Plates, and numerous Woodcuts; and accompanied by several folding plates of Tables, etc. 7*s*.

Vol. I., No. 2. October, 1871. 8vo. pp. 121–264, sewed. 4*s*.

Vol. I., No. 3. January, 1872. 8vo. pp. 265–427, sewed. 16 full-page Plates. 4*s*.

Vol. II., No. 1. April, 1872. 8vo. pp. 136, sewed. Eight two-page plates and two four-page plates. 4*s*.

Vol. II., No. 2. July and Oct, 1872. 8vo. pp. 137–312. 9 plates and a map. 6*s*.

Vol. II., No. 3. January, 1873. 8vo. pp. 143. With 4 plates. 4*s*.

Vol. III., No. 1. April, 1873. 8vo. pp. 136. With 8 plates and two maps. 4*s*.

Vol. III., No. 2. July and October, 1873. 8vo. pp. 168, sewed. With 9 plates. 4*s*.

Vol. III., No. 3. January, 1874. 8vo. pp. 238, sewed. With 8 plates, etc. 6*s*.

Vol. IV., No. 1. April and July, 1874. 8vo. pp. 308, sewed. With 22 plates. 8*s*.

Vol. IV., No. 2. April, 1875. 8vo. pp. 200, sewed. With 11 plates. 6*s*.

Vol. V., No. 1. July, 1875. 8vo. pp. 120, sewed. With 3 plates. 4*s*.

Vol. V., No. 2. October, 1875. 8vo. pp. 132, sewed. With 8 plates. 4*s*.

Vol. V., No. 3. January, 1876. 8vo. pp. 156, sewed. With 8 plates. 5*s*.

Vol. V., No. 4. April, 1876. 8vo. pp. 128, sewed. With 2 plates. 5*s*.

Vol. VI., No. 1. July, 1876. 8vo. pp. 100, sewed. With 5 plates. 5*s*.

Arabic and Persian Books (A Catalogue of). Printed in the East. Constantly for sale by Trübner and Co., 57 and 59, Ludgate Hill, London. 16mo. pp. 46, sewed. 1*s*.

Archæological Survey of India.—See under BURGESS and CUNNINGHAM.

Arden.—A PROGRESSIVE GRAMMAR OF THE TELUGU LANGUAGE, with Copious Examples and Exercises. In Three Parts. Part I. Introduction.—On the Alphabet and Orthography.—Outline Grammar, and Model Sentences.

Price One Shilling.

Part II. A Complete Grammar of the Colloquial Dialect. Part III. On the Grammatical Dialect used in Books. By A. H. ARDEN, M.A., Missionary of the C. M. S. Masulipatam. 8vo. sewed, pp. xiv. and 380. 14*s.*

Arnold.—THE ILIAD AND ODYSSEY OF INDIA. By EDWIN ARNOLD, M.A., F.R.G.S., etc. Fcap. 8vo. sd., pp. 24. 1*s.*

Arnold.—THE INDIAN SONG OF SONGS. From the Sanskrit of the Gita Govinda of Jayadeva. By EDWIN ARNOLD, M.A., F.R.G.S. (of University College, Oxford), formerly Principal of Poona College, and Fellow of the University of Bombay. Cr. 8vo. cl., pp. xvi. and 144. 1875. 5*s.*

Asher.—ON THE STUDY OF MODERN LANGUAGES IN GENERAL, and of the English Language in particular. An Essay. By DAVID ASHER, Ph.D. 12mo. pp. viii. and 80, cloth. 2*s.*

Asiatic Society.—JOURNAL OF THE ROYAL ASIATIC SOCIETY OF GREAT BRITAIN AND IRELAND, from the Commencement to 1863. First Series, complete in 20 Vols. 8vo., with many Plates. Price £10; or, in Single Numbers, as follows:—Nos. 1 to 14, 6*s.* each; No. 15, 2 Parts, 4*s.* each; No. 16, 2 Parts, 4*s.* each; No. 17, 2 Parts, 4*s.* each, No. 18, 6*s.* These 18 Numbers form Vols. I. to IX.—Vol. X., Part 1, op.; Part 2, 5*s.*; Part 3, 5*s.*—Vol. XI., Part 1, 6*s.*; Part 2 not published.—Vol. XII., 2 Parts, 6*s.* each —Vol. XIII., 2 Parts, 6*s.* each.—Vol. XIV., Part 1, 5*s.*; Part 2 not published.—Vol. XV., Part 1, 6*s.*; Part 2, with 3 Maps, £2 2*s.*—Vol. XVI., 2 Parts, 6*s.* each.—Vol. XVII., 2 Parts, 6*s.* each.—Vol. XVIII., 2 Parts, 6*s.* each.—Vol. XIX., Parts 1 to 4, 16*s.*—Vol. XX., Parts 1 and 2, 4*s.* each. Part 3, 7*s.* 6*d.*

Asiatic Society.—JOURNAL OF THE ROYAL ASIATIC SOCIETY OF GREAT BRITAIN AND IRELAND. *New Series.* Vol. I. In Two Parts. pp. iv. and 490, sewed. 16*s.*

CONTENTS.—I. Vajra-chhedikâ, the "Kin Kong King," or Diamond Sûtra. Translated from the Chinese by the Rev. S. Beal, Chaplain, R.N.—II. The Pâramitâ-hridaya Sûtra, or, in Chinese, "Mo ho-pô-ye-po-lo-mih-to-sin-king," *i.e.* "The Great Pâramitâ Heart Sûtra." Translated from the Chinese by the Rev. S. Beal, Chaplain, R.N.—III. On the Preservation of National Literature in the East. By Colonel F. J. Goldsmid.—IV. On the Agricultural, Commercial, Financial, and Military Statistics of Ceylon. By E. R. Power, Esq.—V. Contributions to a Knowledge of the Vedic Theogony and Mythology. By J. Muir, D.C.L., LL.D.—VI. A Tabular List of Original Works and Translations, published by the late Dutch Government of Ceylon at their Printing Press at Colombo. Compiled by Mr. Mat. P. J. Ondaatje, of Colombo.—VII. Assyrian and Hebrew Chronology compared, with a view of showing the extent to which the Hebrew Chronology of Ussher must be modified, in conformity with the Assyrian Canon. By J. W. Bosanquet, Esq.—VIII. On the existing Dictionaries of the Malay Language. By Dr. H. N. van der Tuuk.—IX. Bilingual Readings: Cuneiform and Phœnician. Notes on some Tablets in the British Museum, containing Bilingual Legends (Assyrian and Phœnician). By Major-General Sir H. Rawlinson, K.C.B., Director R.A.S.—X. Translations of Three Copper-plate Inscriptions of the Fourth Century A.D., and Notices of the Châlukya and Gurjjara Dynasties By Professor J. Dowson, Staff College, Sandhurst.—XI. Yama and the Doctrine of a Future Life, according to the Rig-Yajur-, and Atharva-Vedas. By J. Muir, Esq., D.C.L., LL.D.—XII. On the Jyotisha Observation of the Place of the Colures, and the Date derivable from it. By William D. Whitney, Esq., Professor of Sanskrit in Yale College, New Haven, U.S.—Note on the preceding Article. By Sir Edward Colebrooke, Bart., M.P., President R.A.S.—XIII. Progress of the Vedic Religion towards Abstract Conceptions of the Deity. By J. Muir, Esq., D.C.L., LL.D.—XIV. Brief Notes on the Age and Authenticity of the Work of Aryabhata, Varâhamihira, Brahmagupta, Bhattotpala, and Bhâskarâchârya. By Dr. Bhâu Dâji, Honorary Member R.A.S.—XV. Outlines of a Grammar of the Malagasy Language. By H. N. Van der Tuuk.—XVI. On the Identity of Xandrames and Krananda. By Edward Thomas, Esq.

Vol. II. In Two Parts. pp. 522, sewed. 16*s.*

CONTENTS.—I. Contributions to a Knowledge of Vedic Theogony and Mythology. No. 2. By J. Muir, Esq.—II. Miscellaneous Hymns from the Rig- and Atharva-Vedas. By J. Muir, Esq.—III. Five hundred questions on the Social Condition of the Natives of Bengal. By the Rev. J. Long.—IV. Short account of the Malay Manuscripts belonging to the Royal Asiatic Society. By Dr. H. N. van der Tuuk.—V. Translation of the Amitâbha Sûtra from the Chinese. By the Rev. S. Beal, Chaplain Royal Navy.—VI. The initial coinage of Bengal. By Edward Thomas, Esq.—VII. Specimens of an Assyrian Dictionary. By Edwin Norris, Esq.—VIII. On the Relations of the Priests to the other classes of Indian Society in the Vedic age. By J. Muir, Esq.—IX. On the Interpretation of the Veda. By the same.—X. An attempt to Translate from the Chinese a work known as the Confessional Services of the great compassionate Kwan Yin, possessing 1000 hands and 1000 eyes. By the Rev. S. Beal, Chaplain Royal Navy.—XI. The Hymns of the Gaupâyanas and the Legend of King Asamâti. By Professor Max Müller, M.A., Honorary Member Royal Asiatic Society.—XII. Specimen Chapters of an Assyrian Grammar. By the Rev. E. Hincks, D.D., Honorary Member Royal Asiatic Society.

Vol. III. In Two Parts. pp. 516, sewed. With Photograph. 22s.

CONTENTS.—I. Contributions towards a Glossary of the Assyrian Language. By H. F. Talbot.—II. Remarks on the Indo-Chinese Alphabets. By Dr. A. Bastian.—III. The poetry of Mohamed Rabadan, Arragonese. By the Hon. H. E. J. Stanley.—IV. Catalogue of the Oriental Manuscripts in the Library of King's College, Cambridge. By Edward Henry Palmer, B.A., Scholar of St. John's College, Cambridge; Member of the Royal Asiatic Society; Membre de la Société Asiatique de Paris.—V. Description of the Amravati Tope in Guntur. By J. Fergusson, Esq., F.R.S.—VI. Remarks on Prof. Brockhaus' edition of the Kathâsarit-sâgara, Lambaka IX. XVIII. By Dr. H. Kern, Professor of Sanskrit in the University of Leyden.—VII. The source of Colebrooke's Essay "On the Duties of a Faithful Hindu Widow." By Fitzedward Hall, Esq., M.A., D.C.L. Oxon. Supplement: Further detail of proofs that Colebrooke's Essay, "On the Duties of a Faithful Hindu Widow," was not indebted to the Vivâdabhangârnava. By Fitzedward Hall, Esq.—VIII. The Sixth Hymn of the First Book of the Rig Veda. By Professor Max Müller, M.A. Hon. M.R.A.S.—IX. Sassanian Inscriptions. By E. Thomas, Esq.—X. Account of an Embassy from Morocco to Spain in 1690 and 1691. By the Hon. H. E. J. Stanley.—XI. The Poetry of Mohamed Rabadan, of Arragon. By the Hon. H. E. J. Stanley.—XII. Materials for the History of India for the Six Hundred Years of Mohammadan rule, previous to the Foundation of the British Indian Empire. By Major W. Nassau Lees, LL.D., Ph.D.—XIII. A Few Words concerning the Hill people inhabiting the Forests of the Cochin State. By Captain G. E. Fryer, Madras Staff Corps, M.R.A.S.—XIV. Notes on the Bhojpurí Dialect of Hindí, spoken in Western Behar. By John Beames, Esq., B.C.S., Magistrate of Chumparun.

Vol. IV. In Two Parts. pp. 521, sewed. 16s.

CONTENTS.—I. Contribution towards a Glossary of the Assyrian Language. By H. F. Talbot. Part II.—II. On Indian Chronology. By J. Fergusson, Esq., F.R.S.—III. The Poetry of Mohamed Rabadan of Arragon. By the Hon. H. E. J. Stanley.—IV. On the Magar Language of Nepal. By John Beames, Esq., B.C.S.—V. Contributions to the Knowledge of Parsee Literature. By Edward Sachau, Ph.D.—VI. Illustrations of the Lamaist System in Tibet, drawn from Chinese Sources. By Wm. Frederick Mayers, Esq., of H.B.M. Consular Service, China.—VII. Khuddaka Pátha, a Páli Text, with a Translation and Notes. By R. C. Childers, late of the Ceylon Civil Service.—VIII. An Endeavour to elucidate Rashiduddin's Geographical Notices of India. By Col. H. Yule, C.B.—IX. Sassanian Inscriptions explained by the Pahlaví of the Pârsis. By E. W. West, Esq.—X. Some Account of the Senbyû Pagoda at Mengûn, near the Burmese Capital, in a Memorandum by Capt. E. H. Sladan, Political Agent at Mandalé; with Remarks on the Subject by Col. Henry Yule, C.B.—XI. The Brhat-Sanhitâ; or, Complete System of Natural Astrology of Varâha-Mihira. Translated from Sanskrit into English by Dr. H. Kern.—XII. The Mohammedan Law of Evidence, and its influence on the Administration of Justice in India. By N. B. E. Baillie, Esq.—XIII. The Mohammedan Law of Evidence in connection with the Administration of Justice to Foreigners. By N. B. E. Baillie, Esq.—XIV. A Translation of a Bactrian Páli Inscription. By Prof. J. Dowson.—XV. Indo-Parthian Coins. By E. Thomas, Esq.

Vol. V. In Two Parts. pp. 463, sewed. 18s. 6*d.* With 10 full-page and folding Plates.

CONTENTS.—I. Two Játakas. The original Páli Text, with an English Translation. By V. Fausböll.—II. On an Ancient Buddhist Inscription at Keu-yung kwan, in North China. By A. Wylie.—III. The Brhat Sanhitâ; or, Complete System of Natural Astrology of Varâha-Mihira Translated from Sanskrit into English by Dr. H. Kern.—IV. The Pongol Festival in Southern India. By Charles E. Gover.—V. The Poetry of Mohamed Rabadan, of Arragon. By the Right Hon. Lord Stanley of Alderley.—VI. Essay on the Creed and Customs of the Jangams. By Charles P. Brown.—VII. On Malabar, Coromandel, Quilon, etc. By C. P. Brown.—VIII. On the Treatment of the Nexus in the Neo-Aryan Languages of India. By John Beames, B.C.S.—IX. Some Remarks on the Great Tope at Sânchi. By the Rev. S. Beal.—X. Ancient Inscriptions from Mathura. Translated by Professor J. Dowson.—Note to the Mathura Inscriptions. By Major-General A. Cunningham.—XI. Specimen of a Translation of the Adi Granth. By Dr. Ernest Trumpp.—XII. Notes on Dhammapada, with Special Reference to the Question of Nirvâna. By R. C. Childers, late of the Ceylon Civil Service.—XIII. The Brhat-Sanhitâ; or, Complete System of Natural Astrology of Varâha-mihira. Translated from Sanskrit into English by Dr. H. Kern.—XIV. On the Origin of the Buddhist Arthakathâs. By the Mudliar L. Comrilla Vijasinha, Government Interpreter to the Ratnapura Court, Ceylon. With an Introduction by R. C. Childers, late of the Ceylon Civil Service.—XV. The Poetry of Mohamed Rabadan, of Arragon. By the Right Hon. Lord Stanley of Alderley.—XVI. Proverbia Communia Syriaca. By Captain R. F. Burton. XVII. Notes on an Ancient Indian Vase, with an Account of the Engraving thereupon. By Charles Horne, M.R.A.S., late of the Bengal Civil Service.—XVIII. The Bhar Tribe. By the Rev. M. A. Sherring, LL.D., Benares. Communicated by C. Horne, M.R.A.S., late B.C.S.—XIX. Of *Jihad* in Mohammedan Law, and its application to British India. By N. B. E. Baillie.—XX. Comments on Recent Pehlvi Decipherments. With an Incidental Sketch of the Derivation of Aryan Alphabets. And Contributions to the Early History and Geography of Tabaristán. Illustrated by Coins. By E. Thomas, F.R.S.

Vol. VI., Part 1, pp. 212, sewed, with two plates and a map. 8s.

CONTENTS.—The Ishmaelites, and the Arabic Tribes who Conquered their Country. By A. Sprenger.—A Brief Account of Four Arabic Works on the History and Geography of Arabia. By Captain S. B. Miles.—On the Methods of Disposing of the Dead at Llassa, Thibet, etc. By Charles Horne, late B.C.S. The Brhat-Sanhitâ; or, Complete System of Natural Astrology of Varâha-mihira, Translated from Sanskrit into English by Dr. H. Kern.—Notes on Hwen Thsang's Account of the Principalities of Tokháristán, in which some Previous Geographical Identifications are Reconsidered. By Colonel Yule, C.B.—The Campaign of Ælius Gallus in

Arabia. By A. Sprenger.—An Account of Jerusalem, Translated for the late Sir H. M. Elliott from the Persian Text of Násir ibn Khusrû's Safanámah by the late Major A. R. Fuller.—The Poetry of Mohamed Rabadan, of Arragon. By the Right Hon. Lord Stanley of Alderley.

Vol. VI., Part II., pp. 213 to 400 and lxxxiv., sewed. Illustrated with a Map, Plates, and Woodcuts. 8*s*.

CONTENTS.—On Hiouen-Thsang's Journey from Patna to Ballabhi. By James Fergusson, D.C.L., F.R.S.—Northern Buddhism. [Note from Colonel H. Yule, addressed to the Secretary.] —Hwen Thsang's Account of the Principalities of Tokhâristân, etc. By Colonel H. Yule, C.B.—The Bṛhat-Sañhitâ; or, Complete System of Natural Astrology of Varâha-mihira. Translated from Sanskrit into English by Dr. H. Kern.—The Initial Coinage of Bengal, under the Early Muhammadan Conquerors. Part II. Embracing the preliminary period between A.H. 614-634 (A.D. 1217-1236-7). By Edward Thomas, F.R.S.—The Legend of Dipañkara Buddha. Translated from the Chinese (and intended to illustrate Plates XXIX. and L., 'Tree and Serpent Worship'). By S. Beal.—Note on Art. IX., antè pp. 213-274, on Hiouen-Thsang's Journey from Patna to Ballabhi. By James Fergusson, D.C.L., F.R.S.—Contributions towards a Glossary of the Assyrian Language. By H. F. Talbot.

Vol. VII., Part I., pp. 170 and 24, sewed. With a plate. 8*s*.

CONTENTS.—The *Upasampadâ-Kammavâcâ*, being the Buddhist Manual of the Form and Manner of Ordering of Priests and Deacons. The Páli Text, with a Translation and Notes. By J. F. Dickson, B.A., sometime Student of Christ Church, Oxford, now of the Ceylon Civil Service.—Notes on the Megalithic Monuments of the Coimbatore District, Madras. By M. J. Walhouse, late Madras C.S.—Notes on the Sinhalese Language. No. 1. On the Formation of the Plural of Neuter Nouns. By R. C. Childers, late of the Ceylon Civil Service.—The Pali Text of the *Mahâparinibbâna Sutta* and Commentary, with a Translation. By R. C. Childers, late of the Ceylon Civil Service.—The Brihat-Sanhitâ; or, Complete System of Natural Astrology of Varâha-mihira. Translated from Sanskrit into English by Dr. H. Kern.—Note on the Valley of Choombi. By Dr. A. Campbell, late Superintendent of Darjeeling.—The Name of the Twelfth Imâm on the Coinage of Egypt. By H. Sauvaire and Stanley Lane Poole.—Three Inscriptions of Parâkrama Bâhu the Great from Pulastipura, Ceylon (date circa 1180 A.D.). By T. W. Rhys Davids.—Of the Kharâj or Muhammadan Land Tax; its Application to British India, and Effect on the Tenure of Land. By N. B. E. Baillie.—Appendix: A Specimen of a Syriac Version of the Kalilah wa-Dimnah, with an English Translation. By W. Wright.

Vol. VII., Part II., pp. 191 to 394, sewed. With seven plates and a map. 8*s*.

CONTENTS.—Sigiri, the Lion Rock, near Pulastipura, Ceylon; and the Thirty-ninth Chapter of the Mahâvamsa. By T. W. Rhys Davids.—The Northern Frontagers of China. Part I. The Origines of the Mongols. By H. H. Howorth.—Inedited Arabic Coins. By Stanley Lane Poole.—Notice on the Dinârs of the Abbasside Dynasty. By Edward Thomas Rogers.—The Northern Frontagers of China. Part II. The Origines of the Manchus. By H. H. Howorth.—Notes on the Old Mongolian Capital of Shangtu. By S. W. Bushell, B.Sc., M.D.—Oriental Proverbs in their Relations to Folklore, History, Sociology; with Suggestions for their Collection, Interpretation, Publication. By the Rev. J. Long.—Two Old Simhalese Inscriptions. The Sahasa Malla Inscription, date 1200 A.D., and the Ruwanwæli Dagaba Inscription, date 1191 A.D. Text, Translation, and Notes. By T. W. Rhys Davids.—Notes on a Bactrian Pali Inscription and the Samvat Era. By Prof. J. Dowson.—Note on a Jade Drinking Vessel of the Emperor Jahángír. By Edward Thomas, F.R.S.

Vol. VIII., Part I., pp. 156, sewed, with three plates and a plan. 8*s*.

CONTENTS.—Catalogue of Buddhist Sanskrit Manuscripts in the Possession of the Royal Asiatic Society (Hodgson Collection). By Professors E. B. Cowell and J. Eggeling.—On the Ruins of Sigiri in Ceylon. By T. H. Blakesley, Esq., Public Works Department, Ceylon.—The Pâtimokkha, being the Buddhist Office of the Confession of Priests. The Pali Text, with a Translation, and Notes. By J. F. Dickson, M.A., sometime Student of Christ Church, Oxford, now of the Ceylon Civil Service.—Notes on the Sinhalese Language. No. 2. Proofs of the Sanskritic Origin of Sinhalese. By R. C. Childers, late of the Ceylon Civil Service.

Vol. VIII., Part II., pp. 157-308, sewed. 8*s*.

CONTENTS.—An Account of the Island of Bali. By R. Friederich.—The Pali Text of the Mahâparinibbâna Sutta and Commentary, with a Translation. By R. C. Childers, late of the Ceylon Civil Service.—The Northern Frontagers of China. Part III. The Kara Khitai. By H. H. Howorth.—Inedited Arabic Coins. II. By Stanley Lane Poole.—On the Form of Government under the Native Sovereigns of Ceylon. By A. de Silva Ekanâyaka, Mudaliyar of the Department of Public Instruction, Ceylon.

Asiatic Society.—TRANSACTIONS OF THE ROYAL ASIATIC SOCIETY OF GREAT BRITAIN AND IRELAND. Complete in 3 vols. 4to., 80 Plates of Facsimiles, etc., cloth. London, 1827 to 1835. Published at £9 5*s*.; reduced to £5 5*s*.

The above contains contributions by Professor Wilson, G. C. Haughton, Davis, Morrison, Colebrooke, Humboldt, Dorn, Grotefend, and other eminent Oriental scholars.

Asiatic Society of Bengal.—JOURNAL OF THE ASIATIC SOCIETY OF BENGAL. Edited by the Honorary Secretaries. 8vo. 8 numbers per annum. 4*s*. each number.

Asiatic Society of Bengal.—PROCEEDINGS OF THE ASIATIC SOCIETY OF BENGAL. Published Monthly. 1*s*. each number.

Asiatic Society (Bombay Branch).—THE JOURNAL OF THE BOMBAY BRANCH OF THE ROYAL ASIATIC SOCIETY. Edited by the Secretary. Nos. 1 to 33. 7*s*. 6*d*. each number.

Asiatic Society.—JOURNAL OF THE CEYLON BRANCH OF THE ROYAL ASIATIC SOCIETY. 8vo. Published irregularly. 7*s*. 6*d*. each part.

Asiatic Society of Japan.—TRANSACTIONS OF THE ASIATIC SOCIETY OF JAPAN. Vol. I. From 30th October, 1872, to 9th October, 1873. 8vo. pp. 110, with plates. 1874. Vol. II. From 22nd October, 1873, to 15th July, 1874. 8vo. pp. 249. 1874. Vol. III. Part I. From 16th July, 1874, to December, 1874, 1875. Vol. III. Part II. From 13th January, 1875, to 30th June, 1875. Each Part 7*s*. 6*d*.

Asiatic Society (North China Branch).—JOURNAL OF THE NORTH CHINA BRANCH OF THE ROYAL ASIATIC SOCIETY. New Series. Parts 1 to 8. Each part 7*s*. 6*d*.

Aston.—A SHORT GRAMMAR OF THE JAPANESE SPOKEN LANGUAGE. By W. G. ASTON, M.A., Interpreter and Translator, H. B. M.'s Legation, Yedo, Japan. Third edition. 12mo. cloth, pp. 96. 12*s*.

Atharva Veda Prátiçákhya.—See under WHITNEY.

Auctores Sanscriti. Edited for the Sanskrit Text Society, under the supervision of THEODOR GOLDSTÜCKER. Vol. I., containing the Jaiminîya-Nyâya-Mâlâ-Vistara. Parts I. to V., pp. 1 to 400, large 4to. sewed. 10*s*. each part.

Axon.—THE LITERATURE OF THE LANCASHIRE DIALECT. A Bibliographical Essay. By WILLIAM E. A. AXON, F.R.S.L. Fcap. 8vo. sewed. 1870. 1*s*.

Baba.—AN ELEMENTARY GRAMMAR OF THE JAPANESE LANGUAGE, with Easy Progressive Exercises. By TATUI BABA. Crown 8vo. cloth, pp. xii. and 92. 5*s*.

Bachmaier.—PASIGRAPHICAL DICTIONARY AND GRAMMAR. By ANTON BACHMAIER, President of the Central Pasigraphical Society at Munich. 18mo. cloth, pp. viii.; 26; 160. 1870. 3*s*.

Bachmaier.—PASIGRAPHISCHES WÖRTERBUCH ZUM GEBRAUCHE FÜR DIE DEUTSCHE SPRACHE. Verfasst von ANTON BACHMAIER, Vorsitzendem des Central-Vereins für Pasigraphie in München. 18mo. cloth, pp. viii.; 32; 128; 120. 1870. 2*s*. 6*d*

Bachmaier.—DICTIONNAIRE PASIGRAPHIQUE, PRÉCÉDÉ DE LA GRAMMAIRE. Redigé par ANTOINE BACHMAIER, Président de la Société Centrale de Pasigraphie à Munich. 18mo. cloth, pp. vi. 26; 168; 150. 1870. 2*s*. 6*d*.

Ballad Society's Publications. — Subscriptions—Small paper, one guinea, and large paper, three guineas, per annum.

1868.

1. BALLADS AND POEMS FROM MANUSCRIPTS. Vol. I. Part I. On the Condition of England in the Reigns of Henry VIII. and Edward VI. (including the state of the Clergy, Monks, and Friars), contains (besides a long Introduction) the following poems, etc.: Now a Dayes, ab. 1520 A.D.; Vox Populi Vox Dei, A.D. 1547–8; The Ruyn' of a Ream'; The Image of Ypocresye, A D. 1533; Against the Blaspheming English Lutherans and the Poisonous Dragon Luther; The Spoiling of the Abbeys; The Overthrowe of the Abbeys, a Tale of Robin Hoode; De Monasteriis Dirutis. Edited by F. J. FURNIVALL, M.A. 8vo.
2. BALLADS FROM MANUSCRIPTS. Vol. II. Part I. The Poore Mans Pittance. By RICHARD WILLIAMS. Contayninge three severall subjects:—(1.) The firste, the fall and complaynte of Anthonie Babington, whoe, with others, weare executed for highe treason in the feildes nere lyncolns Inne, in the yeare of our lorde—1586. (2.) The seconde contaynes the life and Deathe of Roberte, lorde Deverox, Earle of Essex: whoe was beheaded in the towre of london on ash-wensdaye mornynge, *Anno*—1601. (3.) The

laste, Intituled "acclamatio patrie," contayninge the horrib[l]e treason that weare pretended agaynste your Maiestie, to be donne on the parliament howse The seconde [third] yeare of your Maiestis Raygne [1605]. Edited by F. J. FURNIVALL, M.A. 8vo. (*The Introductions, by Professor W. R. Morfill, M.A., of Oriel Coll., Oxford, and the Index, are published in No. 10.*)

1869.

3. THE ROXBURGHE BALLADS. Part I. With short Notes by W. CHAPPELL, Esq., F.S.A., author of "Popular Music of the Olden Time," etc., etc., and with copies of the Original Woodcuts, drawn by Mr. RUDOLPH BLIND and Mr. W. H. HOOPER, and engraved by Mr. J. H. RIMBAULT and Mr. HOOPER. 8vo.

1870.

4. THE ROXBURGHE BALLADS. Vol. I. Part II.

1871.

5. THE ROXBURGHE BALLADS. Vol. I. Part III. With an Introduction and short Notes by W. CHAPPELL, Esq., F.S.A.
6. CAPTAIN COX, HIS BALLADS AND BOOKS; or, ROBERT LANEHAM'S Letter: Whearin part of the entertainment untoo the Queenz Majesty at Killingworth Castl, in Warwik Sheer in this Soomerz Progress, 1575, is signified; from a freend Officer attendant in the Court, unto hiz freend, a Citizen and Merchant of London. Re-edited, with accounts of all Captain Cox's accessible Books, and a comparison of them with those in the COMPLAYNT OF SCOTLAND, 1548–9 A.D. By F. J. FURNIVALL, M.A. 8vo.

1872.

7. BALLADS FROM MANUSCRIPTS. Vol. I. Part II. Ballads on Wolsey, Anne Boleyn, Somerset, and Lady Jane Grey; with Wynkyn de Worde's Treatise of a Galaunt (A.B. 1520 A.D.). Edited by FREDERICK J. FURNIVALL, M.A. With Forewords to the Volume, Notes, and an Index. 8vo.
8. THE ROXBURGHE BALLADS. Vol. II. Part I.

1873.

9. THE ROXBURGHE BALLADS. Vol. II. Part II.
10. BALLADS FROM MANUSCRIPTS. Vol. II. Part II. Containing Ballads on Queen Elizabeth, Essex, Campion, Drake, Raleigh, Frobisher, Warwick, and Bacon, "the Candlewick Ballads," Poems from the Jackson MS., etc. Edited by W. R. MORFILL, Esq., M.A., with an Introduction to No. 3.

1874.

11. LOVE-POEMS AND HUMOUROUS ONES, written at the end of a volume of small printed books, A.D. 1614–1619, in the British Museum, labelld "Various Poems," and markt $\frac{\text{C. 39. a.}}{\text{1-6.}}$. Put forth by FREDERICK J. FURNIVALL.
12. THE ROXBURGHE BALLADS. Vol. II. Part III.

1875.

13. THE ROXBURGHE BALLADS. Vol. III. Part I.

1876.

14. THE BAGFORD BALLADS. Edited with Introduction and Notes, by JOSEPH WOODFALL EBSWORTH, M.A., Camb., Editor of the Reprinted "'Drolleries' of the Restoration." Part I.

Ballantyne.—ELEMENTS OF HINDÍ AND BRAJ BHÁKÁ GRAMMAR. By the late JAMES R. BALLANTYNE, LL.D. Second edition, revised and corrected Crown 8vo., pp. 44, cloth. 5*s*.

Ballantyne.—FIRST LESSONS IN SANSKRIT GRAMMAR; together with an Introduction to the Hitopadésa. Second edition. Second Impression. By JAMES R. BALLANTYNE, LL.D., Librarian of the India Office. 8vo. pp. viii. and 110, cloth. 1873. 3*s*. 6*d*.

Banerjea.—THE ARIAN WITNESS, or the Testimony of Arian Scriptures in corroboration of Biblical History and the Rudiments of Christian Doctrine. Including Dissertations on the Original Home and Early Adventures of Indo-Arians. By the Rev. K. M. BANERJEA. 8vo. sewed, pp. xviii. and 236. 8*s.* 6*d.*

Bate.—A DICTIONARY OF THE HINDEE LANGUAGE. Compiled by J. D. BATE. 8vo. cloth, pp. 806. £2 12*s.* 6*d.*

Beal.—TRAVELS OF FAH HIAN AND SUNG-YUN, Buddhist Pilgrims from China to India (400 A.D. and 518 A.D.) Translated from the Chinese, by S. BEAL (B.A. Trinity College, Cambridge), a Chaplain in Her Majesty's Fleet, a Member of the Royal Asiatic Society, and Author of a Translation of the Pratimôksha and the Amithâba Sûtra from the Chinese. Crown 8vo. pp. lxxiii. and 210, cloth, ornamental, with a coloured map. 10*s.* 6*d.*

Beal.—A CATENA OF BUDDHIST SCRIPTURES FROM THE CHINESE. By S. BEAL, B.A., Trinity College, Cambridge; a Chaplain in Her Majesty's Fleet, etc. 8vo. cloth, pp. xiv. and 436. 1871. 15*s.*

Beal.—THE ROMANTIC LEGEND OF SÂKHYA BUDDHA. From the Chinese-Sanscrit by the Rev. SAMUEL BEAL, Author of "Buddhist Pilgrims," etc. Crown 8vo. cloth, pp. 400. 1875. 12*s.*

Beal.—THE BUDDHIST TRIPITAKA, as it is known in China and Japan. A Catalogue and Compendious Report. By SAMUEL BEAL, B.A. Folio, sewed, pp. 117. 7*s.* 6*d.*

Beames.—OUTLINES OF INDIAN PHILOLOGY. With a Map, showing the Distribution of the Indian Languages. By JOHN BEAMES. Second enlarged and revised edition. Crown 8vo. cloth, pp. viii. and 96. 5*s.*

Beames.—NOTES ON THE BHOJPURÍ DIALECT OF HINDÍ, spoken in Western Behar. By JOHN BEAMES, Esq., B.C.S., Magistrate of Chumparun. 8vo. pp. 26, sewed. 1868. 1*s.* 6*d.*

Beames.—A COMPARATIVE GRAMMAR OF THE MODERN ARYAN LANGUAGES OF INDIA (to wit), Hindi, Panjabi, Sindhi, Gujarati, Marathi, Uriya, and Bengali. By JOHN BEAMES, Bengal C.S., M.R.A.S., &c.
Vol. I. On Sounds. 8vo. cloth, pp. xvi and 360. 16*s.*
Vol. II. The Noun and the Pronoun. 8vo. cloth, pp. xii. and 348. 16*s.*

Bellairs.—A GRAMMAR OF THE MARATHI LANGUAGE. By H. S. K. BELLAIRS, M.A., and LAXMAN Y. ASHKEDKAR, B.A. 12mo. cloth, pp. 90. 5*s.*

Bellew.—A DICTIONARY OF THE PUKKHTO, OR PUKSHTO LANGUAGE, on a New and Improved System. With a reversed Part, or English and Pukkhto, By H. W. BELLEW, Assistant Surgeon, Bengal Army. Super Royal 8vo. op. xii. and 356, cloth. 42*s.*

Bellew.—A GRAMMAR OF THE PUKKHTO OR PUKSHTO LANGUAGE, on a New and Improved System. Combining Brevity with Utility, and Illustrated by Exercises and Dialogues. By H. W. BELLEW, Assistant Surgeon, Bengal Army. Super-royal 8vo., pp. xii. and 156, cloth. 21*s.*

Bellew.—FROM THE INDUS TO THE TIGRIS: a Narrative of a Journey through the Countries of Balochistan, Afghanistan, Khorassan, and Iran, in 1872; together with a Synoptical Grammar and Vocabulary of the Brahoe Language, and a Record of the Meteorological Observations and Altitudes on the March from the Indus to the Tigris. By H. W. BELLEW, C.S.I., Surgeon Bengal Staff Corps, Author of "A Journal of a Mission to Afghanistan in 1857-58," and "A Grammar and Dictionary of the Pukkhto Language." Demy 8vo. cloth. 14*s.*

Bellew.—KASHMIR AND KASHGHAR. A Narrative of the Journey of the Embassy to Kashghar in 1873-74. By H. W. BELLEW, C.S.I. Demy 8vo. cl., pp. xxxii. and 420. 16*s.*

Bellows.—ENGLISH OUTLINE VOCABULARY, for the use of Students of the Chinese, Japanese, and other Languages. Arranged by JOHN BELLOWS. With Notes on the writing of Chinese with Roman Letters. By Professor SUMMERS, King's College, London. Crown 8vo., pp. 6 and 368, cloth. 6*s.*

Bellows.—OUTLINE DICTIONARY, FOR THE USE OF MISSIONARIES, Explorers, and Students of Language. By MAX MÜLLER, M.A., Taylorian Professor in the University of Oxford. With an Introduction on the proper use of the ordinary English Alphabet in transcribing Foreign Languages. The Vocabulary compiled by JOHN BELLOWS. Crown 8vo. Limp morocco, pp. xxxi. and 368. 7*s.* 6*d.*

Bellows.—DICTIONARY FOR THE POCKET, French and English, English and French. Both Divisions on same page. By JOHN BELLOWS. Masculine and Feminine Words shown by Distinguishing Types. Conjugations of all the Verbs; Liaison marked in French Part, and Hints to aid Pronunciation. Together with Tables and Maps. Revised by ALEXANDRE BELJAME, M.A., and Fellow of the University, Paris. Second Edition. 32mo. roan, with tuck, gilt edges. 10*s.* 6*d.*

Benfey.—A GRAMMAR OF THE LANGUAGE OF THE VEDAS. By Dr. THEODOR BENFEY. In 1 vol. 8vo., of about 650 pages. [*In preparation.*

Benfey.—A PRACTICAL GRAMMAR OF THE SANSKRIT LANGUAGE, for the use of Early Students. By THEODOR BENFEY, Professor of Sanskrit in the University of Göttingen. Second, revised and enlarged, edition. Royal 8vo. pp. viii. and 296, cloth. 10*s.* 6*d.*

Beschi.—CLAVIS HUMANIORUM LITTERARUM SUBLIMIORIS TAMULICI IDIOMATIS. Auctore R. P. CONSTANTIO JOSEPHO BESCHIO, Soc. Jesu, in Madurensi Regno Missionario. Edited by the Rev. K. IHLEFELD, and printed for A. Burnell, Esq., Tranquebar. 8vo. sewed, pp. 171. 10*s.* 6*d.*

Beurmann.—VOCABULARY OF THE TIGRÉ LANGUAGE. Written down by MORITZ VON BEURMANN. Published with a Grammatical Sketch. By Dr. A. MERX, of the University of Jena. pp. viii. and 78, cloth. 3*s.* 6*d.*

Beveridge.—THE DISTRICT OF BAKARGANJ; its History and Statistics. By H. BEVERIDGE, B.C.S. 8vo. cloth, pp. xx. and 460. 21*s.*

Bhagavat-Geeta.—See under WILKINS.

Bibliotheca Indica. A Collection of Oriental Works published by the Asiatic Society of Bengal. Old Series. Fasc. 1 to 235. New Series. Fasc. 1 to 348. (Special List of Contents to be had on application.) Each Fsc in 8vo., 2*s.*; in 4to., 4*s.*

Bigandet.—THE LIFE OR LEGEND OF GAUDAMA, the Buddha of the Burmese, with Annotations. The ways to Neibban, and Notice on the Phongyies, or Burmese Monks. By the Right Reverend P. BIGANDET, Bishop of Ramatha, Vicar Apostolic of Ava and Pegu. 8vo. sewed, pp. xi., 538, and v. £2 2*s.*

Birch.—FASTI MONASTICI AEVI SAXONICI: or, an Alphabetical List of the Heads of Religious Houses in England, previous to the Norman Conquest, to which is prefixed a Chronological Catalogue of Contemporary Foundations. By W. DE GREY BIRCH. 8vo. cloth, pp. viii. and 114. 5*s.*

Bleek.—A COMPARATIVE GRAMMAR OF SOUTH AFRICAN LANGUAGES. By W. H. I. BLEEK, Ph.D. Volume I. I. Phonology. II. The Concord. Section 1. The Noun. 8vo. pp. xxxvi. and 322, cloth. 16*s.*

Bleek.—A BRIEF ACCOUNT OF BUSHMAN FOLK LORE AND OTHER TEXTS. By W. H. I. BLEEK, Ph.D., etc., etc. Folio sd., pp. 21. 1875. 2*s.* 6*d.*

Bleek.—REYNARD IN SOUTH AFRICA; or, Hottentot Fables. Translated from the Original Manuscript in Sir George Grey's Library. By Dr. W. H. I. BLEEK, Librarian to the Grey Library, Cape Town, Cape of Good Hope. In one volume, small 8vo., pp. xxxi. and 94, cloth. 3*s.* 6*d.*

Blochmann.—THE PROSODY OF THE PERSIANS, according to Saifi, Jmi, and other Writers. By H. BLOCHMANN, M.A. Assistant Professor, Calcutta Madrasah. 8vo. sewed, pp. 166. 10*s.* 6*d.*

Blochmann.—SCHOOL GEOGRAPHY OF INDIA AND BRITISH BURMAH. By H. BLOCHMANN, M.A. 12mo. pp. vi. and 100. 2*s.* 6*d.*

Blochmann.—A TREATISE ON THE RUBA'I entitled Risalah i Taranah. By AGHA AHMAD 'ALI. With an Introduction and Explanatory Notes, by H. BLOCHMANN, M.A. 8vo. sewed, pp. 11 and 17. 2*s.* 6*d.*

Blochmann.—The Persian Metres by Saifi, and a Treatise on Persian Rhyme by Jami. Edited in Persian, by H. Blochmann, M.A. 8vo. sewed, pp. 62. 3*s*. 6*d*.

Bombay Sanskrit Series. Edited under the superintendence of G. Bühler, Ph. D., Professor of Oriental Languages, Elphinstone College, and F. Kielhorn, Ph. D., Superintendent of Sanskṛit Studies, Deccan College. 1868–70.

1. Panchatantra iv. and v. Edited, with Notes, by G. Bühler, Ph. D. Pp. 84, 16. 6*s*.
2. Nágojíbhaṭṭa's Paribháshendusékhara. Edited and explained by F. Kielhorn, Ph. D. Part I., the Sanskṛit Text and Various Readings. pp. 116. 10*s*. 6*d*.
3. Panchatantra ii. and iii. Edited, with Notes, by G. Bühler, Ph. D. Pp. 86, 14, 2. 7*s*. 6*d*.
4. Panchatantra i. Edited, with Notes, by F. Kielhorn, Ph.D. Pp. 114, 53. 7*s*. 6*d*.
5. Kálidása's Raghuvaṃśa. With the Commentary of Mallinátha. Edited, with Notes, by Shankar P. Paṇḍit, M.A. Part I. Cantos I.–VI. 10*s*. 6*d*.
6. Kálidása's Málavikágnimitra. Edited, with Notes, by Shankar P. Paṇḍit, M.A. 10*s*. 6*d*.
7. Nágojíbhaṭṭa's Paribháshendusékhara Edited and explained by F. Kielhorn, Ph.D. Part II. Translation and Notes. (Paribhâshâs, i.–xxxvii.) pp. 184. 10*s*. 6*d*.
8. Kálidása's Raghuvaṃśa. With the Commentary of Mallinátha. Edited, with Notes, by Shankar P. Paṇḍit, M.A. Part II. Cantos VII.–XIII. 10*s*. 6*d*.
9. Nágojíbhaṭṭa's Paribháshenduṣekhara. Edited and explained by F. Kielhorn. Part II Translation and Notes. (Paribhâshâs xxxviii.–lxix.) 7*s*. 6*d*.
10. Dandin's Dasakumaracharita. Edited with critical and explanatory Notes by G. Bühler. Part I. 7*s*. 6*d*.
11. Bhartrihari's Nitisataka and Vairagyasataka, with Extracts from Two Sanskrit Commentaries. Edited, with Notes, by Kasinath T. Telang. 9*s*.
12. Nagojibhatta's Paribháshendusekhara. Edited and explained by F. Kielhorn. Part II. Translation and Notes. (Paribhâshâs lxx.–cxxii.) 7*s*. 6*d*.
13. Kalidasa's Raghuvaṃṣa, with the Commentary of Mallinátha. Edited, with Notes, by Shankar P. Paṇḍit. Part III. Cantos XIV.–XIX. 10*s*. 6*d*.
14. Vikramâṅkadevacharita. Edited, with an Introduction, by G. Bühler. 7*s*. 6*d*.

Bottrell.—Traditions and Hearthside Stories of West Cornwall. By W. Bottrell (an old Celt). Demy 12mo. pp. vi. 292, cloth. 1870. Scarce.

Bottrell.—Traditions and Hearthside Stories of West Cornwall. By William Bottrell. With Illustrations by Mr. Joseph Blight. Second Series. Crown 8vo. cloth, pp. iv. and 300. 6*s*.

Boyce.—A Grammar of the Kaffir Language.—By William B. Boyes, Wesleyan Missionary. Third Edition, augmented and improved, with Exercises, by William J. Davis, Wesleyan Missionary. 12mo. pp. xii. and 164, cloth. 8*s*.

Bowditch.—Suffolk Surnames. By N. I. Bowditch. Third Edition, 8vo. pp. xxvi. and 758, cloth. 7*s*. 6*d*.

Bretschneider.—On the Knowledge Possessed by the Ancient

CHINESE OF THE ARABS AND ARABIAN COLONIES, and other Western Countries mentioned in Chinese Books. By E. BRETSCHNEIDER, M.D., Physician of the Russian Legation at Peking. 8vo. pp. 28, sewed. 1871. 1*s*.

Bretschneider.—NOTES ON CHINESE MEDIÆVAL TRAVELLERS TO THE WEST. By E. BRETSCHNEIDER, M.D. Demy 8vo. sd., pp. 130. 5*s*.

Bretschneider.—ARCHÆOLOGICAL AND HISTORICAL RESEARCHES ON PEKING AND ITS ENVIRONS. By E. BRETSCHNEIDER, M.D., Physician to the Russian Legation at Peking. Imp. 8vo. sewed, pp. 64, with 4 Maps. 5*s*.

Bretschneider.—NOTICES OF THE MEDIÆVAL GEOGRAPHY AND HISTORY OF CENTRAL AND WESTERN ASIA. Drawn from Chinese and Mongol Writings, and Compared with the Observations of Western Authors in the Middle Ages. By E. BRETSCHNEIDER, M.D. 8vo. sewed, pp. 233, with two Maps. 12*s*. 6*d*.

Brhat-Sanhita (The).—See under Kern.

Brinton.—THE MYTHS OF THE NEW WORLD A Treatise on the Symbolism and Mythology of the Red Race of America. By DANIEL G. BRINTON, A.M., M.D. Second Edition, revised. Cr. 8vo. cloth, pp. viii. and 331. 12*s*. 6*d*.

British Museum.—CATALOGUE OF SANSKRIT AND PALI BOOKS in the British Museum. By Dr. ERNST HAAS. Printed by permission of the Trustees of the British Museum. 4to pp. viii. and 188, boards. 21*s*.

Brockie.—INDIAN PHILOSOPHY. Introductory Paper. By WILLIAM BROCKIE, Author of "A Day in the Land of Scott," etc., etc. 8vo. pp. 26, sewed. 1872. 6*d*.

Bronson.—A DICTIONARY IN ASSAMESE AND ENGLISH. Compiled by M. BRONSON, American Baptist Missionary. 8vo. calf, pp. viii. and 609. £2 2*s*.

Brown.—THE DERVISHES; or, ORIENTAL SPIRITUALISM. By JOHN P. BROWN, Secretary and Dragoman of the Legation of the United States of America at Constantinople. With twenty-four Illustrations. 8vo. cloth, pp. viii. and 415. 14*s*.

Brown.—SANSKRIT PROSODY AND NUMERICAL SYMBOLS EXPLAINED. By CHARLES PHILIP BROWN, Author of the Telugu Dictionary, Grammar, etc., Professor of Telugu in the University of London. Demy 8vo. pp. 64, cloth. 3*s*. 6*d*.

Buddhaghosha's Parables: translated from Burmese by Captain H. T. ROGERS, R.E. With an Introduction containing Buddha's Dhammapadam, or, Path of Virtue; translated from Pali by F. MAX MÜLLER. 8vo. pp. 378, cloth. 12*s*. 6*d*.

Burgess.—ARCHÆOLOGICAL SURVEY OF WESTERN INDIA. Report of the First Season's Operations in the Belgâm and Kaladgi Districts. Jan. to May, 1874. By JAMES BURGESS. With 56 photographs and lith. plates. Royal 4to. pp. viii. and 45. £2 2*s*.

Burnell.—CATALOGUE OF A COLLECTION OF SANSKRIT MANUSCRIPTS. By A. C. BURNELL, M.R.A.S., Madras Civil Service. PART 1. *Vedic Manuscripts.* Fcap. 8vo. pp. 64, sewed. 1870. 2*s*.

Burnell.—THE SÂMAVIDHÂNABRÂHMAṆA (being the Third Brâhmaṇa) of the Sâma Veda. Edited, together with the Commentary of Sâyaṇa, an English Translation, Introduction, and Index of Words, by A. C. BURNELL. Volume I.—Text and Commentary, with Introduction. 8vo. pp. xxxviii. and 104. 12*s*. 6*d*.

Burnell.—THE VAṂÇABRÂHMAṆA (being the Eighth Brâhmaṇa) of the Sâma Veda. Edited, together with the Commentary of Sâyaṇa, a Preface and Index of Words, by A. C. BURNELL, M.R.A.S., etc. 8vo. sewed, pp. xliii., 12, and xii., with 2 coloured plates. 10*s*. 6*d*.

Burnell.—THE DEVATĀDHYĀYABRĀHMAṆA (being the Fifth Brāhmaṇa) of the Sama Veda. The Sanskrit Text edited, with the Commentary of Sāyaṇa, an Index of Words, etc., by A. C. BURNELL, M.R.A.S. 8vo. and Trans., pp. 34. 5*s*.

Burnell.—ON THE AINDRA SCHOOL OF SANSKRIT GRAMMARIANS. Their Place in the Sanskrit and Subordinate Literatures. By A. C. BURNELL. 8vo. pp. 120. 10*s*. 6*d*.

Burnell.—DAYADAÇAÇLOKI. TEN SLOKAS IN SANSKRIT, with English Translation. By A. C. BURNELL. 8vo. pp. 11. 2*s*.

Burnell.—ELEMENTS OF SOUTH-INDIAN PALÆOGRAPHY, from the 4th to the 17th century A.D. By A. C. BURNELL. 4to. boards, pp. 98. With 30 plates. 1875.

Buttmann.—A GRAMMAR OF THE NEW TESTAMENT GREEK. By A. BUTTMANN. Authorized translation by Prof J. H. Thayer, with numerous additions and corrections by the author. Demy 8vo. cloth, pp. xx. and 474. 1873. 14*s*.

Calcutta Review.—THE CALCUTTA REVIEW. Published Quarterly. Price 8*s*. 6*d*.

Caldwell.—A COMPARATIVE GRAMMAR OF THE DRAVIDIAN, OR SOUTH-INDIAN FAMILY OF LANGUAGES. By the Rev. R. CALDWELL, LL.D. A Second, corrected, and enlarged Edition. Demy 8vo. pp. 805. 1875. 28*s*.

Callaway.—IZINGANEKWANE, NENSUMANSUMANE, NEZINDABA, ZABANTU (Nursery Tales, Traditions, and Histories of the Zulus). In their own words, with a Translation into English, and Notes. By the Rev. HENRY CALLAWAY, M.D. Volume I., 8vo. pp. xiv. and 378, cloth. Natal, 1866 and 1867. 16*s*.

Callaway.—THE RELIGIOUS SYSTEM OF THE AMAZULU.

Part I.—Unkulunkulu; or, the Tradition of Creation as existing among the Amazulu and other Tribes of South Africa, in their own words, with a translation into English, and Notes. By the Rev. Canon CALLAWAY, M.D. 8vo. pp. 128, sewed. 1868. 4*s*.

Part II.—Amatongo; or, Ancestor Worship, as existing among the Amazulu, in their own words, with a translation into English, and Notes. By the Rev. CANON CALLAWAY, M.D. 1869. 8vo. pp. 127, sewed. 1869. 4*s*.

Part III.—Izinyanga Zokubula; or, Divination, as existing among the Amazulu, in their own words. With a Translation into English, and Notes. By the Rev. Canon CALLAWAY, M.D. 8vo. pp. 150, sewed. 1870. 4*s*.

Part IV.—Abatakati, or Medical Magic and Witchcraft. 8vo. pp. 40, sewed. 1*s*. 6*d*.

Calligaris.—LE COMPAGNON DE TOUS, OU DICTIONNAIRE POLYGLOTTE. Par le Colonel LOUIS CALLIGARIS, Grand Officier, etc. (French—Latin—Italian—Spanish—Portuguese—German—English—Modern Greek—Arabic—Turkish.) 2 vols. 4to., pp. 1157 and 746. Turin. £4 4*s*.

Campbell.—SPECIMENS OF THE LANGUAGES OF INDIA, including Tribes of Bengal, the Central Provinces, and the Eastern Frontier. By Sir G. CAMPBELL, M.P. Folio, paper, pp. 308. 1874. £1 11*s*. 6*d*.

Carpenter.—THE LAST DAYS IN ENGLAND OF THE RAJAH RAMMOHUN ROY. By MARY CARPENTER, of Bristol. With Five Illustrations. 8vo. pp. 272, cloth. 7*s*. 6*d*.

Carr.—ఆంధ్రలోకోక్తిచంద్రిక. A COLLECTION OF TELUGU PROVERBS, Translated, Illustrated, and Explained; together with some Sanscrit Proverbs printed in the Devnâgarî and Telugu Characters. By Captain M. W. CARR, Madras Staff Corps. One Vol. and Supplemnt, royal 8vo. pp. 488 and 148. 31*s*. 6*d*

Catlin.—O-KEE-PA. A Religious Ceremony of the Mandans. By GEORGE CATLIN. With 13 Coloured Illustrations. 4to pp. 60, bound in cloth, gilt edges. 14*s*.

Chalmers.—THE ORIGIN OF THE CHINESE; an Attempt to Trace the connection of the Chinese with Western Nations in their Religion, Superstitions, Arts, Language, and Traditions. By JOHN CHALMERS, A.M. Foolscap 8vo. cloth, pp. 78. 5*s*.

Chalmers.—The Speculations on Metaphysics, Polity, and Morality of "The Old Philosopher" Lau Tsze. Translated from the Chinese, with an Introduction by John Chalmers, M.A. Fcap. 8vo. cloth, xx. and 62. 4*s.* 6*d.*

Charnock.—Ludus Patronymicus; or, the Etymology of Curious Surnames. By Richard Stephen Charnock, Ph.D., F.S.A., F.R.G.S. Crown 8vo., pp. 182, cloth. 7*s.* 6*d.*

Charnock.—Verba Nominalia; or Words derived from Proper Names. By Richard Stephen Charnock, Ph. Dr. F.S.A., etc. 8vo. pp. 326, cloth. 14*s.*

Charnock.—The Peoples of Transylvania. Founded on a Paper read before The Anthropological Society of London, on the 4th of May, 1869. By Richard Stephen Charnock, Ph.D., F.S.A., F.R.G.S. Demy 8vo. pp. 36, sewed. 1870. 2*s.* 6*d.*

Chaucer Society's Publications. Subscription, two guineas per annum.

1868. *First Series.*

Canterbury Tales. Part I.

I. The Prologue and Knight's Tale, in 6 parallel Texts (from the 6 MSS. named below), together with Tables, showing the Groups of the Tales, and their varying order in 38 MSS. of the Tales, and in the old printed editions, and also Specimens from several MSS. of the "Moveable Prologues" of the Canterbury Tales,—The Shipman's Prologue, and Franklin's Prologue,—when moved from their right places, and of the substitutes for them.

II. The Prologue and Knight's Tale from the Ellesmere MS.
III. „ „ „ „ „ „ „ Hengwrt „ 154.
IV. „ „ „ „ „ „ „ Cambridge „ Gg. 4. 27.
V. „ „ „ „ „ „ „ Corpus „ Oxford.
VI. „ „ „ „ „ „ „ Petworth „
VII. „ „ „ „ „ „ „ Lansdowne „ 851.

Nos. II. to VII. are separate Texts of the 6-Text edition of the Canterbury Tales, Part I.

1868. *Second Series.*

1. On Early English Pronunciation, with especial reference to Shakspere and Chaucer, containing an investigation of the Correspondence of Writing with Speech in England, from the Anglo-Saxon period to the present day, preceded by a systematic notation of all spoken sounds, by means of the ordinary printing types. Including a re-arrangement of Prof. F. J. Child's Memoirs on the Language of Chaucer and Gower, and Reprints of the Rare Tracts by Salesbury on English, 1547, and Welsh, 1567, and by Barcley on French, 1521. By Alexander J. Ellis, F.R.S., etc., etc. Part I. On the Pronunciation of the xivth, xvith, xviith, and xviiith centuries.

2. Essays on Chaucer; His Words and Works. Part I. 1. Ebert's Review of Sandras's *E'tude sur Chaucer, considére comme Imitateur des Trouvères,* translated by J. W. Van Rees Hoets, M.A., Trinity Hall, Cambridge, and revised by the Author.—II. A Thirteenth Century Latin Treatise on the *Chilindre*: "For by my *chilindre* it is prime of day" (*Shipmannes Tale*). Edited, with a Translation, by Mr. Edmund Brock, and illustrated by a Woodcut of the Instrument from the Ashmole MS. 1522.

3. A Temporary Preface to the Six-Text Edition of Chaucer's Canterbury Tales. Part I. Attempting to show the true order of the Tales, and the Days and Stages of the Pilgrimage, etc., etc. By F. J. Furnivall, Esq., M.A., Trinity Hall, Cambridge.

Chauncer Society's Publications—*continued.*

1869. *First Series.*

VIII.	The Miller's, Reeve's, Cook's, and Gamelyn's Tales:	Ellesmere MS.
IX.	,, ,, ,, ,, ,, ,, ,,	Hengwrt ,,
X.	,, ,, ,, ,, ,, ,, ,,	Cambridge ,,
XI.	,, ,, ,, ,, ,, ,, ,,	Corpus ,,
XII.	,, ,, ,, ,, ,, ,, ,,	Petworth ,,
XIII.	,, ,, ,, ,, ,, ,, ,,	Lansdowne ,,

These are separate issues of the 6-Text Chaucer's Canterbury Tales, Part II.

1869. *Second Series.*

4. English Pronunciation, with especial reference to Shakspere and Chaucer. By Alexander J. Ellis, F.R.S. Part II.

1870. *First Series.*

XIV. Canterbury Tales. Part II. The Miller's, Reeve's, and Cook's Tales, with an Appendix of the Spurious Tale of Gamelyn, in Six parallel Texts.

1870. *Second Series.*

5. On Early English Pronunciation, with especial reference to Shakspere and Chaucer. By A. J. Ellis, F.R.S., F.S.A. Part III. Illustrations on the Pronunciation of xivth and xvith Centuries. Chaucer, Gower, Wycliffe, Spenser, Shakespere, Salesbury, Barcley, Hart, Bullokar, Gill. Pronouncing Vocabulary.

1871. *First Series.*

XV. The Man of Law's, Shipman's, and Prioress's Tales, with Chaucer's own Tale of Sir Thopas, in 6 parallel Texts from the MSS. above named, and 10 coloured drawings of Tellers of Tales, after the originals in the Ellesmere MS.

XVI.	The Man of Law's Tale, &c., &c.:	Ellesmere MS.
XVII.	,, ,, ,, ,,	Cambridge ,,
XVIII.	,, ,, ,, ,,	Corpus ,,

XIX. The Shipman's, Prioress's, and Man of Law's Tales, from the Petworth MS.

XX. The Man of Law's Tales, from the Lansdowne MS. (each with woodcuts of fourteen drawings of Tellers of Tales in the Ellesmere MS.)

XXI. A Parallel-Text edition of Chaucer's Minor Poems, Part I.:—'The Dethe of Blaunche the Duchesse,' from Thynne's ed. of 1532, the Fairfax MS. 16, and Tanner MS. 346; 'the compleynt to Pite,' 'the Parlament of Foules,' and 'the Compleynt of Mars,' each from six MSS.

XXII. Supplementary Parallel-Texts of Chaucer's Minor Poems, Part I., containing 'The Parlament of Foules,' from three MSS.

XXIII. Odd Texts of Chaucer's Minor Poems, Part I., containing 1. two MS. fragments of 'The Parlament of Foules;' 2. the two differing versions of 'The Prologue to the Legende of Good Women,' arranged so as to show their differences; 3. an Appendix of Poems attributed to Chaucer, i. 'The Balade of Pitee by Chauciers;' ii. 'The Cronycle made by Chaucer,' both from MSS. written by Shirley, Chaucer's contemporary.

XXIV. A One-Text Print of Chaucer's Minor Poems, being the best Text from the Parallel-Text Edition, Part I., containing: 1. The Dethe of Blaunche the Duchesse; 2. The Compleynt to Pite; 3. The Parlament of Foules; 4. The Compleynt of Mars; 5. The A B C, with its original from De Guileville's *Pèlerinage de la Vie humaine* (edited from the best Paris MSS. by M. Paul Meyer).

1871. *Second Series.*

6. Trial Fore-words to my Parallel-Text edition of Chaucer's Minor

Chauncer Society's Publications—*continued.*

Poems for the Chaucer Society (with a try to set Chaucer's Works in their right order of Time). By Fredk. J. Furnivall. Part 1. (This Part brings out, for the first time, Chaucer's long early but hopeless love.)

1872. *First Series.*

XXV. Chaucer's Tale of Melibe, the Monk's, Nun's Priest's, Doctor's, Pardoner's, Wife of Bath's, Friar's, and Summoner's Tales, in 6 parallel Texts from the MSS. above named, and with the remaining 13 coloured drawings of Tellers of Tales, after the originals in the Ellesmere MS.

XXVI. The Wife's, Friar's, and Summoner's Tales, from the Ellesmere MS., with 9 woodcuts of Tale-Tellers. (Part IV.)

XXVII. The Wife's, Friar's, Summoner's, Monk's, and Nun's Priest's Tales, from the Hengwrt MS., with 23 woodcuts of the Tellers of the Tales. (Part III.)

XXVIII. The Wife's, Friar's, and Summoner's Tales, from the Cambridge MS., with 9 woodcuts of Tale-Tellers. (Part IV.)

XXIX. A Treatise on the Astrolabe; otherwise called Bred and Mylk for Children, addressed to his Son Lowys by Geoffrey Chaucer. Edited by the Rev. Walter W. Skeat, M.A.

1872. *Second Series.*

7. Originals and Analogues of some of Chaucer's Canterbury Tales. Part 1. 1. The original of the Man of Law's Tale of Constance, from the French Chronicle of Nicholas Trivet, Arundel MS. 56, ab. 1340 A.D., collated with the later copy, ab. 1400, in the National Library at Stockholm; copied and edited. with a trnslation, by Mr. Edmund Brock. 2. The Tale of "Merelaus the Emperor," from the Early-English version of the *Gesta Romanorum* in Harl. MS. 7333; and 3. Part of Matthew Paris's *Vita Offæ Primi*, both stories, illustrating incidents in the Man of Law's Tale. 4. Two French Fabliaux like the Reeve's Tale. 5. Two Latin Stories like the Friar's Tale.

1873. *First Series.*

XXX. The Six-Text Canterbury Tales, Part V., containing the Clerk's and Merchant's Tales.

1873. *Second Series.*

8. Albertano of Brescia's *Liber Consilii et Consolationis*, A.D. 1246 (the Latin source of the French original of Chaucer's *Melibe*), edited from the MSS. by Dr. Thor Sundby.

1874. *First Series.*

XXXI. The Six-Text, Part VI., containing the Squire's and Franklin's Tales.

XXXII. to XXXVI. Large Parts of the separate issues of the Six MSS.

1874. *Second Series.*

9. Essays on Chaucer, his Words and Works, Part II.: 3. John of Hoveden's *Practica Chilindri*, edited from the MS. with a translation, by Mr. E. Brock. 4. Chaucer's use of the final *-e*, by Joseph Payne, Esq. 5. Mrs. E. Barrett-Browning on Chaucer: being those parts of her review of the *Book of the Poets*, 1842, which relate to him; here reprinted by leave of Mr. Robert Browning. 6. Professor Bernhard Ten-Brink's critical edition of Chaucer's *Compleynte to Pite.*

1875. *First Series.*

XXXVII. The Six-Text, Part VII., the Second Nun's, Canon's-Yeoman's, and Manciple's Tales, with the Blank-Parson Link.

XXXVIII. to XLIII. Large Parts of the separate issues of the Six MSS. bringing all up to the Parson's Tale.

Chauncer Society's Publications—*continued.*

XLIV. A detailed Comparison of the *Troylus and Cryseyde* with Boccaccio's *Filostrato*, with a Translation of all Passages used by Chaucer, and an Abstract of the Parts not used, by W. MICHAEL ROSSETTI, Esq., and with a print of the *Troylus* from the Harleian MS. 3943. Part I.

XLV., XLVI. Ryme-Index to the Ellesmere MS. of the Canterbury Tales, by HENRY CROMIE, Esq., M.A. Both in Royal 4to. for the *Six-Text*, and in 8vo. for the separate Ellesmere MS.

1875. *Second Series.*

10. Originals and Analogues of Chaucer's Canterbury Tales, Part II. 6. Alphonsus of Lincoln, a Story like the *Prioress's Tale.* 7. How Reynard caught Chanticleer, the source of the *Nun's-Priest's Tale.* 8. Two Italian Stories, and a Latin one, like the *Pardoner's Tale.* 9. The Tale of the Priest's Bladder, a story like the *Summoner's Tale*, being 'Li dis de le Vescie a Prestre,' par Jakes de Basiw. 10. Petrarch's Latin Tale of Griseldis (with Boccaccio's Story from which it was re-told), the original of the *Clerk's Tale.* 11. Five Versions of a Pear-tree Story like that in the *Merchant's Tale.* 12. Four Versions of The Life of Saint Cecilia, the original of the *Second Nun's Tale.*

11. Early English Pronunciation, with especial reference to Shakspere and Chaucer. By ALEXANDER J. ELLIS, Esq., F.R.S. Part IV.

12. Life Records of Chaucer. Part I., The Robberies of Chaucer by Richard Brerelay and others at Westminster, and at Hatcham, Surrey, on Tuesday, Sept. 6, 1390, with some account of the Robbers, from the Enrolments in the Public Record Office. By WALFORD D. SELBY, Esq., of the Public Record Office.

13. THYNNE'S ANIMADVERSIONS (1599) ON SPEGHT'S *Chaucer's Workes*, re-edited from the unique MS., by FREDK. J. FURNIVALL, with fresh Lives of William and Francis Thynne, and the only known fragment of *The Pilgrim's Tale.*

Childers.—A PALI-ENGLISH DICTIONARY, with Sanskrit Equivalents, and with numerous Quotations, Extracts, and References. Compiled by ROBERT CÆSAR CHILDERS, late of the Ceylon Civil Service. Imperial 8vo. Double Columns. Complete in 1 Vol., pp. xxii. and 622, cloth. 1875. £3 3*s.*
The first Pali Dictionary ever published.

Childers.—A PÁLI GRAMMAR FOR BEGINNERS. By ROBERT C. CHILDERS. In 1 vol. 8vo. cloth. [*In preparation.*

Childers.—NOTES ON THE SINHALESE LANGUAGE. No. 1. On the Formation of the Plural of Neuter Nouns. By R. C. CHILDERS. Demy 8vo. sd., pp. 16. 1873. 1*s.*

China Review; OR, NOTES AND QUERIES ON THE FAR EAST. Published bi-monthly. Edited by E. J. EITEL. 4to. Subscription, £1 10*s.* per volume.

Chinese and Japanese Literature (A Catalogue of), and of Oriental Periodicals. On Sale by Trübner & Co., 57 and 59, Ludgate Hill, London. 8vo. pp. 28. *Gratis.*

Chintamon.—A COMMENTARY ON THE TEXT OF THE BHAGAVAD-GÍTÁ; or, the Discourse between Krishna and Arjuna of Divine Matters. A Sanscrit Philosophical Poem. With a few Introductory Papers. By HURRYCHUND CHINTAMON, Political Agent to H. H. the Guicowar Mulhar Rao Maharajah of Baroda. Post 8vo. cloth, pp. 118. 6*s.*

Christaller.—A DICTIONARY, ENGLISH, TSHI, (ASANTE), AKRA; Tshi (Chwee), comprising as dialects Akán (Asànté, Akém, Akuapém, etc.) and Fànté; Akra (Accra), connected with Adangme; Gold Coast, West Africa.

Enyiresi, Twi né Nkrań nsẹm - asekyerẹ - ńhõma.	Eǹliši, Otšūi kẹ Gã wiemọi - ašišitšõmọ- wolo.

By the Rev. J. G. CHRISTALLER, Rev. C. W. LOCHER, Rev. J. ZIMMERMANN. 16mo. 7*s.* 6*d.*

Christaller.—A GRAMMAR OF THE ASANTE AND FANTE LANGUAGE, called Tshi (Chwee, Twi): based on the Akuapem Dialect, with reference to the other (Akan and Fante) Dialects. By Rev. J. G. CHRISTALLER. 8vo. pp. xxiv. and 203. 1875. 10*s.* 6*d.*

Clarke.—TEN GREAT RELIGIONS: an Essay in Comparative Theology. By JAMES FREEMAN CLARKE. 8vo. cloth, pp. x. and 528. 1871. 14*s.*

Clarke.—MEMOIR ON THE COMPARATIVE GRAMMAR OF EGYPTIAN, COPTIC, AND UDE. By HYDE CLARKE, Cor. Member American Oriental Society; Mem. German Oriental Society, etc., etc. Demy 8vo. sd., pp. 32. 2*s.*

Clarke.—RESEARCHES IN PRE-HISTORIC AND PROTO-HISTORIC COMPARATIVE PHILOLOGY, MYTHOLOGY, AND ARCHÆOLOGY, in connexion with the Origin of Culture in America and the Accad or Sumerian Families. By HYDE CLARKE. Demy 8vo. sewed, pp. xi. and 74. 1875. 2*s.* 6*d.*

Cleasby.—AN ICELANDIC-ENGLISH DICTIONARY. Based on the MS. Collections of the late Richard Cleasby. Enlarged and completed by G. VIGFÚSSON. With an Introduction, and Life of Richard Cleasby, by G. WEBBE DASENT, D.C.L. 4to. £3 7*s.*

Colebrooke.—THE LIFE AND MISCELLANEOUS ESSAYS OF HENRY THOMAS COLEBROOKE. The Biography by his Son, Sir T. E. COLEBROOKE, Bart., M.P., The Essays edited by Professor Cowell. In 3 vols.

Vol. I. The Life. With Portrait and Map. Demy 8vo. cloth, pp. xii. and 492. 14*s.*

Vols. II. and III. The Essays. A New Edition, with Notes by E. B. COWELL, Professor of Sanskrit in the University of Cambridge. Demy 8vo. cloth, pp. xvi.–544, and x.–520. 1873. 28*s.*

Colleccao de Vocabulos e Frases usados na Provincia de S. Pedro, do Rio Grande do Sul, no Brasil. 12mo. pp. 32, sewed. 1*s.*

Contopoulos.—A LEXICON OF MODERN GREEK-ENGLISH AND ENGLISH MODERN GREEK. By N. CONTOPOULOS.

Part I. Modern Greek-English. 8vo. cloth, pp. 460. 12*s.*
Part II. English-Modern Greek. 8vo. cloth, pp. 582. 15*s.*

Conway.—THE SACRED ANTHOLOGY. A Book of Ethnical Scriptures. Collected and edited by M. D. CONWAY. 4th edition. Demy 8vo. cloth, pp. xvi. and 480. 12*s.*

Cotton.—ARABIC PRIMER. Consisting of 180 Short Sentences containing 30 Primary Words prepared according to the Vocal System of Studying Language. By General SIR ARTHUR COTTON, K.C.S.I. Cr. 8vo. cloth, pp. 38. 2*s.* 6*d.*

Cowell and Eggeling.—CATALOGUE OF BUDDHIST SANSKRIT MANUSCRIPTS in the Possession of the Royal Asiatic Society (Hodgson Collection). By Professors E. B. COWELL and J. EGGELING. 8vo. sd., pp. 56. 2*s.* 6*d.*

Cowell.—A SHORT INTRODUCTION TO THE ORDINARY PRAKRIT OF THE SANSKRIT DRAMAS. With a List of Common Irregular Prakrit Words. By Prof. E. B. COWELL. Cr. 8vo. limp cloth, pp. 40. 1875. 3*s.* 6*d.*

Cunningham.—THE ANCIENT GEOGRAPHY OF INDIA. I. The Buddhist Period, including the Campaigns of Alexander, and the Travels of Hwen-Thsang. By ALEXANDER CUNNINGHAM, Major-General, Royal Engineers (Bengal Retired). With thirteen Maps. 8vo. pp. xx. 590, cloth. 1870. 28*s.*

Cunningham.—THE BHILSA TOPES; or, Buddhist Monuments of Central India: comprising a brief Historical Sketch of the Rise, Progress, and Decline of Buddhism; with an Account of the Opening and Examination of the various Groups of Topes around Bhilsa. By Brev.-Major Alexander Cunningham, Bengal Engineers. Illustrated with thirty-three Plates. 8vo. pp. xxxvi. 370, cloth. 1854. £2 2*s.*

Cunningham.—ARCHÆOLOGICAL SURVEY OF INDIA. Four Reports, made during the years 1862-63-64-65. By ALEXANDER CUNNINGHAM, C S.I., Major-General, etc. With Maps and Plates. Vols. 1 to 5. 8vo. cloth. £6.

Dalton.—DESCRIPTIVE ETHNOLOGY OF BENGAL. By EDWARD TUITE DALTON, C.S.I., Colonel, Bengal Staff Corps, etc. Illustrated by Lithograph Portraits copied from Photographs. 33 Lithograph Plates. 4to. half-calf, pp. 340. £6 6*s*.

D'Alwis.—BUDDHIST NIRVÁNA; a Review of Max Müller's Dhammapade. By JAMES D'ALWIS, Member of the Royal Asiatic Society. 8vo. sewed, pp. x. and 140. 6*s*.

D'Alwis.—PALI TRANSLATIONS. Part First. By JAMES D'ALWIS, Member of the Royal Asiatic Society. 8vo. sewed, pp. 24. 1*s*.

D'Alwis.—A DESCRIPTIVE CATALOGUE OF SANSKRIT, PALI, AND SINHALESE LITERARY WORKS OF CEYLON. By JAMES D'ALWIS, M.R.A.S., Advocate of the Supreme Court, &c., &c. In Three Volumes. Vol. I., pp. xxxii. and 244, sewed. 1870. 8*s*. 6*d*. [*Vols. II. and III. in preparation.*

Davids.—THREE INSCRIPTIONS OF PARÂKRAMA BÂHU THE GREAT, from Pulastipura, Ceylon. By T. W. RHYS DAVIDS. 8vo. pp. 20. 1*s*. 6*d*.

Davids.—SÎGIRI, THE LION ROCK, NEAR PULASTIPURA, AND THE 39TH CHAPTER OF THE MAHÂVAMSA. By T. W. RHYS DAVIDS. 8vo. pp. 30. 1*s*. 6*d*.

Delepierre. — SUPERCHERIES LITTERAIRES, PASTICHES SUPPOSITIONS D'AUTEUR, DANS LES LETTRES ET DANS LES ARTS. Par OCTAVE DELEPIERRE. Fcap. 4to. paper cover, pp. 328. 14*s*.

Delepierre.—TABLEAU DE LA LITTÉRATURE DU CENTON, CHEZ LES ANCIENS et chez les Modernes. Par Octave Delepierre. 2 vols. small 4to. paper cover, pp. 324 and 318. 21*s*.

Delepierre.—ESSAI HISTORIQUE ET BIBLIOGRAPHIQUE SUR LES RÉBUS. Par Octave Delepierre. 8vo. pp. 24, sewed. With 15 pages of Woodcuts. 1870. 3*s*. 6*d*.

Dennys.—CHINA AND JAPAN. A complete Guide to the Open Ports of those countries, together with Pekin, Yeddo, Hong Kong, and Macao; forming a Guide Book and Vade Mecum for Travellers, Merchants, and Residents in general; with 56 Maps and Plans. By WM. FREDERICK MAYERS, F.R.G.S. H.M.'s Consular Service; N. B. DENNYS, late H.M.'s Consular Service; and CHARLES KING, Lieut. Royal Marine Artillery. Edited by N. B. DENNYS. In one volume. 8vo. pp. 600, cloth. £2 2*s*.

Dennys.—A HANDBOOK OF THE CANTON VERNACULAR OF THE CHINESE LANGUAGE. Being a Series of Introductory Lessons, for Domestic and Business Purposes. By N. B. DENNYS, M.R.A.S., Ph.D. 8vo. cloth, pp. 4, 195, and 31. £1 10*s*.

Dickson.—THE PÂTIMOKKHA, being the Buddhist Office of the Confession of Priests. The Pali Text, with a Translation, and Notes, by J. F. DICKSON, M.A. 8vo. sd., pp. 69. 2*s*.

Dinkard (The).—The Original Pehlwi Text, the same transliterated in Zend Characters. Translations of the Text in the Gujrati and English Languages; a Commentary and Glossary of Select Terms. By PESHOTUN DUSTOOR BEHRAMJEE SUNJANA. Vol. I. 8vo. cloth. £1 1*s*.

Döhne.—A ZULU-KAFIR DICTIONARY, etymologically explained, with copious Illustrations and examples, preceded by an introduction on the Zulu-Kafir Language. By the Rev. J. L. DÖHNE. Royal 8vo. pp. xlii. and 418, sewed. Cape Town, 1857. 21*s*.

Döhne.—THE FOUR GOSPELS IN ZULU. By the Rev. J. L. DÖHNE, Missionary to the American Board, C.F.M. 8vo. pp. 208, cloth. Pietermaritzburg, 1866. 5*s*.

2

Doolittle.—A VOCABULARY AND HANDBOOK OF THE CHINESE LANGUAGE. Romanized in the Mandarin Dialect. In Two Volumes comprised in Three arts. By Rev. JUSTUS DOOLITTLE, Author of "Social Life of the Chinese." Vol. I. 4to. pp. viii. and 548. Vol. II. Parts II. and III., pp. vii. and 695. £1 11*s*. 6*d*. each vol.

Douglas.—CHINESE-ENGLISH DICTIONARY OF THE VERNACULAR OR SPOKEN LANGUAGE OF AMOY, with the principal variations of the Chang-Chew and Chin-Chew Dialects. By the Rev. CARSTAIRS DOUGLAS, M.A., LL.D., Glasg., Missionary of the Presbyterian Church in England. 1 vol. High quarto, cloth, double columns, pp. 632. 1873. £3 3*s*.

Douglas.—CHINESE LANGUAGE AND LITERATURE. Two Lectures delivered at the Royal Institution, by R. K. DOUGLAS, of the British Museum, and Professor of Chinese at King's College. Cr. 8vo. cl., pp. 118. 1875. 5*s*.

Douse.—GRIMM'S LAW; A STUDY: or, Hints towards an Explanation of the so-called "Lautverschiebung." To which are added some Remarks on the Primitive Indo-European *K*, and several Appendices. By T. LE MARCHANT DOUSE. 8vo. cloth, pp. xvi. and 230. 10*s*. 6*d*.

Dowson.—A GRAMMAR OF THE URDU OR HINDUSTANI LANGUAGE. By JOHN DOWSON, M.R.A.S. 12mo. cloth, pp. xvi. and 264. 10*s*. 6*d*.

Dowson.—A HINDUSTANI EXERCISE BOOK. Containing a Series of Passages and Extracts adapted for Translation into Hindustani. By JOHN DOWSON, M.R.A.S., Professor of Hindustani, Staff College. Crown 8vo. pp. 100. Limp cloth, 2*s*. 6*d*.

Early English Text Society's Publications. Subscription, one guinea per annum.

1. EARLY ENGLISH ALLITERATIVE POEMS. In the West-Midland Dialect of the Fourteenth Century. Edited by R. MORRIS, Esq., from an unique Cottonian MS. 16*s*.
2. ARTHUR (about 1440 A.D.). Edited by F. J. FURNIVALL, Esq., from the Marquis of Bath's unique MS. 4*s*.
3. ANE COMPENDIOUS AND BREUE TRACTATE CONCERNYNG YE OFFICE AND DEWTIE OF KYNGIS, etc. By WILLIAM LAUDER. (1556 A.D.) Edited by F. HALL, Esq., D.C.L. 4*s*.
4. SIR GAWAYNE AND THE GREEN KNIGHT (about 1320-30 A.D.). Edited by R. MORRIS, Esq., from an unique Cottonian MS. 10*s*.
5. OF THE ORTHOGRAPHIE AND CONGRUITIE OF THE BRITAN TONGUE; a treates, noe shorter than necessarie, for the Schooles, be ALEXANDER HUME. Edited for the first time from the unique MS. in the British Museum (about 1617 A.D.), by HENRY B. WHEATLEY, Esq. 4*s*.
6. LANCELOT OF THE LAIK. Edited from the unique MS. in the Cambridge University Library (ab. 1500), by the Rev. WALTER W. SKEAT, M.A. 8*s*.
7. THE STORY OF GENESIS AND EXODUS, an Early English Song, of about 1250 A.D. Edited for the first time from the unique MS. in the Library of Corpus Christi College, Cambridge, by R. MORRIS, Esq. 8*s*.
8. MORTE ARTHURE; the Alliterative Version. Edited from ROBERT THORNTON'S unique MS. (about 1440 A.D.) at Lincoln, by the Rev. GEORGE PERRY, M.A., Prebendary of Lincoln. 7*s*.
9. ANIMADVERSIONS UPPON THE ANNOTACIONS AND CORRECTIONS OF SOME IMPERFECTIONS OF IMPRESSIONES OF CHAUCER'S WORKES, reprinted in 1598; by FRANCIS THYNNE. Edited from the unique MS. in the Bridgewater Library. By G. H. KINGSLEY, Esq., M.D., and F. J. FURNIVALL, Esq., M.A. 10*s*.
10. MERLIN, OR THE EARLY HISTORY OF KING ARTHUR. Edited for the first time from the unique MS. in the Cambridge University Library (about 1450 A.D.), by HENRY B. WHEATLEY, Esq. Part I. 2*s*. 6*d*.

Early English Text Society's Publications—*continued.*

11. THE MONARCHE, and other Poems of Sir David Lyndesay. Edited from the first edition by JOHNE SKOTT, in 1552, by FITZEDWARD HALL, Esq., D.C.L. Part I. *3s.*
12. THE WRIGHT'S CHASTE WIFE, a Merry Tale, by Adam of Cobsam (about 1462 A.D.), from the unique Lambeth MS. 306. Edited for the first time by F. J. FURNIVALL, Esq., M.A. *1s.*
13. SEINTE MARHERETE, ÞE MEIDEN ANT MARTYR. Three Texts of ab. 1200, 1310, 1330 A.D. First edited in 1862, by the Rev. OSWALD COCKAYNE, M.A., and now re-issued. *2s.*
14. KYNG HORN, with fragments of Floriz and Blauncheflur, and the Assumption of the Blessed Virgin. Edited from the MSS. in the Library of the University of Cambridge and the British Museum, by the Rev. J. RAWSON LUMBY. *3s. 6d.*
15. POLITICAL, RELIGIOUS, AND LOVE POEMS, from the Lambeth MS. No. 306, and other sources. Edited by F. J. FURNIVALL, Esq., M.A. *7s. 6d.*
16. A TRETICE IN ENGLISH breuely drawe out of þ book of Quintis essencijs in Latyn, þ Hermys þ prophete and king of Egipt after þ flood of Noe, fader of Philosophris, hadde by reuelacioun of an aungil of God to him sente. Edited from the Sloane MS. 73, by F. J. FURNIVALL, Esq., M.A. *1s.*
17. PARALLEL EXTRACTS from 29 Manuscripts of PIERS PLOWMAN, with Comments, and a Proposal for the Society's Three-text edition of this Poem. By the Rev. W. SKEAT, M.A. *1s.*
18. HALI MEIDENHEAD, about 1200 A.D. Edited for the first time from the MS. (with a translation) by the Rev. OSWALD COCKAYNE, M.A. *1s.*
19. THE MONARCHE, and other Poems of Sir David Lyndesay. Part II., the Complaynt of the King's Papingo, and other minor Poems. Edited from the First Edition by F. HALL, Esq., D.C.L. *3s. 6d.*
20. SOME TREATISES BY RICHARD ROLLE DE HAMPOLE. Edited from Robert of Thornton's MS. (ab. 1440 A.D.), by Rev. GEORGE G. PERRY, M.A. *1s.*
21. MERLIN, OR THE EARLY HISTORY OF KING ARTHUR. Part II. Edited by HENRY B. WHEATLEY, Esq. *4s.*
22. THE ROMANS OF PARTENAY, OR LUSIGNEN. Edited for the first time from the unique MS. in the Library of Trinity College, Cambridge, by the Rev. W. W. SKEAT. M.A. *6s.*
23. DAN MICHEL'S AYENBITE OF INWYT, or Remorse of Conscience, in the Kentish dialect, 1340 A.D. Edited from the unique MS. in the British Museum, by RICHARD MORRIS, Esq. *10s. 6d.*
24. HYMNS OF THE VIRGIN AND CHRIST; THE PARLIAMENT OF DEVILS, and Other Religious Poems. Edited from the Lambeth MS. 853, by F. J. FURNIVALL, M.A. *3s.*
25. THE STACIONS OF ROME, and the Pilgrim's Sea-Voyage and Sea-Sickness, with Clene Maydenhod. Edited from the Vernon and Porkington MSS., etc., by F. J. FURNIVALL, Esq., M.A. *1s.*
26. RELIGIOUS PIECES IN PROSE AND VERSE. Containing Dan Jon Gaytrigg's Sermon; The Abbaye of S. Spirit; Sayne Jon, and other pieces in the Northern Dialect. Edited from Robert of Thorntone's MS. (ab. 1460 A.D.), by the Rev. G. PERRY, M.A. *2s.*
27. MANIPULUS VOCABULORUM: a Rhyming Dictionary of the English Language, by PETER LEVINS (1570). Edited, with an Alphabetical Index, by HENRY B. WHEATLEY. *12s.*
28. THE VISION OF WILLIAM CONCERNING PIERS PLOWMAN, together with Vita de Dowel, Dobet et Dobest. 1362 A.D., by WILLIAM LANGLAND. The earliest or Vernon Text; Text A. Edited from the Vernon MS., with full Collations, by Rev. W. W. SKEAT, M.A. *7s.*

Early English English Text Society's Publications—*continued.*

29. OLD ENGLISH HOMILIES AND HOMILETIC TREATISES. (Sawles Warde and the Wohunge of Ure Lauerd: Ureisuns of Ure Louerd and of Ure Lefdi, etc.) of the Twelfth and Thirteenth Centuries. Edited from MSS. in the British Museum, Lambeth, and Bodleian Libraries; with Introduction, Translation, and Notes. By RICHARD MORRIS. *First Series.* Part I. 7*s.*

30. PIERS, THE PLOUGHMAN'S CREDE (about 1394). Edited from the MSS. by the Rev. W. W. SKEAT, M.A. 2*s.*

31. INSTRUCTIONS FOR PARISH PRIESTS. By JOHN MYRC. Edited from Cotton MS. Claudius A. II., by EDWARD PEACOCK, Esq., F.S.A., etc., etc. 4*s.*

32. THE BABEES BOOK, Aristotle's A B C, Urbanitatis, Stans Puer ad Mensam, The Lytille Childrenes Lytil Boke. THE BOKES OF NURTURE of Hugh Rhodes and John Russell, Wynkyn de Worde's Boke of Kervynge, The Booke of Demeanor, The Boke of Curtasye, Seager's Schoole of Vertue, etc., etc. With some French and Latin Poems on like subjects, and some Forewords on Education in Early England. Edited by F. J. FURNIVALL, M.A., Trin. Hall, Cambridge 15*s.*

33. THE BOOK OF THE KNIGHT DE LA TOUR LANDRY, 1372. A Father's Book for his Daughters, Edited from the Harleian MS. 1764, by THOMAS WRIGHT Esq., M.A., and Mr. WILLIAM ROSSITER. 8*s.*

34. OLD ENGLISH HOMILIES AND HOMILETIC TREATISES. (Sawles Warde, and the Wohunge of Ure Lauerd: Ureisuns of Ure Louerd and of Ure Lefdi, etc.) of the Twelfth and Thirteenth Centuries. Edited from MSS. in the British Museum, Lambeth, and Bodleian Libraries; with Introduction, Translation, and Notes, by RICHARD MORRIS. *First Series.* Part 2. 8*s.*

35. SIR DAVID LYNDESAY'S WORKS. PART 3. The Historie of ane Nobil and Wailzeand Sqvyer, WILLIAM MELDRUM, umqvhyle Laird of Cleische and Bynnis, compylit be Sir DAUID LYNDESAY of the Mont *alias* Lyoun King of Armes. With the Testament of the said Williame Meldrum, Squyer, compylit alswa be Sir Dauid Lyndesay, etc. Edited by F. HALL, D.C.L. 2*s.*

36. MERLIN, OR THE EARLY HISTORY OF KING ARTHUR. A Prose Romance (about 1450–1460 A.D.), edited from the unique MS. in the University Library, Cambridge, by HENRY B. WHEATLEY. With an Essay on Arthurian Localities, by J. S. STUART GLENNIE, Esq. Part III. 1869. 12*s.*

37. SIR DAVID LYNDESAY'S WORKS. Part IV. Ane Satyre of the thrie estaits, in commendation of vertew and vitvperation of vyce. Maid be Sir DAVID LINDESAY, of the Mont, *alias* Lyon King of Armes. At Edinbvrgh. Printed be Robert Charteris, 1602. Cvm privilegio regis. Edited by F. HALL, Esq., D.C.L. 4*s.*

38. THE VISION OF WILLIAM CONCERNING PIERS THE PLOWMAN, together with Vita de Dowel, Dobet, et Dobest, Secundum Wit et Resoun, by WILLIAM LANGLAND (1377 A.D.). The "Crowley" Text; or Text B. Edited from MS. Laud Misc. 581, collated with MS. Rawl. Poet. 38, MS. B. 15. 17. in the Library of Trinity College, Cambridge, MS. Dd. 1. 17. in the Cambridge University Library, the MS. in Oriel College, Oxford, MS. Bodley 814, etc. By the Rev. WALTER W. SKEAT, M.A., late Fellow of Christ's College, Cambridge. 10*s.* 6*d.*

39. THE "GEST HYSTORIALE" OF THE DESTRUCTION OF TROY. An Alliterative Romance, translated from Guido De Colonna's "Hystoria Troiana." Now first edited from the unique MS. in the Hunterian Museum, University of Glasgow, by the Rev. GEO A. PANTON and DAVID DONALDSON. Part I. 10*s.* 6*d.*

40. ENGLISH GILDS. The Original Ordinances of more than One Hundred Early English Gilds: Together with the olde usages of the cite of Wynchestre; The Ordinances of Worcester; The Office of the Mayor of Bristol; and the Customary of the Manor of Tettenhall-Regis. From

Early English Text Society's Publications—*continued.*

Original MSS. of the Fourteenth and Fifteenth Centuries. Edited with Notes by the late TOULMIN SMITH, Esq., F.R.S. of Northern Antiquaries (Copenhagen). With an Introduction and Glossary, etc., by his daughter, LUCY TOULMIN SMITH. And a Preliminary Essay, in Five Parts, ON THE HISTORY AND DEVELOPMENT OF GILDS, by LUJO BRENTANO, Doctor Juris Utriusque et Philosophiæ. 21*s.*

41. THE MINOR POEMS OF WILLIAM LAUDER, Playwright, Poet, and Minister of the Word of God (mainly on the State of Scotland in and about 1568 A.D., that year of Famine and Plague). Edited from the Unique Originals belonging to S. CHRISTIE-MILLER, Esq., of Britwell, by F. J. FURNIVALL, M.A., Trin. Hall, Camb. 3*s.*

42. BERNARDUS DE CURA REI FAMULIARIS, with some Early Scotch Prophecies, etc. From a MS., KK 1. 5, in the Cambridge University Library. Edited by J. RAWSON LUMBY, M.A., late Fellow of Magdalen College, Cambridge. 2*s.*

43. RATIS RAVING, and other Moral and Religious Pieces, in Prose and Verse. Edited from the Cambridge University Library MS. KK 1. 5, by J. RAWSON LUMBY, M.A., late Fellow of Magdalen College, Cambridge. 3*s.*

44. JOSEPH OF ARIMATHIE: otherwise called the Romance of the Seint Graal, or Holy Grail: an alliterative poem, written about A.D. 1350, and now first printed from the unique copy in the Vernon MS. at Oxford. With an appendix, containing "The Lyfe of Joseph of Armathy," reprinted from the black-letter copy of Wynkyn de Worde; "De sancto Joseph ab Arimathia," first printed by Pynson, A.D. 1516; and "The Lyfe of Joseph of Arimathia," first printed by Pynson, A.D. 1520. Edited, with Notes and Glossarial Indices, by the Rev. WALTER W. SKEAT, M.A. 5*s.*

45. KING ALFRED'S WEST-SAXON VERSION OF GREGORY'S PASTORAL CARE. With an English translation, the Latin Text, Notes, and an Introduction Edited by HENRY SWEET, Esq., of Balliol College, Oxford. Part I. 10*s.*

46. LEGENDS OF THE HOLY ROOD; SYMBOLS OF THE PASSION AND CROSS-POEMS. In Old English of the Eleventh, Fourteenth, and Fifteenth Centuries. Edited from MSS. in the British Museum and Bodleian Libraries; with Introduction, Translations, and Glossarial Index. By RICHARD MORRIS, LL.D. 10*s.*

47. SIR DAVID LYNDESAY'S WORKS. PART V. The Minor Poems of Lyndesay. Edited by J. A. H. MURRAY, Esq. 3*s.*

48. THE TIMES' WHISTLE: or, A Newe Daunce of Seven Satires, and other Poems: Compiled by R. C., Gent. Now first Edited from MS. Y. 8. 3. in the Library of Canterbury Cathedral; with Introduction, Notes, and Glossary, by J. M. COWPER. 6*s.*

49. AN OLD ENGLISH MISCELLANY, containing a Bestiary, Kentish Sermons, Proverbs of Alfred, Religious Poems of the 13th century. Edited from the MSS. by the Rev. R. MORRIS, LL.D. 10*s.*

50. KING ALFRED'S WEST-SAXON VERSION OF GREGORY'S PASTORAL CARE. Edited from 2 MSS., with an English translation. By HENRY SWEET, Esq., Balliol College, Oxford. Part II. 10*s.*

51. ÞE LIFLADE OF ST. JULIANA, from two old English Manuscripts of 1230 A.D. With renderings into Modern English, by the Rev. O. COCKAYNE and EDMUND BROCK. Edited by the Rev. O. COCKAYNE, M.A. Price 2*s.*

52. PALLADIUS ON HUSBONDRIE, from the unique MS., ab. 1420 A.D., ed. Rev. B. LODGE. Part I. 10*s.*

53. OLD ENGLISH HOMILIES, Series II., from the unique 13th-century MS. in Trinity Coll. Cambridge, with a photolithograph; three Hymns to the Virgin and God, from a unique 13th-century MS. at Oxford, a photolithograph of the music to two of them, and transcriptions of it in modern notation by Dr. RIMBAULT, and A. J. ELLIS, Esq., F.R.S.; the whole edited by the Rev. RICHARD MORRIS, LL.D. 8*s.*

Early English Text Society's Publications—*continued.*

54. The Vision of Piers Plowman, Text C (completing the three versions of this great poem), with an Autotype; and two unique alliterative Poems: Richard the Redeles (by William, the author of the *Vision*); and The Crowned King; edited by the Rev. W. W. Skeat, M.A. 18*s.*

55. Generydes, a Romance, edited from the unique MS., ab. 1440 A.D., in Trin. Coll. Cambridge, by W. Aldis Wright, Esq., M.A., Trin. Coll. Cambr. Part I. 3*s.*

56. The Gest Hystoriale of the Destruction of Troy, translated from Guido de Colonna, in alliterative verse; edited from the unique MS. in the Hunterian Museum, Glasgow, by D. Donaldson, Esq., and the late Rev. G. A. Panton. Part II. 10*s.* 6*d.*

57. The Early English Version of the "Cursor Mundi," in four Texts, from MS. Cotton, Vesp. A. iii. in the British Museum; Fairfax MS. 14. in the Bodleian; the Göttingen MS. Theol. 107; MS. R. 3, 8, in Trinity College, Cambridge. Edited by the Rev. R. Morris, LL.D. Part I. with two photo-lithographic facsimiles by Cooke and Fotheringham. 10*s.* 6*d.*

58. The Blickling Homilies, edited from the Marquis of Lothian's Anglo-Saxon MS. of 971 A.D., by the Rev. R. Morris, LL.D. (With a Photolithograph). Part I. 8*s.*

59. The Early English Version of the "Cursor Mundi;" in four Texts, from MS. Cotton Vesp. A. iii. in the British Museum; Fairfax MS. 14. in the Bodleian; the Göttingen MS. Theol. 107; MS. R. 3, 8, in Trinity College, Cambridge. Edited by the Rev. R. Morris, LL.D. Part II. 15*s.*

60. Meditacyuns on the Soper of our Lorde (perhaps by Robert of Brunne). Edited from the MSS. by J. M. Cowper, Esq. 2*s.* 6*d.*

61. The Romance and Prophecies of Thomas of Erceldoune, printed from Five MSS. Edited by Dr. James A. H. Murray. 10*s.* 6*d.*

62. The Early English Version of the "Cursor Mundi," in Four Texts. Edited by the Rev. R. Morris, M.A., LL.D. Part III. 15*s.*

63. The Blickling Homilies. Edited from the Marquis of Lothian's Anglo-Saxon MS. of 971 A.D., by the Rev. R. Morris, LL.D. Part II. 4*s.*

64. Francis Thynne's Emblemes and Epigrams, A.D. 1600, from the Earl of Ellesmere's unique MS. Edited by F. J. Furnivall, M.A. 4*s.*

65. Be Domes Dæge (Bede's De Die Judicii) and other short Anglo-Saxon Pieces. Edited from the unique MS. by the Rev. J. Rawson Lumby, B.D. 2*s.*

Extra Series. Subscriptions—Small paper, one guinea; large paper two guineas, per annum.

1. The Romance of William of Palerne (otherwise known as the Romance of William and the Werwolf). Translated from the French at the command of Sir Humphrey de Bohun, about A.D. 1350, to which is added a fragment of the Alliterative Romance of Alisaunder, translated from the Latin by the same author, about A.D. 1340; the former re-edited from the unique MS. in the Library of King's College, Cambridge, the latter now first edited from the unique MS. in the Bodleian Library, Oxford. By the Rev. Walter W. Skeat, M.A. 8vo. sewed, pp. xliv. and 328. £1 6*s.*

2. On Early English Pronunciation, with especial reference to Shakspere and Chaucer; containing an investigation of the Correspondence of Writing with Speech in England, from the Anglo-Saxon period to the present day, preceded by a systematic Notation of all Spoken Sounds by means of the ordinary Printing Types; including a re-arrangement of Prof. F. J. Child's Memoirs on the Language of Chaucer and Gower, and reprints of the rare Tracts by Salesbury on English, 1547, and Welsh, 1567, and by

Early English Text Society's Publications—*continued.*

Barcley on French, 1521 By Alexander J. Ellis, F.R.S. Part I. On the Pronunciation of the xivth, xvith, xviith, and xviiith centuries. 8vo. sewed, pp. viii. and 416. 10*s.*

3. Caxton's Book of Curtesye, printed at Westminster about 1477–8, A.D., and now reprinted, with two MS. copies of the same treatise, from the Oriel MS. 79, and the Balliol MS. 354. Edited by Frederick J. Furnivall, M.A. 8vo. sewed, pp. xii. and 58. 5*s.*

4. The Lay of Havelok the Dane; composed in the reign of Edward I., about A.D. 1280. Formerly edited by Sir F. Madden for the Roxburghe Club, and now re-edited from the unique MS. Laud Misc. 108, in the Bodleian Library, Oxford, by the Rev. Walter W. Skeat, M.A. 8vo. sewed, pp. lv. and 160. 10*s.*

5. Chaucer's Translation of Boethius's "De Consolatione Philosophie." Edited from the Additional MS. 10,340 in the British Museum. Collated with the Cambridge Univ. Libr. MS. Ii. 3. 21. By Richard Morris. 8vo. 12*s.*

6 The Romance of the Chevelere Assigne. Re-edited from the unique manuscript in the British Museum, with a Preface, Notes, and Glossarial Index, by Henry H. Gibbs, Esq., M.A. 8vo. sewed, pp. xviii. and 38. 3*s.*

7. On Early English Pronunciation, with especial reference to Shakspere and Chaucer. By Alexander J. Ellis, F.R.S., etc., etc. Part II. On the Pronunciation of the xiiith and previous centuries, of Anglo-Saxon, Icelandic, Old Norse and Gothic, with Chronological Tables of the Value of Letters and Expression of Sounds in English Writing. 10*s.*

8. Queene Elizabethes Achademy, by Sir Humphrey Gilbert. A Booke of Precedence, The Ordering of a Funerall, etc. Varying Versions of the Good Wife, The Wise Man, etc., Maxims, Lydgate's Order of Fools, A Poem on Heraldry, Occleve on Lords' Men, etc., Edited by F. J. Furnivall, M.A., Trin. Hall, Camb. With Essays on Early Italian and German Books of Courtesy, by W. M. Rossetti, Esq., and E. Oswald, Esq. 8vo. 13*s.*

9. The Fraternitye of Vacabondes, by John Awdeley (licensed in 1560-1, imprinted then, and in 1565), from the edition of 1575 in the Bodleian Library. A Caueat or Warening for Commen Cursetors vulgarely called Vagabones, by Thomas Harman, Esquiere. From the 3rd edition of 1567, belonging to Henry Huth, Esq., collated with the 2nd edition of 1567, in the Bodleian Library, Oxford, and with the reprint of the 4th edition of 1573. A Sermon in Praise of Thieves and Thievery, by Parson Haben or Hyberdyne, from the Lansdowne MS. 98, and Cotton Vesp. A. 25. Those parts of the Groundworke of Conny-catching (ed. 1592), that differ from *Harman's Caueat.* Edited by Edward Viles & F. J. Furnivall. 8vo. 7*s.* 6*d.*

10. The Fyrst Boke of the Introduction of Knowledge, made by Andrew Borde, of Physycke Doctor. A Compendyous Regyment of a Dyetary of Helth made in Mountpyllier, compiled by Andrewe Boorde, of Physycke Doctor. Barnes in the Defence of the Berde: a treatyse made, answerynge the treatyse of Doctor Borde upon Berdes. Edited, with a life of Andrew Boorde, and large extracts from his Breuyary, by F. J Furnivall, M.A., Trinity Hall, Camb. 8vo. 18*s.*

11. The Bruce; or, the Book of the most excellent and noble Prince, Robert de Broyss, King of Scots: compiled by Master John Barbour, Archdeacon of Aberdeen. A.D. 1375. Edited from MS. G 23 in the Library of St. John's College, Cambridge, written A.D. 1487; collated with the MS. in the Advocates' Library at Edinburgh, written A.D. 1489, and with Hart's Edition, printed A.D. 1616; with a Preface, Notes, and Glossarial Index, by the Rev. Walter W. Skeat, M.A. Part I 8vo. 12*s.*

Early English Text Society's Publications—*continued.*

12. ENGLAND IN THE REIGN OF KING HENRY THE EIGHTH. A Dialogue between Cardinal Pole and Thomas Lupset, Lecturer in Rhetoric at Oxford. By THOMAS STARKEY, Chaplain to the King. Edited, with Preface, Notes, and Glossary, by J. M. COWPER. And with an Introduction, containing the Life and Letters of Thomas Starkey, by the Rev. J. S. BREWER, M.A. Part II. 12*s.*
(*Part I., Starkey's Life and Letters, is in preparation.*

13. A SUPPLICACYON FOR THE BEGGARS. Written about the year 1529, by SIMON FISH. Now re-edited by FREDERICK J. FURNIVALL. With a Supplycacion to our moste Soueraigne Lorde Kynge Henry the Eyght (1544 A.D.), A Supplication of the Poore Commons (1546 A.D.), The Decaye of England by the great multitude of Shepe (1550–3 A.D.). Edited by J. MEADOWS COWPER. 6*s.*

14. ON EARLY ENGLISH PRONUNCIATION, with especial reference to Shakspere and Chaucer. By A. J. ELLIS, F.R.S., F.S.A. Part III. Illustrations of the Pronunciation of the XIVth and XVIth Centuries. Chaucer, Gower, Wycliffe, Spenser, Shakspere, Salesbury, Barcley, Hart, Bullokar, Gill. Pronouncing Vocabulary. 10*s.*

15. ROBERT CROWLEY'S THIRTY-ONE EPIGRAMS, Voyce of the Last Trumpet, Way to Wealth, etc., 1550–1 A.D. Edited by J. M. COWPER, Esq. 12*s.*

16. A TREATISE ON THE ASTROLABE; addressed to his son Lowys, by Geoffrey Chaucer, A.D. 1391. Edited from the earliest MSS. by the Rev. WALTER W. SKEAT, M.A., late Fellow of Christ's College, Cambridge. 10*s.*

17. THE COMPLAYNT OF SCOTLANDE, 1549, A.D., with an Appendix of four Contemporary English Tracts. Edited by J. A. H. MURRAY, Esq. Part I. 10*s.*

18. THE COMPLAYNT OF SCOTLANDE, etc. Part II. 8*s.*

19. OURE LADYES MYROURE, A.D. 1530, edited by the Rev. J. H. BLUNT, M.A., with four full-page photolithographic facsimiles by Cooke and Fotheringham. 24*s.*

20. LONELICH'S HISTORY OF THE HOLY GRAIL (ab. 1450 A.D.), translated from the French Prose of SIRES ROBIERS DE BORRON. Re-edited from the Unique MS. in Corpus Christi College, Cambridge, by F. J. Furnivall, Esq., M.A. Part I. 8*s.*

21. BARBOUR'S BRUCE. Part II. Edited from the MSS. and the earliest printed edition by the Rev. W. W. SKEAT, M.A. 4*s.*

22. HENRY BRINKLOW'S COMPLAYNT OF RODERYCK MORS, somtyme a gray Fryre, unto the Parliament Howse of Ingland his naturall Country, for the Redresse of certen wicked Lawes, euel Customs, and cruel Decreys (ab. 1542); and THE LAMENTACION OF A CHRISTIAN AGAINST THE CITIE OF LONDON, made by Roderigo Mors, A.D. 1545. Edited by J. M. COWPER, Esq. 9*s.*

23. ON EARLY ENGLISH PRONUNCIATION, with especial reference to Shakspere and Chaucer. By A. J. ELLIS, Esq., F.R.S. Part IV. 10*s.*

24. LONELICH'S HISTORY OF THE HOLY GRAIL (ab. 1450 A.D.), translated from the French Prose of SIRES ROBIERS DE BORRON. Re-edited from the Unique MS. in Corpus Christi College, Cambridge, by F. J. FURNIVALL, Esq., M.A. Part II. 10*s.*

25. THE ROMANCE OF GUY OF WARWICK. Edited from the Cambridge University MS. by Prof. J. ZUPITZA, Ph.D. Part I. 20*s.*

Edda Saemundar Hinns Froda—The Edda of Saemund the Learned. From the Old Norse or Icelandic. By BENJAMIN THORPE. Part I. with a Mythological Index. 12mo. pp. 152, cloth, 3*s.* 6*d.* Part II. with Index of Persons and Places. 12mo. pp. viii. and 172, cloth. 1866. 4*s.*; or in 1 Vol. complete, 7*s.* 6*d.*

Edkins.—INTRODUCTION TO THE STUDY OF THE CHINESE CHARACTERS. By J. EDKINS, D.D., Peking, China. Roy. 8vo. pp. 340, paper boards. 18*s.*

Edkins.—CHINA'S PLACE IN PHILOLOGY. An attempt to show that the Languages of Europe and Asia have a common origin. By the Rev. JOSEPH EDKINS. Crown 8vo, pp. xxiii.—403, cloth. 10*s.* 6*d.*

Edkins.—A VOCABULARY OF THE SHANGHAI DIALECT. By J. EDKINS. 8vo. half-calf, pp. vi. and 151. Shanghai, 1869. 21*s.*

Edkins.—A GRAMMAR OF COLLOQUIAL CHINESE, as exhibited in the Shanghai Dialect. By J. EDKINS, B.A. Second edition, corrected. 8vo. half-calf, pp. viii. and 225. Shanghai, 1868. 21*s.*

Edkins.—A GRAMMAR OF THE CHINESE COLLOQUIAL LANGUAGE, commonly called the Mandarin Dialect. By JOSEPH EDKINS. Second edition. 8vo. half-calf, pp. viii. and 279. Shanghai, 1864. £1 10*s.*

Eger and Grime; an Early English Romance. Edited from Bishop Percy's Folio Manuscript, about 1650 A.D. By JOHN W. HALES, M.A., Fellow and late Assistant Tutor of Christ's College, Cambridge, and FREDERICK J. FURNIVALL, M.A., of Trinity Hall, Cambridge. 1 vol. 4to., pp. 64, (only 100 copies printed), bound in the Roxburghe style. 10*s.* 6*d.*

Eitel.—HANDBOOK FOR THE STUDENT OF CHINESE BUDDHISM. By the Rev. E. J. EITEL, of the London Missionary Society. Crown 8vo. pp. viii., 224, cl., 18*s*

Eitel.—FENG-SHUI: or, The Rudiments of Natural Science in China. By Rev. E. J. EITEL, M.A., Ph.D. Demy 8vo. sewed, pp. vi. and 84. 6*s.*

Eitel.—BUDDHISM: its Historical, Theoretical, and Popular Aspects. In Three Lectures. By Rev. E. J. EITEL, M.A. Ph.D. Second Edition. Demy 8vo. sewed, pp. 130. 5*s.*

Elliot.—THE HISTORY OF INDIA, as told by its own Historians. The Muhammadan Period. Edited from the Posthumous Papers of the late Sir H. M. ELLIOT, K.C.B., East India Company's Bengal Civil Service, by Prof. JOHN DOWSON, M.R.A.S., Staff College, Sandhurst.

Vols. I. and II. With a Portrait of Sir H. M. Elliot. 8vo. pp xxxii. and 542, x. and 580, cloth. 18*s.* each.
Vol. III. 8vo. pp. xii. and 627, cloth. 24*s.*
Vol. IV. 8vo. pp. x. and 563 cloth 21*s*
Vol. V. 8vo. pp. xii. and 576, cloth. 21*s.*
Vol. VI. 8vo. pp. viii. and 574, cloth. 21*s.*
Vol. VII. 8vo. pp. viii. and 574, cloth.
Vol. VIII. 8vo. [*In the Press.*

Elliot.—MEMOIRS ON THE HISTORY, FOLKLORE, AND DISTRIBUTION OF THE RACES OF THE NORTH WESTERN PROVINCES OF INDIA; being an amplified Edition of the original Supplementary Glossary of Indian Terms. By the late Sir HENRY M. ELLIOT, K.C.B., of the Hon. East India Company's Bengal Civil Service. Edited, revised, and re-arranged, by JOHN BEAMES, M.R.A.S., Bengal Civil Service; Member of the German Oriental Society, of the Asiatic Societies of Paris and Bengal, and of the Philological Society of London. In 2 vols. demy 8vo., pp. xx., 370, and 396, cloth. With two Lithographic Plates, one full-page coloured Map, and three large coloured folding Maps. 36*s.*

Ellis.—ON NUMERALS, as Signs of Primeval Unity among Mankind. By ROBERT ELLIS, B.D., Late Fellow of St. John's College, Cambridge. Demy 8vo. cloth, pp. viii. and 94. 3*s.* 6*d.*

Ellis.—THE ASIATIC AFFINITIES OF THE OLD ITALIANS. By ROBERT ELLIS, B.D., Fellow of St. John's College, Cambridge, and author of "Ancient Routes between Italy and Gaul." Crown 8vo. pp. iv. 156, cloth. 1870. 5*s.*

Ellis.—PERUVIA SCYTHICA. The Quichua Language of Peru: its derivation from Central Asia with the American languages in general, and with the Turanian and Iberian languages of the Old World, including the Basque, the Lycian, and the Pre-Aryan language of Etruria. By ROBERT ELLIS, B.D. 8vo. cloth, pp. xii. and 219. 1875. 6*s.*

Ellis.—ETRUSCAN NUMERALS. By ROBERT ELLIS, B.D. 8vo. sewed, pp. 52. 2*s*. 6*d*.

English and Welsh Languages.—THE INFLUENCE OF THE ENGLISH AND Welsh Languages upon each other, exhibited in the Vocabularies of the two Tongues. Intended to suggest the importance to Philologers, Antiquaries, Ethnographers, and others, of giving due attention to the Celtic Branch of the Indo-Germanic Family of Languages. Square, pp. 30, sewed. 1869. 1*s*.

English Dialect Society's Publications. Subscription, 10*s*. 6*d*. per annum.

1873.

1. Series B. Part 1. Reprinted Glossaries. Containing a Glossary of North of England Words, by J. H.; five Glossaries, by Mr. MARSHALL; and a West-Riding Glossary, by Dr. WILLAN. 7*s*. 6*d*.
2. Series A. Bibliographical. A List of Books illustrating English Dialects. Part I. Containing a General List of Dictionaries, etc.; and a List of Books relating to some of the Counties of England. 4*s*.
3. Series C. Original Glossaries. Part I. Containing a Glossary of Swaledale Words. By Captain HARLAND. 4*s*.

1874.

4. Series D. The History of English Sounds. By H. SWEET, Esq. 4*s*. 6*d*.
5. Series B. Part II. Reprinted Glossaries. Containing seven Provincial English Glossaries, from various sources. 7*s*.
6. Series B. Part III. Ray's Collection of English Words not generally used, from the edition of 1691; together with Thoresby's Letter to Ray, 1703. Re-arranged and newly edited by Rev. WALTER W. SKEAT. 8*s*.

6*. Subscribers to the English Dialect Society for 1874 also receive a copy of 'A Dictionary of the Sussex Dialect.' By the Rev. W. D. PARISH.

1875.

7. Series D. Part II. The Dialect of West Somerset. By F. T. ELWORTHY, Esq. 3*s*. 6*d*.
8. Series A. Part II. Containing a List of Books Relating to some of the Counties of England. 6*s*.
9. Series C. A Glossary of Words used in the Neighbourhood of Whitby. By F. K. ROBINSON. Part I. 7*s*. 6*d*.
10. Series C. A Glossary of the Dialect of Lancashire. By J. H. NODAL and G. MILNER. Part I. 2*s*. 6*d*.

1876.

11. On the Survival of Old English Words in our Dialects. By Dr. R. MORRIS. 6*d*.
12. Series C. Original Glossaries. Part III. Containing Five Original Provincial English Glossaries. 7*s*.
13. Series C. A Glossary of Words used in the Neighbourhood of Whitby. By F. K. Robinson. Part II. 6*s* 6*d*.
14. A Glossary of Mid-Yorkshire Words, with a Grammar. By C. CLOUGH ROBINSON. 9*s*.

Etherington.—THE STUDENT'S GRAMMAR OF THE HINDÍ LANGUAGE. By the Rev. W. ETHERINGTON, Missionary, Benares. Second edition. Crown 8vo. pp. xiv., 255, and xiii., cloth. 1873. 12*s*.

Faber.—A SYSTEMATICAL DIGEST OF THE DOCTRINES OF CONFUCIUS, according to the ANALECTS, GREAT LEARNING, and DOCTRINE of the MEAN, with an Introduction on the Authorities upon CONFUCIUS and Confucianism. By ERNST FABER, Rhenish Missionary. Translated from the German by P. G. von Moellendorff. 8vo. sewed, pp. viii. and 131. 1875. 12*s*. 6*d*.

Facsimiles of Two Papyri found in a Tomb at Thebes. With a Translation by SAMUEL BIRCH, LL.D., F.S.A., Corresponding Member of the Institute of France, Academies of Berlin, Herculaneum, etc., and an Account of their Discovery. By A. HENRY RHIND, Esq., F.S.A., etc. In large folio, pp. 30 of text, and 16 plates coloured, bound in cloth. 21*s*.

Fallon.—A NEW HINDUSTANI-ENGLISH DICTIONARY. By S. W. FALLON, Ph.D. Halle. Parts I. to IV. Roy. 8vo. Price 4*s*. 6*d*. each Part. To be completed in about 25 Parts of 48 pages each Part, forming together One Volume.

Fausböll.—THE DASARATHA-JÁTAKA, being the Buddhist Story of King Râma. The original Pâli Text, with a Translation and Notes by V. FAUSBÖLL. 8vo. sewed, pp. iv. and 48. 2*s*. 6*d*.

Fausböll.—FIVE JÁTAKAS, containing a Fairy Tale, a Comical Story, and Three Fables. In the original Pâli Text, accompanied with a Translation and Notes. By V. FAUSBÖLL. 8vo. sewed, pp. viii. and 72. 6*s*.

Fausböll.—TEN JÁTAKAS. The Original Páli Text, with a Translation and Notes. By V. FAUSBÖLL. 8vo. sewed, pp. xiii. and 128. 7*s*. 6*d*.

Fausböll.—JÁTAKA. See under JÁTAKA.

Fiske.—MYTHS AND MYTH-MAKERS: Old Tales and Superstitions interpreted by Comparative Mythology. By JOHN FISKE, M.A., Assistant Librarian, and late Lecturer on Philosophy at Harvard University. Crown 8vo. cloth, pp. viii. and 252. 10*s*. 6*d*.

Foss.—NORWEGIAN GRAMMAR, with Exercises in the Norwegian and and English Languages, and a List of Irregular Verbs. By FRITHJOF FOSS, Graduate of the University of Norway. Crown 8vo., pp. 50, cloth limp. 2*s*.

Foster.—PRE-HISTORIC RACES OF THE UNITED STATES OF AMERICA. By J. W. FOSTER, LL.D., Author of the "Physical Geography of the Mississippi Valley," etc. With 72 Illustrations. 8vo. cloth, pp. xvi. and 416. 14*s*.

Furnivall.—EDUCATION IN EARLY ENGLAND. Some Notes used as Forewords to a Collection of Treatises on "Manners and Meals in the Olden Time," for the Early English Text Society. By FREDERICK J. FURNIVALL, M.A., Trinity Hall, Cambridge, Member of Council of the Philological and Early English Text Societies. 8vo. sewed, pp. 74. 1*s*.

Fu So Mimi Bukuro.—A BUDGET OF JAPANESE NOTES. By CAPT. PFOUNDES, of Yokohama. 8vo. sewed, pp. 184. 7*s*. 6*d*.

Gautama.—THE INSTITUTES OF GAUTAMA. Edited with an Index of Words. By Adolf. Friederich Stenzler, Ph.D., Prof. of Oriental Languages in the University of Breslau. 8vo. cloth, pp. iv. and 78. 4*s*. 6*d*.

Garrett.—A CLASSICAL DICTIONARY OF INDIA, illustrative of the Mythology, Philosophy, Literature, Antiquities, Arts, Manners, Customs, etc., of the Hindus. By JOHN GARRETT. 8vo. pp. x. and 798. cloth. 28s.

Garrett.—SUPPLEMENT TO THE ABOVE CLASSICAL DICTIONARY OF INDIA. By JOHN GARRETT, Director of Public Instruction at Mysore. 8vo. cloth, pp. 160. 7*s*. 6*d*.

Giles.—CHINESE SKETCHES. By HERBERT A. GILES, of H.B.M.'s China Consular Service. 8vo. cl., pp. 204. 10*s*. 6*d*.

Giles.—A DICTIONARY OF COLLOQUIAL IDIOMS IN THE MANDARIN DIALECT. By HERBERT A. GILES. 4to. pp. 65. £1 8*s*.

Giles.—SYNOPTICAL STUDIES IN CHINESE CHARACTER. By HERBERT A. GILES. 8vo. pp. 118. 15*s*.

Giles.—CHINESE WITHOUT A TEACHER. Being a Collection of Easy and Useful Sentences in the Mandarin Dialect. With a Vocabulary. By HERBERT A. GILES. 12mo. pp. 60. 5*s*.

Giles.—THE SAN TZU CHING; or, Three Character Classic; and the Ch'Jen Tsu Wen; or, Thousand Character Essay. Metrically Translated by HERBERT A. GILES. 12mo. pp. 28. Price 2*s*. 6*d*.

God.—Book of God. By ⊙. 8vo. cloth. Vol. I.: The Apocalypse. pp. 647. 12*s.* 6*d.*—Vol. II. An Introduction to the Apocalypse, pp. 752. 14*s.*—Vol. III. A Commentary on the Apocalypse, pp. 854. 16*s.*

Goldstücker.—A Dictionary, Sanskrit and English, extended and improved from the Second Edition of the Dictionary of Professor H. H. Wilson, with his sanction and concurrence. Together with a Supplement, Grammatical Appendices, and an Index, serving as a Sanskrit-English Vocabulary. By Theodor Goldstücker. Parts I. to VI. 4to. pp. 400. 1856-1863. 6*s.* each.

Goldstücker.—Panini: His Place in Sanskrit Literature. An Investigation of some Literary and Chronological Questions which may be settled by a study of his Work. A separate impression of the Preface to the Facsimile of MS. No. 17 in the Library of Her Majesty's Home Government for India, which contains a portion of the Manava-Kalpa-Sutra, with the Commentary of Kumarila-Swamin. By Theodor Goldstücker. Imperial 8vo. pp. 268, cloth. £2 2*s.*

Goldstücker.—On the Deficiencies in the Present Administration of Hindu Law; being a paper read at the Meeting of the East India Association on the 8th June, 1870. By Theodor Goldstücker, Professor of Sanskrit in University College, London, &c. Demy 8vo. pp. 56, sewed. 1*s.* 6*d.*

Gover.—The Folk-Songs of Southern India. By Charles E. Gover. 8vo. pp. xxiii. and 299, cloth 10*s.* 6*d.*

Grammatography.—A Manual of Reference to the Alphabets of Ancient and Modern Languages. Based on the German Compilation of F. Ballhorn. Royal 8vo. pp. 80, cloth. 7*s.* 6*d.*

The "Grammatography" is offered to the public as a compendious introduction to the reading of the most important ancient and modern languages. Simple in its design, it will be consulted with advantage by the philological student, the amateur linguist, the bookseller, the corrector of the press, and the diligent compositor.

ALPHABETICAL INDEX.

Afghan (or Pushto).	Czechian (or Bohemian).	Hebrew (current hand).	Polish.
Amharic.	Danish.	Hebrew (Judæo-German).	Pushto (or Afghan).
Anglo-Saxon.	Demotic.	Hungarian.	Romaic (Modern Greek
Arabic.	Estrangelo.	Illyrian.	Russian.
Arabic Ligatures.	Ethiopic.	Irish.	Runes.
Aramaic.	Etruscan.	Italian (Old).	Samaritan.
Archaic Characters.	Georgian.	Japanese.	Sanscrit.
Armenian.	German.	Javanese.	Servian.
Assyrian Cuneiform.	Glagolitic.	Lettish.	Slavonic (Old).
Bengali.	Gothic.	Mantshu.	Sorbian (or Wendish).
Bohemian (Czechian).	Greek.	Median Cuneiform.	Swedish.
Búgis.	Greek Ligatures.	Modern Greek (Romaic)	Syriac.
Burmese.	Greek (Archaic).	Mongolian.	Tamil.
Canarese (or Carnâtaca).	Gujerati (or Guzzeratte).	Numidian.	Telugu.
Chinese.	Hieratic.	Old Slavonic (or Cyrillic).	Tibetan.
Coptic.	Hieroglyphics.	Palmyrenian.	Turkish.
Croato-Glagolitic.	Hebrew.	Persian.	Wallachian.
Cufic.	Hebrew (Archaic).	Persian Cuneiform.	Wendish (or Sorbian).
Cyrillic (or Old Slavonic).	Hebrew (Rabbinical).	Phœnician.	Zend.

Grassmann.—Wörterbuch zum Rig-Veda. Von Hermann Grassmann, Professor am Marienstifts-Gymnasium zu Stettin. 8vo. pp. 1775. £1 10*s.*

Green.—Shakespeare and the Emblem-Writers: an Exposition of their Similarities of Thought and Expression. Preceded by a View of the Emblem-Book Literature down to A.D. 1616. By Henry Green, M.A. In one volume, pp. xvi. 572, profusely illustrated with Woodcuts and Photolith. Plates, elegantly bound in cloth gilt, large medium 8vo. £1 11*s.* 6*d*; large imperial 8vo. 1870. £2 12*s.* 6*d.*

Grey.—Handbook of African, Australian, and Polynesian Philology, as represented in the Library of His Excellency Sir George Grey, K.C.B., Her Majesty's High Commissioner of the Cape Colony. Classed, Annotated, and Edited by Sir George Grey and Dr. H. I. Bleek.

Vol. I. Part 1.—South Africa. 8vo. pp. 186. 7*s.* 6*d.*
Vol. I. Part 2.—Africa (North of the Tropic of Capricorn). 8vo. pp. 70. 2*s.*

Vol. I. Part 3.—Madagascar. 8vo. pp. 24. 1*s.*
Vol. II. Part 1.—Australia. 8vo. pp. iv. and 44. 1*s.* 6*d.*
Vol. II. Part 2.—Papuan Languages of the Loyalty Islands and New Hebrides, comprising those of the Islands of Nengone, Lifu, Aneitum, Tana, and others. 8vo. p. 12. 6*d.*
Vol. II. Part 3.—Fiji Islands and Rotuma (with Supplement to Part II., Papuan Languages, and Part I., Australia). 8vo. pp. 34. 1*s.*
Vol. II. Part 4.—New Zealand, the Chatham Islands, and Auckland Islands. 8vo. pp. 76. 3*s.* 6*d.*
Vol. II. Part 4 (*continuation*).—Polynesia and Borneo. 8vo. pp. 77-154. 3*s.* 6*d.*
Vol. III. Part 1.—Manuscripts and Incunables. 8vo. pp. viii. and 24. 2*s.*
Vol. IV. Part 1.—Early Printed Books. England. 8vo. pp. vi. and 266.

Grey.—MAORI MEMENTOS: being a Series of Addresses presented by the Native People to His Excellency Sir George Grey, K.C.B., F.R.S. With Introductory Remarks and Explanatory Notes; to which is added a small Collection of Laments, etc. By CH. OLIVER B. DAVIS. 8vo. pp. iv. and 228, cloth. 12*s.*

Griffin.—THE RAJAS OF THE PUNJAB. Being the History of the Principal States in the Punjab, and their Political Relations with the British Government. By LEPEL H. GRIFFIN, Bengal Civil Service; Under Secretary to the Government of the Punjab, Author of "The Punjab Chiefs," etc. Second edition. Royal 8vo., pp. xiv. and 630. 21*s.*

Griffith.—SCENES FROM THE RAMAYANA, MEGHADUTA, ETC. Translated by RALPH T. H. GRIFFITH, M.A., Principal of the Benares College. Second Edition. Crown 8vo. pp. xviii., 244, cloth. 6*s.*

CONTENTS.—Preface—Ayodhya—Ravan Doomed—The Birth of Rama—The Heir apparent—Manthara's Guile—Dasaratha's Oath—The Step-mother—Mother and Son—The Triumph of Love—Farewell?—The Hermit's Son—The Trial of Truth—The Forest—The Rape of Sita—Rama's Despair—The Messenger Cloud—Khumbakarna—The Suppliant Dove—True Glory—Feed the Poor—The Wise Scholar.

Griffith.—THE RÁMÁYAN OF VÁLMÍKI. Translated into English verse. By RALPH T. H. GRIFFITH, M.A., Principal of the Benares College. 5 vols.

Vol. I., containing Books I. and II. Demy 8vo. pp. xxxii. 440, cloth. 1870. 18*s.*

Vol. II., containing Book II., with additional Notes and Index of Names. Demy 8vo. pp. 504, cloth. 18*s.*

Vol. III. Demy 8vo. pp. v. and 371, cloth. 1872. 15*s.*

Vol. IV. Demy 8vo. pp. viii. and 432. 1873. 18*s.*

Vol. V. Demy 8vo. pp. 368, cloth. 1875. 15*s.*

Grout.—THE ISIZULU: a Grammar of the Zulu Language; accompanied with an Historical Introduction, also with an Appendix. By Rev. LEWIS GROUT. 8vo. pp. lii. and 432, cloth. 21*s.*

Gubernatis.—ZOOLOGICAL MYTHOLOGY; or, the Legends of Animals. By ANGELO DE GUBERNATIS, Professor of Sanskrit and Comparative Literature in the Instituto di Studii Superiori e di Perfezionamento at Florence, etc. In 2 vols. 8vo. pp. xxvi. and 432, vii. and 442. 28*s.*

Gundert.—A MALAYALAM AND ENGLISH DICTIONARY. By Rev. H. GUNDERT, D. Ph. Royal 8vo. pp. viii. and 1116. £2 10*s.*

Haas.—CATALOGUE OF SANSKRIT AND PALI BOOKS IN THE LIBRARY OF THE BRITISH MUSEUM. By Dr. ERNST HAAS. Printed by Permission of the Trustees of the British Museum. 4to. cloth, pp. 200. £1 1*s.*

Háfiz of Shíráz.—SELECTIONS FROM HIS POEMS. Translated from the Persian by HERMAN BICKNELL. With Preface by A. S. BICKNELL. Demy 4to., pp. xx. and 384, printed on fine stout plate-paper, with appropriate Oriental Bordering in gold and colour, and Illustrations by J. R. HERBERT, R.A. £2 2*s.*

Haldeman.—PENNSYLVANIA DUTCH: a Dialect of South Germany with an Infusion of English. By S. S. HALDEMAN, A.M., Professor of Comparative Philology in the University of Pennsylvania, Philadelphia. 8vo. pp. viii. and 70, cloth. 1872. 3*s.* 6*d.*

Hall.—MODERN ENGLISH. By FITZEDWARD HALL, M.A., Hon. D.C.L., Oxon. Cr. 8vo. cloth, pp. xvi. and 394. 10*s.* 6*d.*

Hall.—ON "RELIABLE." With a General Survey of English Adjectives in *-able.* By FITZEDWARD HALL, M.A., D.C.L., Oxon. 8vo. cloth. [*Nearly Ready.*

Hans Breitmann Ballads.—See under LELAND.

Hardy.—CHRISTIANITY AND BUDDHISM COMPARED. By the late REV. R. SPENCE HARDY, Hon. Member Royal Asiatic Society. 8vo. sd. pp. 138. 6*s.*

Hassoun.—THE DIWAN OF HATIM TAI. An Old Arabic Poet of the Sixth Century of the Christian Era. Edited by R. HASSOUN. With Illustrations. 4to. pp. 43. 3*s.* 6*d.*

Haswell.—GRAMMATICAL NOTES AND VOCABULARY OF THE PEGUAN LANGUAGE. To which are added a few pages of Phrases, etc. By Rev. J. M. HASWELL. 8vo. pp. xvi. and 160. 15*s.*

Haug.—THE BOOK OF ARDA VIRAF. The Pahlavi text prepared by Destur Hoshangji Jamaspji Asa. Revised and collated with further MSS., with an English translation and Introduction, and an Appendix containing the Texts and Translations of the Gosht-i Fryano and Hadokht Nask. By MARTIN HAUG, Ph.D., Professor of Sanskrit and Comparative Philology at the University of Munich. Assisted by E. W. WEST, Ph.D. Published by order of the Bombay Government. 8vo. sewed, pp. lxxx., v., and 316. £1 5*s.*

Haug.—A LECTURE ON AN ORIGINAL SPEECH OF ZOROASTER (Yasna 45), with remarks on his age. By MARTIN HAUG, Ph.D. 8vo. pp. 28, sewed. Bombay, 1865. 2*s.*

Haug.—THE AITAREYA BRAHMANAM OF THE RIG VEDA: containing the Earliest Speculations of the Brahmans on the meaning of the Sacrificial Prayers, and on the Origin, Performance, and Sense of the Rites of the Vedic Religion. Edited, Translated, and Explained by MARTIN HAUG, Ph.D., Superintendent of Sanskrit Studies in the Poona College, etc., etc. In 2 Vols. Crown 8vo. Vol. I. Contents, Sanskrit Text, with Preface, Introductory Essay, and a Map of the Sacrificial Compound at the Soma Sacrifice, pp. 312. Vol. II. Translation with Notes, pp. 544. £2 2*s.*

Haug.—AN OLD ZAND-PAHLAVI GLOSSARY. Edited in the Original Characters, with a Transliteration in Roman Letters, an English Translation, and an Alphabetical Index. By DESTUR HOSHENGJI JAMASPJI, High-priest of the Parsis in Malwa, India. Revised with Notes and Introduction by MARTIN HAUG, Ph.D., late Superintendent of Sanscrit Studies in the Poona College, Foreign Member of the Royal Bavarian Academy. Published by order of the Government of Bombay. 8vo. sewed, pp. lvi. and 132. 15*s.*

Haug.—AN OLD PAHLAVI-PAZAND GLOSSARY. Edited, with an Alphabetical Index, by DESTUR HOSHANGJI JAMASPJI ASA, High Priest of the Parsis in Malwa, India. Revised and Enlarged, with an Introductory Essay on the Pahlavi Language, by MARTIN HAUG, Ph.D. Published by order of the Government of Bombay. 8vo. pp. xvi. 152, 268, sewed. 1870. 28*s.*

Heaviside.—AMERICAN ANTIQUITIES; or, the New World the Old, and the Old World the New. By JOHN T. C. HEAVISIDE. 8vo. pp. 46, sewed. 1*s.* 6*d.*

Hepburn.—A JAPANESE AND ENGLISH DICTIONARY. With an English and Japanese Index. By J. C. HEPBURN, M.D., LL.D. Second edition. Imperial 8vo. cloth, pp. xxxii., 632 and 201. 8*l.* 8*s.*

Hepburn.—JAPANESE-ENGLISH AND ENGLISH-JAPANESE DICTIONARY. By J. C. HEPBURN, M.D., LL.D. Abridged by the Author from his larger work. Small 4to. cloth, pp. vi. and 206. 1873. 12*s.* 6*d.*

Hernisz.—A GUIDE TO CONVERSATION IN THE ENGLISH AND CHINESE LANGUAGES, for the use of Americans and Chinese in California and elsewhere. By STANISLAS HERNISZ. Square 8vo. pp. 274, sewed. 10*s.* 6*d.*

The Chinese characters contained in this work are from the collections of Chinese groups, engraved on steel, and cast into moveable types, by Mr. Marcellin Legrand, engraver of the Imperial Printing Office at Paris. They are used by most of the missions to China.

Hincks.—SPECIMEN CHAPTERS OF AN ASSYRIAN GRAMMAR. By the late Rev. E. HINCKS, D.D., Hon. M.R.A.S. 8vo., pp. 44, sewed. 1*s.*

Hodgson.—ESSAYS ON THE LANGUAGES, LITERATURE, AND RELIGION OF NEPAL AND TIBET; together with further Papers on the Geography, Ethnology, and Commerce of those Countries. By B. H. HODGSON, late British Minister at Nepâl. Reprinted with Corrections and Additions from "Illustrations of the Literature and Religion of the Buddhists," Serampore, 1841; and "Selections from the Records of the Government of Bengal," No. XXVII, Calcutta, 1857. Royal 8vo. cloth, pp. 288. 14*s.*

Hoffmann.—SHOPPING DIALOGUES, in Japanese, Dutch, and English. By Professor J. HOFFMANN. Oblong 8vo. pp. xiii. and 44, sewed. 3*s.*

Hoffmann, J. J.—A JAPANESE GRAMMAR. Second Edition. Large 8vo. cloth, pp. viii. and 368, with two plates. £1 1*s.*

Howse.—A GRAMMAR OF THE CREE LANGUAGE. With which is combined an analysis of the Chippeway Dialect. By JOSEPH HOWSE, Esq., F.R.G.S. 8vo. pp. xx. and 324, cloth. 7*s.* 6*d.*

Hunter.—A COMPARATIVE DICTIONARY OF THE LANGUAGES OF INDIA AND HIGH ASIA, with a Dissertation, based on The Hodgson Lists, Official Records, and Manuscripts. By W. W. HUNTER, B.A., M.R.A.S., Honorary Fellow, Ethnological Society, of Her Majesty's Bengal Civil Service. Folio, pp. vi. and 224, cloth. £2 2*s.*

Hunter.—STATISTICAL ACCOUNT OF THE PROVINCES OF BENGAL. By W. W. HUNTER, LL.D., Director-General of Statistics to the Government of India, etc., Author of 'The Annals of Rural Bengal,' etc. In 6 vols. Demy 8vo. [*Shortly.*

Ikhwánu-s Safá.—IKHWÁNU-S SAFÁ; or, BROTHERS OF PURITY. Describing the Contention between Men and Beasts as to the Superiority of the Human Race. Translated from the Hindustání by Professor J. DOWSON, Staff College, Sandhurst. Crown 8vo. pp. viii. and 156, cloth. 7*s.*

Indian Antiquary (The).—A Journal of Oriental Research in Archæology, History, Literature, Languages, Philosophy, Religion, Folklore, etc. Edited by JAMES BURGESS, M.R.A.S., F.R.G.S. 4to. Published 12 numbers per annum. Subscription £2.

Inman.—ANCIENT PAGAN AND MODERN CHRISTIAN SYMBOLISM EXPOSED AND EXPLAINED. By THOMAS INMAN, M.D. Second Edition. With Illustrations. Demy 8vo. cloth, pp. xl. and 148. 1874. 7*s.* 6*d.*

Inman.—ANCIENT FAITHS EMBODIED IN ANCIENT NAMES. By THOMAS INMAN, M.D. Vol. I. Second edition. With 4 plates and numerous woodcuts. Royal 8vo. cloth, pp. xliv. and 792. 1872. £1 10*s.*

Vol. II. Second Edition. With 9 plates and numerous woodcuts. Royal 8vo. cloth, pp. xvi. and 1028. 1873. £1 10*s.*

Jaiminîya-Nyâya-Mâlâ-Vistara—See under AUCTORES SANSCRITI.

Jataka (The), together with its Commentary. Now first published in Pali, by V. FAUSBÖLL, with a Translation by R. C. CHILDERS, late of the Ceylon Civil Service. To be completed in five volumes. Text. Vol. I. Part I. Roy. 8vo. sewed, pp. 224. 7*s.* 6*d.*

Jenkins's Vest-Pocket Lexicon.—AN ENGLISH DICTIONARY of all except Familiar Words; including the principal Scientific and Technical Terms, and Foreign Moneys, Weights and Masures. By JABEZ JENKINS. 64mo., pp. 564, cloth. 1*s.* 6*d.*

Johnson.—ORIENTAL RELIGIONS, AND THEIR RELATION TO UNIVERSAL RELIGION. By SAMUEL JOHNSON. Large 8vo., pp. vi. and 802, handsomely bound in cloth. 24*s.*

Kalid-i-Afghani.—TRANSLATION OF THE KALID-I-AFGHANI, the Text-book for the Pakkhto Examination, with Notes, Historical, Geographical, Grammatical, and Explanatory. By TREVOR CHICHELE PLOWDEN. Imp. 8vo. pp. xx. and 406, with a Map. *Lahore*, 1875. £2 2*s*.

Kellogg.—A GRAMMAR OF THE HINDI LANGUAGE, in which are treated the Standard Hindî, Braj, and the Eastern Hindî of the Ramayan of Tulsi Das; also the Colloquial Dialects of Marwar, Kumaon, Avadh, Baghelkhand, Bhojpur, etc., with Copious Philological Notes. By the Rev. S. H. KELLOGG, M.A. Royal 8vo. cloth, pp. 400. 21*s*.

Kern.—THE ÂRYABHAṬIYA, with the Commentary Bhatadîpikâ of Paramadiçvara, edited by Dr. H. KERN. 4to. pp. xii. and 107. 9*s*.

Kern.—THE BRHAT-SANHITÁ; or, Complete System of Natural Astrology of Varâha-Mihira. Translated from Sanskrit into English by Dr. H. KERN, Professor of Sanskrit at the University of Leyden. Part I. 8vo. pp. 50, stitched. Parts 2 and 3 pp. 51–154. Part 4 pp. 155–210. Part 5 pp. 211–266. Part 6 pp. 267–330. Price 2*s*. each part. [*Will be completed in Nine Parts.*

Khirad-Afroz (The Illuminator of the Understanding). By Maulaví Hafízu'd-dín. A new edition of the Hindústání Text, carefully revised, with Notes, Critical and Explanatory. By EDWARD B. EASTWICK, M.P., F.R.S., F.S.A., M.R.A.S., Professor of Hindústání at the late East India Company's College at Haileybury. 8vo. cloth, pp. xiv. and 321. 18*s*.

Kidd.—CATALOGUE OF THE CHINESE LIBRARY OF THE ROYAL ASIATIC SOCIETY. By the Rev. S. KIDD. 8vo. pp. 58, sewed. 1*s*.

Kielhorn.—A GRAMMAR OF THE SANSKRIT LANGUAGE. By F. KIELHORN, Ph.D., Superintendent of Sanskrit Studies in Deccan College. Registered under Act xxv. of 1867. Demy 8vo. pp. xvi. 260. cloth. 1870. 10*s*. 6*d*.

Kilgour.—THE HEBREW OR IBERIAN RACE, including the Pelasgians, the Phenicians, the Jews, the British, and others. By HENRY KILGOUR. 8vo. sewed, pp. 76. 1872. 2*s*. 6*d*.

Kistner.—BUDDHA AND HIS DOCTRINES. A Bibliographical Essay. By OTTO KISTNER. Imperial 8vo., pp. iv. and 32, sewed. 2*s*. 6*d*.

Koch.—A HISTORICAL GRAMMAR OF THE ENGLISH LANGUAGE. By C. F. KOCH. Translated into English. Edited, Enlarged, and Annotated by the Rev. R. MORRIS, LL.D., M.A. [*Nearly ready.*

Koran (The). Arabic text, lithographed in Oudh, A.H. 1284 (1867). 16mo. pp. 942. 7*s*. 6*d*.

Kroeger.—THE MINNESINGER OF GERMANY. By A. E. KROEGER. 12mo. cloth, pp. vi. and 284. 7*s*.

CONTENTS.—Chapter I. The Minnesinger and the Minnesong.—II. The Minnelay.—III. The Divine Minnesong.—IV. Walther von der Vogelweide.—V. Ulrich von Lichtenstein.—VI. The Metrical Romances of the Minnesinger and Gottfried von Strassburg's 'Tristan and Isolde."

Lacombe.—DICTIONNAIRE ET GRAMMAIRE DE LA LANGUE DES CRIS, par le Rév. Père ALB. LACOMBE. 8vo. paper, pp. xx. and 713, iv. and 190. 21*s*.

Laghu Kaumudí. A Sanskrit Grammar. By Varadarája. With an English Version, Commentary, and References. By JAMES R. BALLANTYNE, LL D., Principal of the Snskrit College, Benares. 8vo. pp. xxxvi. and 424, cloth. £1 11*s*. 6*d*.

Land.—THE PRINCIPLES OF HEBREW GRAMMAR. By J. P. N. LAND, Professor of Logic and Metaphysic in the University of Leyden. Translated from the Dutch by REGINALD LANE POOLE, Balliol College, Oxford. Part I. Sounds. Part II. Words. Crown 8vo. pp. xx. and 220, cloth. 7*s*. 6*d*.

Legge.—THE CHINESE CLASSICS. With a Translation, Critical and Exegetical Notes, Prolegomena, and Copious Indexes. By JAMES LEGGE, D.D., of the London Missionary Society. In seven vols.

Vol. I. containing Confucian Analects, the Great Learning, and the Doctrine of the Mean. 8vo. pp. 526, cloth. £2 2*s*.

Vol. II., containing the Works of Mencius. 8vo. pp. 634, cloth. £2 2*s*.

Vol. III. Part I. containing the First Part of the Shoo-King, or the Books of Tang, the Books of Yu, the Books of Hea, the Books of Shang, and the Prolegomena. Royal 8vo. pp. viii. and 280, cloth. £2 2*s.*

Vol. III. Part II. containing the Fifth Part of the Shoo-King, or the Books of Chow, and the Indexes. Royal 8vo. pp. 281—736, cloth. £2 2*s*

Vol. IV. Part I. containing the First Part of the She-King, or the Lessons from the States; and the Prolegomena. Royal 8vo. cloth, pp. 182-244. £2 2*s.*

Vol. IV. Part II. containing the First Part of the She-King, or the Minor Odes of the Kingdom, the Greater Odes of the Kingdom, the Sacrificial Odes and Praise-Songs, and the Indexes. Royal 8vo. cloth, pp. 540. £2 2*s.*

Vol. V. Part I. containing Dukes Yin, Hwan, Chwang, Min, He, Wan, Seuen, and Ch'ing; and the Prolegomena. Royal 8vo. cloth, pp. xii., 148 and 410. £2 2*s.*

Vol. V. Part II. Contents:—Dukes Seang, Ch'aon, Ting, and Gal, with Tso's Appendix, and the Indexes. Royal 8vo. cloth, pp. 526. £2 2*s.*

Legge.—THE CHINESE CLASSICS. Translated into English. With Preliminary Essays and Explanatory Notes. By JAMES LEGGE, D.D., LL.D.

Vol. I. The Life and Teachings of Confucius. Crown 8vo. cloth, pp. vi. and 338. 10*s.* 6*d.*

Vol. II. The Life and Works of Mencius. Crown 8vo. cloth, pp. 412. 12*s.*

Vol. III. The She King, or The Book of Poetry. Crown 8vo., cloth, pp. viii. and 432. 12*s.*

Leigh.—THE RELIGION OF THE WORLD. By H. STONE LEIGH. 12mo. pp. xii. 66, cloth. 1869. 2*s.* 6*d.*

Leland.—THE ENGLISH GIPSIES AND THEIR LANGUAGE. By CHARLES G. LELAND. Second Edition. Crown 8vo. cloth, pp. 276. 7*s.* 6*d.*

Leland.—THE BREITMANN BALLADS. THE ONLY AUTHORIZED EDITION. Complete in 1 vol., including Nineteen Ballads illustrating his Travels in Europe (never before printed), with Comments by Fritz Schwackenhammer. By CHARLES G. LELAND. Crown 8vo. handsomely bound in cloth, pp. xxviii. and 292. 6*s.*

HANS BREITMANN'S PARTY. With other Ballads. By CHARLES G. LELAND. Tenth Edition. Square, pp. xvi. and 74, cloth. 2*s.* 6*d.*

HANS BREITMANN'S CHRISTMAS. With other Ballads. By CHARLES G. LELAND. Second edition. Square, pp. 80, sewed. 1*s.*

HANS BREITMANN AS A POLITICIAN. By CHARLES G. LELAND. Second edition. Square, pp. 72, sewed. 1*s.*

HANS BREITMANN IN CHURCH. With other Ballads. By CHARLES G. Leland. With an Introduction and Glossary. Second edition. Square, pp. 80, sewed. 1*s.*

HANS BREITMANN AS AN UHLAN. Six New Ballads, with a Glossary. Square, pp. 72, sewed. 1*s.*

Leland.—FUSANG; or, the Discovery of America by Chinese Buddhist Priests in the Fifth Century. By CHARLES G. LELAND. Cr. 8vo. cloth, pp. xix. and 212. 7*s.* 6*d.*

Leland.—ENGLISH GIPSY SONGS. In Rommany, with Metrical English Translations. By CHARLES G. LELAND, Author of "The English Gipsies," etc.; Prof. E. H. PALMER; and JANET TUCKEY. Crown 8vo. cloth, pp. xii. and 276. 7*s.* 6*d.*

Leland.—PIDGIN-ENGLISH SING-SONG; or Songs and Stories in the China-English Dialect. With a Vocabulary. By CHARLES G. LELAND. Fcap, 8vo. pp. viii. and 140, boards. 1876. 5*s.*

Leonowens.—THE ENGLISH GOVERNESS AT THE SIAMESE COURT-being Recollections of six years in the Royal Palace at Bangkok. By ANNA HARRIETTE LEONOWENS. With Illustrations from Photographs presented to the Author by the King of Siam. 8vo. cloth, pp. x. and 332. 1870. 12*s.*

Leonowens.—THE ROMANCE OF SIAMESE HAREM LIFE. By Mrs. ANNA H. LEONOWENS, Author of "The English Governess at the Siamese Court." With 17 Illustrations, principally from Photographs, by the permission of J. Thomson, Esq. Crown 8vo. cloth, pp. viii. and 278. 14*s.*

Lobscheid.—ENGLISH AND CHINESE DICTIONARY, with the Punti and Mandarin Pronunciation. By the Rev. W. LOBSCHEID, Knight of Francis Joseph, C.M.I.R.G.S.A., N.Z.B.S.V., etc. Folio, pp. viii. and 2016. In Four Parts. £8 8*s.*

Lobscheid.—CHINESE AND ENGLISH DICTIONARY, Arranged according to the Radicals. By the Rev. W. LOBSCHEID, Knight of Francis Joseph, C.M.I.R.G.S.A., N.Z.B.S.V., &c. 1 vol. imp. 8vo. double columns, pp. 600, bound. £2 8*s.*

Ludewig (Hermann E.)—The LITERATURE of AMERICAN ABORIGINAL LANGUAGES. With Additions and Corrections by Professor WM. W. TURNER. Edited by NICOLAS TRÜBNER. 8vo. fly and general Title, 2 leaves; Dr. Ludewig's Preface, pp. v.—viii.; Editor's Preface, pp. iv.—xii.; Biographical Memoir of Dr. Ludewig, pp. xiii.—xiv.; and Introductory Biographical Notices, pp. xiv.—xxiv., followed by List of Contents. Then follow Dr. Ludewig's Bibliotheca Glottica, alphabetically arranged, with Additions by the Editor, pp. 1—209; Professor Turner's Additions, with those of the Editor to the same, also alphabetically arranged, pp. 210—246; Index, pp. 247—256; and List of Errata, pp. 257, 258. Handsomely bound in cloth. 10*s.* 6*d.*

Macgowan.—A MANUAL OF THE AMOY COLLOQUIAL. By Rev. J. MACGOWAN, of the London Missionary Society. 8vo. sewed, pp. xvii. and 200. Amoy, 1871. £1 1*s.*

Maclay and Baldwin.—AN ALPHABETIC DICTIONARY OF THE CHINESE LANGUAGE IN THE FOOCHOW DIALECT. By Rev. R. S. MACLAY, D.D., of the Methodist Episcopal Mission, and Rev. C. C. BALDWIN, A.M., of the American Board of Mission. 8vo. half-bound, pp. 1132. Foochow, 1871. £4 4*s.*

Mahabharata. Translated into Hindi for MADAN MOHUN BHATT, by KRISHNACHANDRADHARMADHIKARIN of Benares. (Containing all but the Harivansá.) 3 vols. 8vo. cloth, pp. 574, 810, and 1106. £3 3*s.*

Maha-Vira-Charita; or, the Adventures of the Great Hero Rama. An Indian Drama in Seven Acts. Translated into English Prose from the Sanskrit of Bhavabhûti. By JOHN PICKFORD, M.A. Crown 8vo. cloth. 5*s.*

Maino-i-Khard (The Book of the).—The Pazand and Sanskrit Texts (in Roman characters) as arranged by Neriosengh Dhaval, in the fifteenth century. With an English translation, a Glossary of the Pazand texts, containing the Sanskrit, Rosian, and Pahlavi equivalents, a sketch of Pazand Grammar, and an Introduction. By E. W. WEST. 8vo. sewed, pp. 484. 1871. 16*s.*

Maltby.—A PRACTICAL HANDBOOK OF THE URIYA OR ODIYA LANGUAGE. 8vo. pp. xiii. and 201. 1874. 10*s.* 6*d.*

Manava-Kalpa-Sutra; being a portion of this ancient Work on Vaidik Rites, together with the Commentary of KUMARILA-SWAMIN. A Facsimile of the MS. No. 17, in the Library of Her Majesty's Home Government for India. With a Preface by THEODOR GOLDSTÜCKER. Oblong folio, pp. 268 of letter-press and 121 leaves of facsimiles. Cloth. £4 4*s.*

Manipulus Vocabulorum; A Rhyming Dictionary of the English Language. By Peter Levins (1570) Edited, with an Alphabetical Index, by HENRY B. WHEATLEY. 8vo. pp. xvi. and 370, cloth. 14*s.*

Manning.—AN INQUIRY INTO THE CHARACTER AND ORIGIN OF THE POSSESSIVE AUGMENT in English and in Cognate Dialects. By the late JAMES MANNING, Q.A.S., Recorder of Oxford. 8vo. pp. iv. and 90. 2*s.*

March.—A COMPARATIVE GRAMMAR OF THE ANGLO-SAXON LANGUAGE in which its forms are illustrated by those of the Sanskrit, Greek, Latin,

Gothic, Old Saxon, Old Friesic, Old Norse, and Old High-German. By FRANCIS A. MARCH, LL.D. Demy 8vo. cloth, pp. xi. and 253. 1873. 10*s.*

Markham.—QUICHUA GRAMMAR and DICTIONARY. Contributions towards a Grammar and Dictionary of Quichua, the Language of the Yncas of Peru; collected by CLEMENTS R. MARKHAM, F.S.A., Corr. Mem. of the University of Chile. Author of "Cuzco and Lima," and "Travels in Peru and India." In one vol. crown 8vo., pp. 223, cloth. £1. 11*s.* 6*d.*

Markham.—OLLANTA: A DRAMA IN THE QUICHUA LANGUAGE. Text, Translation, and Introduction, By CLEMENTS R. MARKHAM, F.R.G.S. Crown 8vo., pp. 128, cloth. 7*s.* 6*d.*

Markham.—A MEMOIR OF THE LADY ANA DE OSORIO, Countess of Chinchon, and Vice-Queen of Peru, A.D. 1629–39. With a Plea for the Correct Spelling of the Chinchona Genus. By CLEMENTS R. MARKHAM, C.B., F.R.S., Commendador da Real Ordem de Christo, Socius Academiæ Cæsareæ Naturæ Curiosorum Cognomen Chinchon. Small 4to, pp. 112. With a Map, 2 Plates, and numerous Illustrations. Roxburghe binding. 28*s.*

Markham.—THE NARRATIVES OF THE MISSION OF GEORGE BOGLE, B.C.S., to the Teshu Lama, and of the Journey of Thomas Manning to Lhasa. Edited, with Notes and Introduction, and lives of Mr. Bogle and Mr. Manning, by CLEMENTS R MARKHAM, C.B., F.R.S. Demy 8vo., with Maps and Illustrations, pp. clxi. 314, cl. 21*s.*

Marsden's Numismata Orientalia. New Edition. Part I. Ancient Indian Weights. By EDWARD THOMAS, F.R.S., etc., etc. With a Plate and Map of the India of Manu. Royal 4to. sewed, pp. 84. 9*s.* 6*d.*

Part II. The Urtuki Turkumans. By STANLEY LANE POOLE. Royal 4to. pp. xii. and 44, and 6 plates. 9*s.*

Mason.—BURMAH: its People and Natural Productions; or Notes on the Nations, Fauna, Flora, and Minerals of Tenasserim, Pegu, and Burmah. By Rev. F. MASON, D.D., M.R.A.S., Corresponding Member of the American Oriental Society, of the Boston Society of Natural History, and of the Lyceum of Natural History, New York. 8vo. pp. xviii. and 914, cl. Rangoon, 1860. 30*s.*

Mason.—THE PALI TEXT OF KACHCHAYANO'S GRAMMAR, WITH ENGLISH ANNOTATIONS. By FRANCIS MASON, D.D. I. The Text Aphorisms, 1 to 673. II. The English Annotations, including the various Readings of six independent Burmese Manuscripts, the Singalese Text on Verbs, and the Cambodian Text on Syntax. To which is added a Concordance of the Aphorisms. In Two Parts. 8vo. sewed, pp. 208, 75, and 28. Toongoo, 1871. £1 11*s.* 6*d.*

Mathews.—ABRAHAM BEN EZRA'S UNEDITED COMMENTARY ON THE CANTICLES, the Hebrew Text after two MS., with English Translation by H. J. MATHEWS, B.A., Exeter College, Oxford. 8vo. cl. limp, pp. x., 34, 24. 2*s.* 6*d.*

Mathuráprasáda Misra.—A TRILINGUAL DICTIONARY, being a comprehensive Lexicon in English, Urdú, and Hindí, exhibiting the Syllabication, Pronunciation, and Etymology of English Words, with their Explanation in English, and in Urdú and Hindí in the Roman Character. By MATHURÁ-PRASÁDA MISRA, Second Master, Queen's College, Benares. 8vo. pp. xv. and 1330, cloth. Benares, 1865. £2 2*s.*

Mayers.—ILLUSTRATIONS OF THE LAMAIST SYSTEM IN TIBET, drawn from Chinese Sources. By WILLIAM FREDERICK MAYERS, Esq., of Her Britannic Majesty's Consular Service, China. 8vo. pp. 24, sewed. 1869. 1*s.* 6*d.*

Mayers—THE CHINESE READER'S MANUAL. A Handbook of Biographical, Historical, Mythological, and General Literary Reference. By W. F. MAYERS, Chinese Secretary to H. B. M.'s Legation at Peking, F.R.G.S., etc., etc. Demy 8vo. pp. xxiv. and 440. £1 5*s.*

Medhurst.—CHINESE DIALOGUES, QUESTIONS, and FAMILIAR SENTENCES, literally translated into English, with a view to promote commercial intercourse and assist beginners in the Language. By the late W. H. MEDHURST, D.D. A new and enlarged Edition. 8vo. pp. 226. 18*s*.

Megha-Duta (The). (Cloud-Messenger.) By Kālidāsa. Translated from the Sanskrit into English verse, with Notes and Illustrations. By the late H. H. WILSON, M.A., F.R.S., Boden Professor of Sanskrit in the University of Oxford, etc., etc. The Vocabulary by FRANCIS JOHNSON, sometime Professor of Oriental Languages at the College of the Honourable the East India Company, Haileybury. New Edition. 4to. cloth, pp. xi. and 180. 10*s*. 6*d*.

Memoirs read before the ANTHROPOLOGICAL SOCIETY OF LONDON, 1863 1864. 8vo., pp. 542, cloth. 21*s*.

Memoirs read before the ANTHROPOLOGICAL SOCIETY OF LONDON, 1865-6. Vol. II. 8vo., pp. x. 464, cloth. 21*s*.

Mitra.—THE ANTIQUITIES OF ORISSA. By RAJENDRALALA MITRA. Vol. I. Published under Orders of the Government of India. Folio, cloth, pp. 180. With a Map and 36 Plates. £4 4*s*.

Moffat.—THE STANDARD ALPHABET PROBLEM; or the Preliminary Subject of a General Phonic System, considered on the basis of some important facts in the Sechwana Language of South Africa, and in reference to the views of Professors Lepsius, Max Müller, and others. A contribution to Phonetic Philology. By ROBERT MOFFAT, junr., Surveyor, Fellow of the Royal Geographical Society. 8vo. pp. xxviii. and 174, cloth. 7*s*. 6*d*.

Molesworth.—A DICTIONARY, MÁRATHI and ENGLISH. Compiled by J. T. MOLESWORTH, assisted by GEORGE and THOMAS CANDY. Second Edition, revised and enlarged. By J. T. MOLESWORTH. Royal 4to. pp. xxx and 922, boards. Bombay, 1857. £3 3*s*.

Molesworth.—A COMPENDIUM OF MOLESWORTH'S MARATHI AND ENGLISH DICTIONARY. By BABA PADMANJI. Second Edition. Revised and Enlarged. Demy 8vo. cloth, pp. xx. and 624. 21*s*.

Morley.—A DESCRIPTIVE CATALOGUE of the HISTORICAL MANUSCRIPTS in the ARABIC and PERSIAN LANGUAGES preserved in the Library of the Royal Asiatic Society of Great Britain and Ireland. By WILLIAM H. MORLEY, M.R.A.S. 8vo. pp. viii. and 160, sewed. London, 1854. 2*s*. 6*d*.

Morrison.—A DICTIONARY OF THE CHINESE LANGUAGE. By the Rev. R. MORRISON, D.D. Two vols. Vol. I. pp. x. and 762; Vol. II. pp. 828, cloth. Shanghae, 1865. £6 6*s*.

Muhammed.—THE LIFE OF MUHAMMED. Based on Muhammed Ibn Ishak By Abd El Malik Ibn Hisham. Edited by Dr. FERDINAND WÜSTENFELD. One volume containing the Arabic Text. 8vo. pp. 1026, sewed. Price 21*s*. Another volume, containing Introduction, Notes, and Index in German. 8vo. pp. lxxii. and 266, sewed. 7*s*. 6*d*. Each part sold separately

The test based on the Manuscripts of the Berlin, Leipsic, Gotha and Leyden Libraries, has en carefully revised by the learned editor, and printed with the utmost exactness.

Muir.—ORIGINAL SANSKRIT TEXTS, on the Origin and History of the People of India, their Religion and Institutions. Collected, Translated, and Illustrated by JOHN MUIR, Esq., D.C.L., LL.D., Ph.D.

Vol. I. Mythical and Legendary Accounts of the Origin of Caste, with an Inquiry into its existence in the Vedic Age. Second Edition, re-written and greatly enlarged. 8vo. pp. xx. 532, cloth. 1868. 21*s*.

Vol. II. The Trans-Himalayan Origin of the Hindus, and their Affinity with the Western Branches of the Aryan Race. Second Edition, revised, with Additions. 8vo. pp. xxxii. and 512, cloth. 1871. 21*s*.

Vol. III. The Vedas: Opinions of their Authors, and of later Indian Writers, on their Origin, Inspiration, and Authority. Second Edition, revised and enlarged. 8vo. pp. xxxii. 312, cloth. 1868. 16*s*.

Vol. IV. Comparison of the Vedic with the later representations of the principal Indian Deities. Second Edition Revised. 8vo. pp. xvi. and 524, cloth. 1873. 21*s*.

Vol. V. Contributions to a Knowledge of the Cosmogony, Mythology, Religious Ideas, Life and Manners of the Indians in the Vedic Age. 8vo. pp. xvi. 492, cloth, 1870. 21*s*.

Müller.—THE SACRED HYMNS OF THE BRAHMINS, as preserved to us in the oldest collection of religious poetry, the Rig-Veda-Sanhita, translated and explained. By F. MAX MÜLLER, M.A., Fellow of All Souls' College; Professor of Comparative Philology at Oxford; Foreign Member of the Institute of France, etc., etc. Volume I. 8vo. pp. clii. and 264. 12*s*. 6*d*.

Müller.—THE HYMNS OF THE RIG-VEDA, in Samhitá and Pada Texts, without the Commentary of Sâyana. Edited by Prof. MAX MÜLLER. In 2 vols. 8vo. pp. 1704, paper. £3 3*s*.

Müller.—LECTURE ON BUDDHIST NIHILISM. By F. MAX MÜLLER, M.A., Professor of Comparative Philology in the University of Oxford; Member of the French Institute, etc. Delivered before the General Meeting of the Association of German Philologists, at Kiel, 28th September, 1869. (Translated from the German.) Sewed. 1869. 1*s*.

Nagananda; OR THE JOY OF THE SNAKE-WORLD. A Buddhist Drama in Five Acts. Translated into English Prose, with Explanatory Notes, from the Sanskrit of Sri-Harsha-Deva. By PALMER BOYD, B.A., Sanskrit Scholar of Trinity College, Cambridge. With an Introduction by Professor COWELL. Crown 8vo., pp. xvi. and 100, cloth. 4*s*. 6*d*.

Naradiya Dharma Sastram; OR, THE INSTITUTES OF NARADA. Translated for the First Time from the unpublished Sanskrit original. By Dr. JULIUS JOLLY, University, Wurzburg. With a Preface, Notes chiefly critical, an Index of Quotations from Narada in the principal Indian Digests, and a general Index. Crown 8vo., pp. xxxv. 144, cloth. 10*s*. 6*d*.

Newman. — A DICTIONARY OF MODERN ARABIC — 1. Anglo-Arabic Dictionary. 2. Anglo-Arabic Vocabulary. 3. Arabo-English Dictionary. By F. W. NEWMAN, Emeritus Professor of University College, London. In 2 vols. crown 8vo., pp. xvi. and 376—464, cloth. £1 1*s*.

Newman.—A HANDBOOK OF MODERN ARABIC, consisting of a Practical Grammar, with numerous Examples, Dialogues, and Newspaper Extracts, in a European Type. By F. W. NEWMAN, Emeritus Professor of University College, London; formerly Fellow of Balliol College, Oxford. Post 8vo. pp. xx. and 192, cloth. London, 1866. 6*s*.

Newman.—THE TEXT OF THE IGUVINE INSCRIPTIONS, with interlinear Latin Translation and Notes. By FRANCIS W. NEWMAN, late Professor of Latin at University College, London. 8vo. pp. xvi. and 54, sewed. 2*s*.

Newman.—ORTHOËPY: or, a simple mode of Accenting English, for the advantage of Foreigners and of all Learners. By FRANCIS W. NEWMAN, Emeritus Professor of University College, London. 8vo. pp. 28, sewed. 1869. 1*s*.

Nodal.—ELEMENTOS DE GRAMÁTICA QUICHUA Ó IDIOMA DE LOS YNCAS. Bajo los Auspicios de la Redentora, Sociedad de Filántropos para mejorar la suerte de los Aboríjenes Peruanos. Por el Dr. JOSE FERNANDEZ NODAL, Abogado de los Tribunales de Justicia de la República del Perú. Royal 8vo. cloth, pp. xvi. and 441. Appendix, pp. 9. £1 1*s*.

Nodal.—LOS VINCULOS DE OLLANTA Y CUSI-KCUYLLOR. DRAMA EN QUICHUA. Obra Compilada y Espurgada con la Version Castellana al Frente de su Testo por el Dr. JOSÉ FERNANDEZ NODAL, Abogado de los Tribunales de Justicia de la República del Perú. Bajo los Auspicios de la Redentora Sociedad de Filántropos para Mejoror la Suerte de los Aboríjenes Peruanos. Roy. 8vo. bds. pp. 70. 1874. 7*s*. 6*d*.

Notley.—A Comparative Grammar of the French, Italian, Spanish, and Portuguese Languages. By Edwin A. Notley. Crown oblong 8vo. cloth, pp. xv. and 396. 7*s.* 6*d.*

Nutt.—Fragments of a Samaritan Targum. Edited from a Bodleian MS With an Introduction, containing a Sketch of Samaritan History, Dogma, and Literature. By J. W. Nutt, M.A. Demy 8vo. cloth, pp. viii., 172, and 84. With Plate. 1874. 15*s.*

Nutt.—A Sketch of Samaritan History, Dogma, and Literature. Published as an Introduction to "Fragments of a Samaritan Targum. By J. W. Nutt, M.A. Demy 8vo. cloth, pp. viii. and 172. 1874. 5*s.*

Nutt.—Two Treatises on Verbs containing Feeble and Double Letters by R. Jehuda Hayug of Fez, translated into Hebrew from the original Arabic by R. Moses Gikatilia, of Cordova; with the Treatise on Punctuation by the same Author, translated by Aben Ezra. Edited from Bodleian MSS. with an English Translation by J. W. Nutt, M.A. Demy 8vo. sewed, pp. 312. 1870. 7*s.* 6*d.*

Oera Linda Book, from a Manuscript of the Thirteenth Century, with the permission of the Proprietor, C. Over de Linden, of the Helder The Original Frisian Text, as verified by Dr. J. O. Ottema; accompanied by an English Version of Dr. Ottema's Dutch Translation, by William R. Sandbach. 8vo. cl. pp. xxvii. and 223. 5*s.*

Ollanta: A Drama in the Quichua Language. See under Markham and under Nodal.

Oriental Congress.—Report of the Proceedings of the Second International Congress of Orientalists held in London, 1874. Roy. 8vo. paper, pp. 76. 5*s.*

Oriental Congress—Transactions of the Second Session of the International Congress of Orientalists, held in London in September, 1874. Edited by Robert K. Douglas, Honorary Secretary. Demy 8vo. cloth, pp. viii. and 456. 21*s.*

Osburn.—The Monumental History of Egypt, as recorded on the Ruins of her Temples, Palaces, and Tombs. By William Osburn. Illustrated with Maps, Plates, etc. 2 vols. 8vo. pp. xii. and 461; vii. and 643, cloth. £2 2*s.*

Vol. I.—From the Colonization of the Valley to the Visit of the Patriarch Abram.
Vol. II.—From the Visit of Abram to the Exodus.

Palmer.—Egyptian Chronicles, with a harmony of Sacred and Egyptian Chronology, and an Appendix on Babylonian and Assyrian Antiquities. By William Palmer, M.A., and late Fellow of Magdalen College, Oxford. vols.. 8vo. cloth, pp. lxxiv. and 428, and viii. and 636. 1861. 12*s.*

Palmer.—A Concise Dictionary of the Persian Language. By E. H. Palmer, M.A., Professor of Arabic in the University of Cambridge. Square 16mo. pp. viii. and 364, cloth. 10*s* 6*d.*

Palmer.—Leaves from a Word Hunter's Note Book. Being some Contributions to English Etymology. By the Rev A. Smythe Palmer, B.A., sometime Scholar in the University of Dublin. Cr. 8vo. cl. pp. xii.–316. 7*s.* 6*d.*

Palmer.—The Song of the Reed; and other Pieces. By E. H. Palmer, M.A., Cambridge. Crown 8vo. pp. 208, handsomely bound in cloth. 5*s.*

Among the Contents will be found translations from Hafiz, from Omer el Kheiyám, and from other Persian as well as Arabic poets.

Pand-Námah.—The Pand-Námah; or, Books of Counsels. By Ádarbád Máráspand. Translated from Pehlevi into Gujerathi, by Harbad Sheriarjee Dadabhoy. And from Gujerathi into English by the Rev. Shapurji Edalji. Fcap. 8vo. sewed. 1870. 6*d.*

Pandit's (A) Remarks on Professor Max Müller's Translation of the "Rig-Veda." Sanskrit and English. Fcap. 8vo. sewed. 1870. 6d.

Paspati.—Études sur les Tchinghianés (Gypsies) ou Bohémiens de L'Empire Ottoman. Par Alexandre G. Paspati, M.D. Large 8vo. sewed, pp. xii. and 652. Constantinople, 1871. 28s.

Patell.—Cowasjee Patell's Chronology, containing corresponding Dates of the different Eras used by Christians, Jews, Greeks, Hindús, Mohamedans, Parsees, Chinese, Japanese, etc. By Cowasjee Sorabjee Patell. 4to. pp. viii. and 184, cloth. 50s.

Peking Gazette.—Translation of the Peking Gazette for 1872, 1873, 1874, and 1875. 8vo. pp. 137, 124, 160, and 177. 10s. 6d each.

Percy.—Bishop Percy's Folio Manuscripts—Ballads and Romances. Edited by John W. Hales, M.A., Fellow and late Assistant Tutor of Christ's College, Cambridge; and Frederick J. Furnivall, M.A., of Trinity Hall, Cambridge; assisted by Professor Child, of Harvard University, Cambridge, U.S.A., W. Chappell, Esq., etc. In 3 volumes. Vol. I., pp. 610; Vol. 2, pp. 681.; Vol. 3, pp. 640. Demy 8vo. half-bound, £4 4s. Extra demy 8vo half-bound, on Whatman's ribbed paper, £6 6s. Extra royal 8vo., paper covers, on Whatman's best ribbed paper, £10 10s. Large 4to., paper covers, on Whatman's best ribbed paper, £12.

Phillips.—The Doctrine of Addai the Apostle Now first Edited in a Complete Form in the Original Syriac, with an English Translation and Notes. By George Phillips, D.D., President of Queen's College, Cambridge. 8vo. pp. 122, cloth. 7s. 6d.

Pierce the Ploughman's Crede (about 1394 Anno Domini). Transcribed and Edited from the MS. of Trinity College, Cambridge, R. 3, 15. Collated with the MS. Bibl. Reg. 18. B. xvii. in the British Museum, and with the old Printed Text of 1553, to which is appended "God spede the Plough" (about 1500 Anno Domini), from the Lansdowne MS. 762. By the Rev. Walter W. Skeat, M.A., late Fellow of Christ's College, Cambridge. pp. xx. and 75, cloth. 1867. 2s. 6d.

Pimentel.—Cuadro descriptivo y comparativo de las Lenguas Indígenas de México, o Tratado de Filologia Mexicana. Par Francisco Pimentel. 2 Edicion unica completa. 3 Vols. 8vo. *Mexico*, 1875. £2 2s.

Pischel.—Hemacandra's Grammatik der Prâkritsprachen (Siddhahemacandram Adhyâya VIII.) mit Kritischen und Erläuternden Anmerkungen. Herausgegeben von Richard Pischel. Part I. Text und Wörtverzeichniss. 8vo. pp. xiv. and 236. 8s.

Prakrita-Prakasa; or, The Prakrit Grammar of Vararuchi, with the Commentary (Manorama) of Bhamaha. The first complete edition of the Original Text with Various Readings from a Collation of Six Manuscripts in the Bodleian Library at Oxford, and the Libraries of the Royal Asiatic Society and the East India House; with copious Notes, an English Translation, and Index of Prakrit words, to which is prefixed an easy Introduction to Prakrit Grammar. By E. B. Cowell. Second issue, with new Preface, and corrections. 8vo. pp. xxxii. and 204. 14s.

Priaulx.—Quæstiones Mosaicæ; or, the first part of the Book of Genesis compared with the remains of ancient religions. By Osmond de Beauvoir Priaulx. 8vo. pp. viii. and 548, cloth. 12s.

Rámâyan of Válmiki.—Vols. I. and II. See under Griffith.

Ram Jasan.—A Sanskrit and English Dictionary. Being an Abridgment of Professor Wilson's Dictionary. With an Appendix explaining the use of Affixes in Sanskrit. By Pandit Ram Jasan, Queen's College, Benares. Published under the Patronage of the Government, N.W.P. Royal 8vo. cloth, pp. ii. and 707. 28s.

Ram Raz.—ESSAY on the ARCHITECTURE of the HINDUS. By RAM RAZ, Native Judge and Magistrate of Bangalore. With 48 plates. 4to. pp. xiv. and 64, sewed. London, 1834. £2 2*s*.

Rask.—A GRAMMAR OF THE ANGLO-SAXON TONGUE. From the Danish of Erasmus Rask, Professor of Literary History in, and Librarian to, the University of Copenhagen, etc. By BENJAMIN THORPE. Second edition, corrected and improved. 18mo. pp. 200, cloth. 5*s*. 6*d*.

Rawlinson.—A COMMENTARY ON THE CUNEIFORM INSCRIPTIONS OF BABYLONIA AND ASSYRIA, including Readings of the Inscription on the Nimrud Obelisk, and Brief Notice of the Ancient Kings of Nineveh and Babylon, by Major H. C. RAWLINSON. 8vo. pp. 84, sewed. London, 1850. 2*s*. 6*d*.

Rawlinson.—OUTLINES OF ASSYRIAN HISTORY, from the Inscriptions of Nineveh. By Lieut. Col. RAWLINSON, C.B., followed by some Remarks by A. H. LAYARD, Esq., D.C.L. 8vo., pp. xliv., sewed. London, 1852. 1*s*.

Rawlinson.—INSCRIPTION OF TIGLATH PILESER I., KING OF ASSYRIA, B.C. 1150, as translated by Sir H. RAWLINSON, FOX TALBOT, Esq., Dr. HINCKS, and Dr. OPPERT. Published by the Royal Asiatic Society. 8vo. sd., pp. 74. 2*s*.

Rawlinson.—NOTES ON THE EARLY HISTORY OF BABYLONIA. By Colonel RAWLINSON, C.B. 8vo. sd., pp. 48. 1*s*.

Renan.—AN ESSAY ON THE AGE AND ANTIQUITY OF THE BOOK OF NABATHÆAN AGRICULTURE. To which is added an Inaugural Lecture on the Position of the Shemitic Nations in the History of Civilization. By M. ERNEST RENAN, Membre de l'Institut. Crown 8vo., pp. xvi. and 148, cloth. 3*s*. 6*d*.

Revue Celtique.—THE REVUE CELTIQUE, a Quarterly Magazine for Celtic Philology, Literature, and History. Edited with the assistance of the Chief Celtic Scholars of the British Islands and of the Continent, and Conducted by H. GAIDOZ. 8vo. Subscription, £1 per Volume.

Rhys.—LECTURES ON WELSH PHILOLOGY. By JOHN RHYS Crown 8vo. cloth. 10*s*. 6*d*. [*In preparation.*

Rig-Veda.—THE HYMNS OF THE RIG-VEDA IN THE SAMHITÁ AND PADA TEXT, without the Commentary of the Sâyana. Edited by Prof. MAX MÜLLER. In 2 vols. 8vo. paper, pp. 1704. £3 3*s*.

Rig-Veda-Sanhita: THE SACRED HYMNS OF THE BRAHMANS. Translated and explained by F. MAX MÜLLER, M.A., LL.D., Fellow of All Souls' College, Professor of Comparative Philology at Oxford, Foreign Member of the Institute of France, etc., etc. Vol. I. HYMNS TO THE MARUTS, OR THE STORM-GODS. 8vo. pp. clii. and 264. cloth. 1869. 12*s*. 6*d*.

Rig-Veda Sanhita.—A COLLECTION OF ANCIENT HINDU HYMNS. Constituting the First Ashtaka, or Book of the Rig-veda; the oldest authority for the religious and social institutions of the Hindus. Translated from the Original Sanskrit by the late H. H. WILSON, M.A. 2nd Ed., with a Postscript by Dr. FITZEDWARD HALL. Vol. I. 8vo. cloth, pp. lii. and 348, price 21*s*.

Rig-veda Sanhita.—A Collection of Ancient Hindu Hymns, constituting the Fifth to Eighth Ashtakas, or books of the Rig-Veda, the oldest Authority for the Religious and Social Institutions of the Hindus. Translated from the Original Sanskrit by the late HORACE HAYMAN WILSON, M.A., F.R.S., etc. Edited by E. B. COWELL, M.A., Principal of the Calcutta Sanskrit College. Vol. IV., 8vo., pp. 214, cloth. 14*s*.

A few copies of Vols. II. and III. still left. [*Vols. V. and VI. in the Press.*

Roe and Fryer.—TRAVELS IN INDIA IN THE SEVENTEENTH CENTURY. By Sir THOMAS ROE and Dr. JOHN FRYER. Reprinted from the "Calcutta Weekly Englishman." 8vo. cloth, pp. 474. 7*s*. 6*d*.

Rœhrig.—THE SHORTEST ROAD TO GERMAN. Designed for the use of both Teachers and Students. By F. L. O. RŒHRIG. Cr. 8vo. cloth, pp. vii. and 225. 1874. 7*s*. 6*d*.

Rogers.—NOTICE ON THE DINARS OF THE ABBASSIDE DYNASTY. By EDWARD THOMAS ROGERS, late H.M. Consul, Cairo. 8vo. pp. 44, with a Map and four Autotype Plates. 5*s*.

Rosny.—A GRAMMAR OF THE CHINESE LANGUAGE. By Professor LEON DE ROSNY. 8vo. pp. 48. 1874. 3*s*.

Rudy.—THE CHINESE MANDARIN LANGUAGE, after Ollendorff's New Method of Learning Languages. By CHARLES RUDY. In 3 Volumes. Vol. I. Grammar. 8vo. pp. 248. £1 1*s*.

Sabdakalpadruma, the well-known Sanskrit Dictionary of RAJAH RADHAKANTA DEVA. In Bengali characters. 4to. Parts 1 to 40. (In course of publication.) 3*s*. 6*d*. each part.

Sakuntala.—KÂLIDÂSA'S ÇAKUNTALÂ. The Bengalí Recension. With Critical Notes. Edited by RICHARD PISCHEL. 8vo. cloth, pp. xi. and 210. 12*s*.

Sale.—THE KORAN; commonly called THE ALCORAN OF MOHAMMED. Translated into English immediately from the original Arabic. By GEORGE SALE, Gent. To which is prefixed the Life of Mohammed. Crown 8vo. cloth, pp. 472. 7*s*.

Sâma-Vidhâna-Brâhmana. With the Commentary of Sâyana. Edited, with Notes, Translation, and Index, by A. C. BURNELL, M.R.A.S. Vol. I. Text and Commentary. With Introduction. 8vo. cloth, pp. xxxviii. and 104. 12*s*. 6*d*.

Sanskrit Works.—A CATALOGUE OF SANSKRIT WORKS PRINTED IN INDIA, offered for Sale at the affixed nett prices by TRÜBNER & Co. 16mo. pp. 52. 1*s*.

Satow.—AN ENGLISH JAPANESE DICTIONARY OF THE SPOKEN LANGUAGE. By ERNEST MASON SATOW, Japanese Secretary to H.M. Legation at Yedo, and ISHIBASHI MASAKATA, of the Imperial Japanese Foreign Office. Imp. 32mo., pp. xx. and 366, cloth. 12*s*.

Sayce.—AN ASSYRIAN GRAMMAR FOR COMPARATIVE PURPOSES. By A. H. SAYCE, M.A. 12mo. cloth, pp. xvi. and 188. 7*s*. 6*d*.

Sayce.—THE PRINCIPLES OF COMPARATIVE PHILOLOGY. By A. H. SAYCE, Fellow and Tutor of Queen's College, Oxford. Second Edition. Cr. 8vo. cl., pp. xxxii. and 416. 10*s*. 6*d*.

Scarborough.—A COLLECTION OF CHINESE PROVERBS. Translated and Arranged by WILLIAM SCARBOROUGH, Wesleyan Missionary, Hankow. With an Introduction, Notes, and Copious Index. Cr. 8vo. pp. xliv. and 278. 12*s*. 6*d*.

Schele de Vere.—STUDIES IN ENGLISH; or, Glimpses of the Inner Life of our Language. By M. SCHELE DE VERE, LL.D., Professor of Modern Languages in the University of Virginia. 8vo. cloth, pp vi. and 365. 10*s*. 6*d*.

Schele de Vere.—AMERICANISMS: THE ENGLISH OF THE NEW WORLD. By M. SCHELE DE VERE, LL.D., Professor of Modern Languages in the University of Virginia. 8vo. pp. 685, cloth. 12*s*.

Schleicher.—COMPENDIUM OF THE COMPARATIVE GRAMMAR OF THE INDO-EUROPEAN, SANSKRIT, GREEK, AND LATIN LANGUAGES. By AUGUST SCHLEICHER. Translated from the Third German Edition by HERBERT BENDALL, B.A., Chr. Coll. Camb. Part I. 8vo. cloth, pp. 184. 7*s*. 6*d*. Part II. Morphology, Roots and Stems: Numerals. 8vo. cloth. [*In the Press*.

Schemeil.—EL MUBTAKER; or, First Born. (In Arabic, printed at Beyrout). Containing Five Comedies, called Comedies of Fiction, on Hopes and Judgments, in Twenty-six Poems of 1092 Verses, showing the Seven Stages of Life, from man's conception unto his death and burial. By EMIN IBRAHIM SCHEMEIL. In one volume, 4to. pp. 166, sewed. 1870. 5*s*.

Schlagintweit.—Buddhism in Tibet. Illustrated by Literary Documents and Objects of Religious Worship. With an Account of the Buddhist Systems preceding it in India. By Emil Schlagintweit, LL.D. With a Folio Atlas of 20 Plates, and 20 Tables of Native Prints in the Text. Royal 8vo., pp. xxiv. and 404. £2 2*s*.

Schlagintweit.—Glossary of Geographical Terms from India and Tibet, with Native Transcription and Transliteration. By Hermann de Schlagintweit. Forming, with a "Route Book of the Western Himalaya, Tibet, and Turkistan," the Third Volume of H., A., and R. de Schlagintweit's "Results of a Scientific Mission to India and High Asia." With an Atlas in imperial folio, of Maps, Panoramas, and Views. Royal 4to., pp. xxiv. and 293. £4.

Shápurjí Edaljí.—A Grammar of the Gujarátí Language. By Shápurjí Edaljí. Cloth, pp. 127. 10*s*. 6*d*.

Shápurjí Edaljí.—A Dictionary, Gujrati and English. By Shápurjí Edaljí. Second Edition. Crown 8vo. cloth, pp. xxiv. and 874. 21*s*.

Shaw.—A Sketch of the Turkí Language as spoken in Eastern Turkistan (Kashgar and Yarkand); together with a Collection of Extracts. Part I. By Robert Barkley Shaw, F.R.G.S. Printed under the authority of the Government of India. Large 8vo. cloth, pp. 174 and 32. Price £1 1*s*.

Sherring.—The Sacred City of the Hindus. An Account of Benares in Ancient and Modern Times. By the Rev. M. A. Sherring, M.A., LL.D.; and Prefaced with an Introduction by Fitzedward Hall, Esq., D.C.L. 8vo. cloth, pp. xxxvi. and 388, with numerous full-page illustrations. 21*s*.

Sherring.—Hindu Tribes and Castes, as represented in Benares. By the Rev. M. A. Sherring, M.A., LL.B., London, Author of "The Sacred City of the Hindus," etc. With Illustrations. 4to. cloth, pp. xxiii. and 405. £4 4*s*.

Sherring.—The History of Protestant Missions in India. From their commencement in 1706 to 1871. By the Rev. M. A. Sherring, M.A., London Mission, Benares. Demy 8vo. cloth, pp. xi. and 482. 16*s*.

Singh.—Sakhee Book; or, The Description of Gooroo Gobind Singh's Religion and Doctrines, translated from Gooroo Mukhi into Hindi, and afterwards into English. By Sirdar Attar Singh, Chief of Bhadour. With the author's photograph. 8vo. pp. xviii. and 205. 15*s*.

Smith.—A Vocabulary of Proper Names in Chinese and English. of Places, Persons, Tribes, and Sects, in China, Japan, Corea, Assam, Siam, Burmah, The Straits, and adjacent Countries. ByF. China. 4to. half-bound, pp. vi., 72, and x. 1870. 10*s*. 6*d*.

Smith.—Contributions towards the Materia Medica and Natural History of China. For the use of Medical Missionaries and Native Medical Students. By F. Porter Smith, M.B. London, Medical Missionary in Central China. Imp. 4to. cloth, pp. viii. and 240. 1870. £1 1*s*.

Sophocles.—A Glossary of Later and Byzantine Greek. By E. A. Sophocles. 4to., pp. iv. and 624, cloth. £2 2*s*.

Sophocles.—Romaic or Modern Greek Grammar. By E. A. Sophocles. 8vo. pp. xxviii. and 196. 7*s*. 6*d*.

Sophocles.—Greek Lexicon of the Roman and Byzantine Periods (from B.C. 146 to A.D. 1100). By E. A. Sophocles. Imp. 8vo. pp. xvi. 1188, cloth. 1870. £2 8*s*.

Steele.—An Eastern Love Story. Kusa Játakaya: a Buddhistic Legendary Poem, with other Stories. By Thomas Steele, Ceylon Civil Service. Crown 8vo. cloth, pp. xii. and 260. 1871. 6*s*.

Stent.—THE JADE CHAPLET, in Twenty-four Beads. A Collection of Songs, Ballads, etc. (from the Chinese). By GEORGE CARTER STENT, M.N.C.B.R.A.S., Author of "Chinese and English Vocabulary," "Chinese and English Pocket Dictionary," "Chinese Lyrics," "Chinese Legends," etc. Cr. 8o. cloth, pp. 176. 5*s*.

Stent.—A CHINESE AND ENGLISH VOCABULARY IN THE PEKINESE DIALECT. By G. E. STENT. 8vo. pp. ix. and 677. 1871. £1 10*s*.

Stent.—A CHINESE AND ENGLISH POCKET DICTIONARY. By G. E. STENT. 16mo. pp. 250. 1874. 10*s*. 6*d*.

Stoddard.—GRAMMAR OF THE MODERN SYRIAC LANGUAGE, as spoken in Oroomiah, Persia, and in Koordistan. By Rev. D. T. STODDARD, Missionary of the American Board in Persia. Demy 8vo. bds., pp. 190. 7*s*. 6*d*.

Stokes.—BEUNANS MERIASEK. The Life of Saint Meriasek, Bishop and Confessor. A Cornish Drama. Edited, with a Translation and Notes, by WHITLEY STOKES. Medium 8vo. cloth, pp. xvi., 280, and Facsimile. 1872. 15*s*.

Stokes.—GOIDELICA—Old and Early-Middle Irish Glosses: Prose and Verse. Edited by WHITLEY STOKES. Second edition. Medium 8vo. cloth, pp. 192. 18*s*.

Stratmann.—A DICTIONARY OF THE OLD ENGLISH LANGUAGE. Compiled from the writings of the XIIIth, XIVth, and XVth centuries. By FRANCIS HENRY STRATMANN. Second Edition. 4to., pp. xii. and 594. 1873. In wrapper, £1 11*s*. 6*d*.; cloth, £1 14*s*.

Stratmann.—AN OLD ENGLISH POEM OF THE OWL AND THE NIGHTINGALE. Edited by FRANCIS HENRY STRATMANN. 8vo. cloth, pp. 60. 3*s*.

Strong.—SELECTIONS FROM THE BOSTAN OF SADI, translated into English Verse. By DAWSONNE MELANCTHON STRONG, Captain H.M. 10th Bengal Lancers. 12mo. cloth, pp. ii, and 56. 2*s*. 6*d*.

Surya-Siddhanta (Translation of the).—A TEXT BOOK OF HINDU ASTRONOMY, with Notes and Appendix, &c. By W. D. WHITNEY. 8vo. boards, pp. iv. and 354. £1 11*s*. 6*d*.

Swamy.—THE DATHÁVANSA; or, the History of the Tooth-Relic of Gotama Buddha. The Pali Text and its Translation into English, with Notes. By M. COOMÁRA SWÁMY, Mudeliár. Demy 8vo. cloth, pp. 174. 1874. 10*s*. 6*d*.

Swamy.—THE DATHÁVANSA; or, the History of the Tooth-Relic of Gotama Buddha. English Translation only. With Notes. Demy 8vo. cloth, pp. 100. 1874. 6*s*.

Swamy.—SUTTA NÍPÁTA; or, the Dialogues and Discourses of Gotama Buddha. Translated from the Pali, with Introduction and Notes. By Sir M. COOMÁRA SWAMY. Cr. 8vo. cloth, pp. xxxvi. and 160. 1874. 6*s*.

Sweet.—A HISTORY OF ENGLISH SOUNDS, from the Earliest Period, including an Investigation of the General Laws of Sound Change, and full Word Lists. By HENRY SWEET. Demy 8vo. cloth, pp. iv. and 164. 4*s*. 6*d*.

Syed Ahmad.—A SERIES OF ESSAYS ON THE LIFE OF MOHAMMED, and Subjects subsidiary thereto. By SYED AHMAD KHAN BAHADOR, C.S.I., Author of the "Mohammedan Commentary on the Holy Bible," Honorary Member of the Royal Asiatic Society, and Life Honorary Secretary to the Allygurh Scientific Society. 8vo. pp. 532, with 4 Genealogical Tables, 2 Maps, and a Coloured Plate, handsomely bound in cloth. 30*s*.

Táittiríya-Pratiçakhya.—See under WHITNEY.

Talmud.—SELECTIONS FROM THE TALMUD. Being Specimens of the Contents of that Ancient Book. Its Commentaries, Teaching, Poetry, and Legends. Also brief Sketches of the Men who made and commented upon it. Translated from the original by H. POLANO. 8vo. cloth, pp. 382. 15*s*.

Tarkavachaspati.—VACHASPATYA, a Comprehensive Dictionary, in Ten Parts. Compiled by TARANATHA TARKAVACHASPATI, Professor of Grammar and Philosophy in the Government Sanskrit College of Calcutta. An Alphabetically Arranged Dictionary, with a Grammatical Introduction and Copious Citations from the Grammarians and Scholiasts, from the Vedas, etc. Parts I. to VII. 4to. paper. 1873–6. 18*s.* each Part.

Technologial Dictionary.—POCKET DICTIONARY OF TECHNICAL TERMS USED IN ARTS AND SCIENCES. English-German-French. Based on the larger Work by KARMARSCH. 3 vols imp. 16mo. 12*s.* cloth.

Technological Dictionary of the terms employed in the Arts and Sciences; Architecture, Civil, Military and Naval; Civil Engineering, including Bridge Building, Road and Railway Making; Mechanics; Machine and Engine Making; Shipbuilding and Navigation; Metallurgy, Mining and Smelting; Artillery; Mathematics; Physics; Chemistry; Mineralogy, etc. With a Preface by Dr. K. KARMARSCH. Second Edition. 3 vols.
Vol. I. English—German—French. 8vo. pp. 666. 12*s.*
Vol. II. German—English—French. 8vo. pp. 646. 10*s.* 6*d.*
Vol. III. French—German—English. 8vo. pp. 618. 12*s.*

The Boke of Nurture. By JOHN RUSSELL, about 1460–1470 Anno Domini. The Boke of Keruynge. By WYNKYN DE WORDE, Anno Domini 1513. The Boke of Nurture. By HUGH RHODES, Anno Domini 1577. Edited from the Originals in the British Museum Library, by FREDERICK J. FURNIVALL, M.A., Trinity Hall, Cambridge, Member of Council of the Philological and Early English Text Societies. 4to. half-morocco, gilt top, pp. xix. and 146, 28, xxviii. and 56. 1867. 1*l.* 11*s.* 6*d*

The Vision of William concerning Piers Plowman, together with Vita de Dowel, Dobet et Dobest, secundum wit et resoun. By WILLIAM LANGLAND (about 1362-1380 anno domini). Edited from numerous Manuscripts, with Prefaces, Notes, and a Glossary. By the Rev. WALTER W. SKEAT, M.A. pp. xliv. and 158, cloth, 1867. Vernon A. Text; Text 7*s.* 6*d.*

Thomas.—EARLY SASSANIAN INSCRIPTIONS, SEALS AND COINS, illustrating the Early History of the Sassanian Dynasty, containing Proclamations of Ardeshir Babek, Sapor I., and his Successors. With a Critical Examination and Explanation of the Celebrated Inscription in the Hâjîâbad Cave, demonstrating that Sapor, the Conqueror of Valerian, was a Professing Christian. By EDWARD THOMAS, F R.S. Illustrated. 8vo. cloth, pp. 148. 7*s.* 6*d.*

Thomas.—THE CHRONICLES OF THE PATHÁN KINGS OF DEHLI. Illustrated by Coins, Inscriptions, and other Antiquarian Remains. By EDWARD THOMAS, F.R.S., late of the East India Company's Bengal Civil Service. With numerous Copperplates and Woodcuts. Demy 8vo. cloth, pp. xxiv. and 467. 1871. 28*s.*

Thomas.—THE REVENUE RESOURCES OF THE MUGHAL EMPIRE IN INDIA, from A.D. 1593 to A.D. 1707. A Supplement to "The Chronicles of the Pathán Kings of Delhi." By EDWARD THOMAS, F.R.S. Demy 8vo., pp. 60, cloth. 3*s.* 6*d.*

Thomas.—COMMENTS ON RECENT PEHLVI DECIPHERMENTS. With an Incidental Sketch of the Derivation of Aryan Alphabets, and contributions to the Early History and Geography of Tabaristân. Illustrated by Coins. By EDWARD THOMAS, F.R.S. 8vo. pp. 56, and 2 plates, cloth, sewed. 3*s.* 6*d.*

Thomas.—SASSANIAN COINS. Communicated to the Numismatic Society of London. By E. THOMAS, F.R.S. Two parts. With 3 Plates and a Woodcut. 12mo. sewed, pp. 43. 5*s.*

Thomas.—RECORDS OF THE GUPTA DYNASTY. Illustrated by Inscriptions, Written History, Local Tradition and Coins. To which is added a Chapter on the Arabs in Sind. By EDWARD THOMAS, F.R.S. . Folio, with a Plate, handsomely bound in cloth, pp. iv. and 64. Price 14*s.*

Thomas.—THE THEORY AND PRACTICE OF CREOLE GRAMMAR. By J. J. THOMAS. Port of Spain (Trinidad), 1869. 1 vol. 8vo. bds. pp. viii. and 135. 12*s.*

Thorburn.—Bannú; or, Our Afghán Frontier. By S. S. Thorburn, I.C.S., Settlement Officer of the Bannú District. 8vo. cloth, pp. x. and 480. 18*s.*

Thorpe.—Diplomatarium Anglicum Ævi Saxonici. A Collection of English Charters, from the reign of King Æthelberht of Kent, A.D., DCV., to that of William the Conqueror. Containing: I. Miscellaneous Charters. II. Wills. III. Guilds. IV. Manumissions and Acquittances. With a Translation of the Anglo-Saxon. By the late Benjamin Thorpe, Member of the Royal Academy of Sciences at Munich, and of the Society of Netherlandish Literature at Leyden. 8vo. pp. xlii. and 682, cloth. 1865. £1 1*s.*

Tindall.—A Grammar and Vocabulary of the Namaqua-Hottentot Language. By Henry Tindall, Wesleyan Missionary. 8vo. pp. 124, sewed. 6*s.*

Trübner's Bibliotheca Sanscrita. A Catalogue of Sanskrit Literature, chiefly printed in Europe. To which is added a Catalogue of Sanskrit Works printed in India; and a Catalogue of Pali Books. Constantly for sale by Trübner & Co. Cr. 8vo. sd., pp. 84. 2*s.* 6*d.*

Trumpp.—Grammar of the Paṣ̌to, or Language of the Afghans, compared with the Irānian and North-Indian Idioms. By Dr. Ernest Trumpp. 8vo. sewed, pp. xvi. and 412. 21*s.*

Trumpp.—Grammar of the Sindhi Language. Compared with the Sanskrit-Prakrit and the Cognate Indian Vernaculars. By Dr. Ernest Trumpp. Printed by order of Her Majesty's Government for India. Demy 8vo. sewed, pp. xvi. and 590. 15*s.*

Van der Tuuk.—Outlines of a Grammar of the Malagasy Language By H. N. van der Tuuk. 8vo., pp. 28, sewed. 1*s.*

Van der Tuuk.—Short Account of the Malay Manuscripts belonging to the Royal Asiatic Society. By H. N. van der Tuuk. 8vo., pp. 52. 2*s* 6*d.*

Vedarthayatna (The); or, an Attempt to Interpret the Vedas. A Marathi and English Translation of the Rig Veda, with the Original Samhitâ and Pada Texts in Sanskrit. Parts I. to V. 8vo. pp. 1—313. Price 3*s.* 6*d.* each.

Vishnu-Purana (The); a System of Hindu Mythology and Tradition. Translated from the original Sanskrit, and Illustrated by Notes derived chiefly from other Purāṇas. By the late H. H. Wilson, M.A., F.R.S., Boden Professor of Sanskrit in the University of Oxford, etc., etc. Edited by Fitzedward Hall. In 6 vols. 8vo. Vol. I. pp. cxl. and 200; Vol. II. pp. 343; Vol. II., pp. 348; Vol IV. pp. 346, cloth; Vol. V. pp. 392, cloth. 10*s.* 6*d.* each.

Vol. V., Part 2, containing the Index, and completing the Work, is in the Press.

Wade.—Yü-Yen Tzŭ-Erh Chi. A progressive course designed to assist the Student of Colloquial Chinese, as spoken in the Capital and the Metropolitan Department. In eight parts, with Key, Syllabary, and Writing Exercises. By Thomas Francis Wade, C.B., Secretary to Her Britannic Majesty's Legation, Peking. 3 vols. 4to. Progressive Course, pp. xx. 296 and 16; Syllabary, pp. 126 and 36; Writing Exercises, pp. 48; Key, pp. 174 and 140, sewed. £4.

Wade.—Wên-Chien Tzŭ-Erh Chi. A series of papers selected as specimens of documentary Chinese, designed to assist Students of the language, as written by the officials of China. In sixteen parts, with Key. Vol. I. By Thomas Francis Wade, C.B., Secretary to Her Britannic Majesty's Legation at Peking. 4to., half-cloth, pp. xii. and 455; and iv, 72, and 52. £1 16*s.*

Wake.—Chapters on Man. With the Outlines of a Science of comparative Psychology. By C. Staniland Wake, Fellow of the Anthropological Society of London. Crown 8vo. pp. viii. and 344, cloth. 7*s.* 6*d.*

Watson.—Index to the Native and Scientific Names of Indian and other Eastern Economic Plants and Products, originally prepared under the authority of the Secretary of State for India in Council. By John Forbes Watson, M.A., M.D., F.L.S., F.R.A.S., etc., Reporter on the Products of India. Imperial 8vo., cloth, pp. 650. £1 11*s.* 6*d.*

Weber.—On the Râmâyana. By Dr. Albrecht Weber, Berlin. Translated from the German by the Rev. D. C. Boyd, M.A. Reprinted from "The Indian Antiquary." Fcap. 8vo. sewed, pp. 130. 5*s.*

Webster.—An Introductory Essay to the Science of Comparative Theology; with a Tabular Synopsis of Scientific Religion. By Edward Webster, of Ealing, Middlesex. Read in an abbreviated form as a Lecture to a public audience at Ealing, on the 3rd of January, 1870, and to an evening congregation at South Place Chapel, Finsbury Square, London, on the 27th of February, 1870. 8vo. pp. 28, sewed. 1870. 1*s.*

Wedgwood.—A Dictionary of English Etymology. By Hensleigh Wedgwood. Second Edition, thoroughly revised and corrected by the Author, and extended to the Classical Roots of the Language. With an Introduction on the Formation of Language. Imperial 8vo., about 800 pages, double column. In Five Monthly Parts, of 160 pages. Price 5*s.* each; or complete in one volume, cl., price 26*s.*

Wedgwood.—On the Origin of Language. By Hensleigh Wedgwood, late Fellow of Christ's College, Cambridge. Fcap. 8vo. pp. 172, cloth. 3*s.* 6*d.*

West.—Glossary and Index of the Pahlavi Texts of the Book of Arda Viraf, The Tale of Gosht-I Fryano, The Hadokht Nask, and to some extracts from the Din-Kard and Nirangistan; prepared from Destur Hoshangji Asa's Glossary to the Arda Viraf Namak, and from the Original Texts, with Notes on Pahlavi Grammar. By E. W. West, Ph.D. Revised by Martin Haug, Ph.D. Published by order of the Government of Bombay. 8vo. sewed, pp. viii. and 352. 25*s.*

Wheeler.—The History of India from the Earliest Ages. By J. Talboys Wheeler, Assistant Secretary to the Government of India in the Foreign Department, Secretary to the Indian Record Commission, author of "The Geography of Herodotus," etc. etc. Demy 8vo. cl.

Vol. I. The Vedic Period and the Maha Bharata. pp. lxxv. and 576. 18*s.*

Vol. II., The Ramayana and the Brahmanic Period. pp. lxxxviii. and 680, with two Maps. 21*s.*

Vol. III. Hindu, Buddhist, Brahmanical Revival. pp. 484, with two maps. 18*s*

Vol. IV. Part I. Mussulman Rule. pp. xxxii. and 320. 14*s.*

Wheeler.—Journal of a Voyage up the Irrawaddy to Mandalay and Bhamo. By J. Talboys Wheeler. 8vo. pp. 104, sewed. 1871. 3*s.* 6*d.*

Whitney.—Oriental and Linguistic Studies. The Veda; the Avesta; the Science of Language. By William Dwight Whitney, Professor of Sanskrit and Comparative Philology in Yale College. Cr. 8vo. cl., pp. x. and 418. 12*s.*

Contents.—The Vedas.—The Vedic Doctrine of a Future Life.—Müller's History of Vedic Literature.—The Translation of the Veda.—Müller's Rig-Veda Translation.—The Avesta.—Indo-European Philology and Ethnology.—Müller's Lectures on Language.—Present State of the Question as to the Origin of Language.—Bleek and the Simious Theory of Language.—Schleicher and the Physical Theory of Language.—Steinthal and the Psychological Theory of Language.—Language and Education.—Index.

Whitney.—Oriental and Linguistic Studies. By W. D. Whitney, Professor of Sanskrit. Second Series. Contents: The East and West—Religion and Mythology—Orthography and Phonology—Hindú Astronomy. Crown 8vo. cloth. pp. 446. 12*s.*

Whitney.—Atharva Veda Prátiçákhya; or, Çáunakíyá Caturádhyáyiká (The). Text, Translation, and Notes. By William D. Whitney, Professor of Sanskrit in Yale College. 8vo. pp. 286, boards. £1 11*s.* 6*d.*

Whitney.—Language and the Study of Language: Twelve Lectures on the Principles of Linguistic Science. By W. D. Whitney. Third Edition, augmented by an Analysis. Crown 8vo. cloth, pp. xii. and 504. 10*s.* 6*d.*

Whitney.—Language and its Study, with especial reference to the Indo-European Family of Languages. Seven Lectures by W. D. Whitney, Professor of Sanskrit, and Instructor in Modern Languages in Yale College. Edited with Introduction, Notes, Tables of Declension and Conjugation, Grimm's Law with Illustration, and an Index, by the Rev. R. Morris, M.A., LL.D. Cr. 8vo. cl., pp. xxii. and 318. *5s.*

Whitney.—Surya-Siddhanta (Translation of the): A Text-book of Hindu Astronomy, with Notes and an Appendix, containing additional Notes and Tables, Calculations of Eclipses, a Stellar Map, and Indexes. By W. D. Whitney. 8vo. pp. iv. and 354, boards. *£1 11s. 6d.*

Whitney.—Táittiríya-Prátiçákhya, with its Commentary, the Tribháshyaratna: Text, Translation, and Notes. By W. D. Whitney, Prof. of Sanskrit in Yale College, New Haven. 8vo. pp. 469. 1871. *25s.*

Williams.—A Dictionary, English and Sanscrit. By Monier Williams, M.A. Published under the Patronage of the Honourable East India Company. 4to. pp. xii. 862, cloth. 1855. *£3 3s.*

Williams.—A Syllabic Dictionary of the Chinese Language, arranged according to the Wu-Fang Yuen Yin, with the pronunciation of the Characters as heard in Peking, Canton, Amoy, and Shanghai. By S. Wells Williams. 4to. cloth, pp. lxxxiv. and 1252. 1874. *£5 5s.*

Williams.—First Lessons in the Maori Language. With a Short Vocabulary. By W. L. Williams, B.A. Fcap. 8vo. pp. 98, cloth. *5s.*

Williams.—A Sanskrit-English Dictionary, Etymologically and Philologically arranged, with special reference to Greek, Latin, German, Anglo-Saxon, English, and other cognate Indo-European Languages. By Monier Williams, M.A., Boden Professor of Sanskrit. 4to. cloth. *£4 14s. 6d.*

Wilson.—Works of the late Horace Hayman Wilson, M.A., F.R.S., Member of the Royal Asiatic Societies of Calcutta and Paris, and of the Oriental Soc. of Germany, etc., and Boden Prof. of Sanskrit in the University of Oxford.

Vols I. and II. Essays and Lectures chiefly on the Religion of the Hindus, by the late H. H. Wilson, M.A., F.R.S., etc. Collected and edited by Dr. Reinhold Rost. 2 vols cloth, pp. xiii. and 399, vi. and 416. *21s.*

Vols. III, IV. and V. Essays Analytical, Critical, and Philological, on Subjects connected with Sanskrit Literature. Collected and Edited by Dr. Reinhold Rost. 3 vols. 8vo. pp. 408, 406, and 390, cloth. Price *36s*

Vols. VI., VII., VIII, IX. and X. Vishnu Purána, a System of Hindu Mythology and Tradition. Translated from the original Sanskrit, and Illustrated by Notes derived chiefly from other Purâṇâs. By the late H. H. Wilson, Edited by Fitzedward Hall, M.A., D.C.L., Oxon. Vols. I. to V. 8vo., pp. cxl. and 200; 344; 344; 346, cloth. *2l. 12s. 6d.*

Vol. V., Part 2, containing the Index, and completing the Work, is in the Press.

Vols. XI. and XII. Select Specimens of the Theatre of the Hindus. Translated from the Original Sanskrit. By the late Horace Hayman Wilson, M.A., F.R.S. 3rd corrected Ed. 2 vols. 8vo. pp. lxi. and 384; and iv. and 418, cl. *21s.*

Wilson.—Select Specimens of the Theatre of the Hindus. Translated from the Original Sanskrit. By the late Horace Hayman Wilson, M.A., F.R.S. Third corrected edition. 2 vols. 8vo., pp. lxxi. and 384; iv. and 418, cloth. *21s.*

CONTENTS.

Vol. I.—Preface—Treatise on the Dramatic System of the Hindus—Dramas translated from the Original Sanskrit—The Mrichchakati, or the Toy Cart—Vikram aand Urvasi, or the Hero and the Nymph—Uttara Ráma Charitra, or continuation of the History of Ráma.

Vol. II.—Dramas translated from the Original Sanskrit—Malâti and Mádhava, or the Stolen Marriage—Mudrá Rakshasa, or the Signet of the Minister—Ratnávalí, or the Necklace—Appendix, containing short accounts of different Dramas.

Wilson.—The Present State of the Cultivation of Oriental Literature. A Lecture delivered at the Meeting of the Royal Asiatic Society. By the Director, Professor H. H. Wilson. 8vo. pp. 26, sewed. London, 1852. *6d.*

Wilson.—A DICTIONARY IN SANSKRIT AND ENGLISH. Translated, amended, and enlarged fram an original compilation prepared by learned Natives for the College of Fort William by H. H. WILSON. The Third Edition edited by Jagunmohana Tarkalankara and Khettramohana Mookerjee. Published by Gyanendrachandra Rayachoudhuri and Brothers. 4to. pp. 1008. Calcutta, 1874. £3 3*s.*

Wise.—COMMENTARY ON THE HINDU SYSTEM OF MEDICINE. By T. A. WISE, M.D., Bengal Medical Service. 8vo., pp. xx. and 432, cloth. 7*s.* 6*d.*

Wise.—REVIEW OF THE HISTORY OF MEDICINE. By THOMAS A. WISE, M.D. 2 vols. 8vo. cloth. Vol. I., pp. xcviii. and 397; Vol. II., pp. 574. 10*s.*

Withers.—THE ENGLISH LANGUAGE SPELLED AS PRONOUNCED, with enlarged Alphabet of Forty Letters. With Specimen. By GEORGE WITHERS. Royal 8vo. sewed, pp. 84. 1*s.*

Wright.—FEUDAL MANUALS OF ENGLISH HISTORY. A Series of Popular Sketches of our National History, compiled at different periods, from the Thirteenth Century to the Fifteenth, for the use of the Feudal Gentry and Nobility. Now first edited from the Original Manuscripts. By THOMAS WRIGHT, Esq., M.A. Small 4to. cloth, pp. xxiv. and 184. 1872. 15*s.*

Wright.—THE HOMES OF OTHER DAYS. A History of Domestic Manners and Sentiments during the Middle Ages. By THOMAS WRIGHT, Esq., M.A., F.S.A. With Illustrations from the Illuminations in contemporary Manuscripts and other Sources, drawn and engraved by F. W. Fairholt, Esq., F.S.A. 1 Vol. medium 8vo. handsomely bound in cloth, pp. xv. and 512. 350 Woodcuts. £1 1*s.*

Wright.—ANGLO-SAXON AND OLD-ENGLISH VOCABULARIES, Illustrating the Condition and Manners of our Forefathers, as well as the History of the Forms of Elementary Education, and of the Languages spoken in this Island from the Tenth Century to the Fifteenth. Edited by THOMAS WRIGHT, Esq., M.A., F.S.A., etc. Second Edition, edited, collated, and corrected by RICHARD WULCKER. [*In the press.*

Wright.—THE CELT, THE ROMAN, AND THE SAXON; a History of the Early Inhabitants of Britain down to the Conversion of the Anglo-Saxons to Christianity. Illustrated by the Ancient Remains brought to Light by Recent Research. By THOMAS WRIGHT, Esq., M.A., F.S.A., etc., etc. Third Corrected and Enlarged Edition. Numerous Illustrations. Crown 8vo. cloth, pp. xiv. and 562. 14*s.*

Wylie.—NOTES ON CHINESE LITERATURE; with introductory Remarks on the Progressive Advancement of the Art; and a list of translations from the Chinese, into various European Languages. By A. WYLIE, Agent of the British and Foreign Bible Society in China. 4to. pp. 296, cloth. Price, 1*l.* 16*s.*

Yates.—A BENGÁLÍ GRAMMAR. By the late Rev. W. YATES, D.D. Reprinted, with improvements, from his Introduction to the Bengálí Language Edited by I. WENGER. Fcap. 8vo., pp. iv. and 150, bds. Calcutta, 1864. 3*s.* 6*d.*